Justice for Children and Families

Justice for Children and Families

A Developmental Perspective

Edited by

Mike Shaw
Tavistock Clinic

Sue Bailey
Academy of Medical Royal Colleges

CAMBRIDGE
UNIVERSITY PRESS

CAMBRIDGE
UNIVERSITY PRESS

University Printing House, Cambridge CB2 8BS, United Kingdom

One Liberty Plaza, 20th Floor, New York, NY 10006, USA

477 Williamstown Road, Port Melbourne, VIC 3207, Australia

314–321, 3rd Floor, Plot 3, Splendor Forum, Jasola District Centre, New Delhi – 110025, India

79 Anson Road, #06-04/06, Singapore 079906

Cambridge University Press is part of the University of Cambridge.

It furthers the University's mission by disseminating knowledge in the pursuit of education, learning, and research at the highest international levels of excellence.

www.cambridge.org
Information on this title: www.cambridge.org/9781108457699
DOI: 10.1017/9781108619554

© Royal College of Psychiatrists 2018

First published 2018

Printed and bound in Great Britain by Clays Ltd, Elcograf S.p.A.

A catalogue record for this publication is available from the British Library.

Library of Congress Cataloging-in-Publication Data
Names: Shaw, Mike (Child psychiatrist), editor. | Bailey, Sue, 1950– editor.
Title: Justice for children and families : a developmental perspective / edited by Mike Shaw,
Tavistock Clinic; Sue Bailey, Academy of Medical Royal Colleges.
Description: Cambridge, United Kingdom; New York, NY, USA:
Cambridge University Press, 2018. | Includes bibliographical references and index.
Identifiers: LCCN 2018014881 | ISBN 9781108457699 (paperback)
Subjects: LCSH: Children – Legal status, laws, etc. – Great Britain. |
Children – Legal status, laws, etc. | Child welfare – Great Britain. |
Child welfare. | BISAC: PSYCHOLOGY / Mental Health.
Classification: LCC KD3305.J87 2018 | DDC 342.4108/772–dc23
LC record available at https://lccn.loc.gov/2018014881

ISBN 978-1-108-45769-9 Paperback

Contents

Contributors

Gwen Adshead
Consultant Forensic Psychiatrist and Psychotherapist, Southern Health Foundation Trust and CNWL Foundation Trust; and Honorary Professor of Psychiatry Gresham College, London

Maggie Atkinson
Children's Commissioner for England 2010–15

Najette Ayadi O'Donnell
Paediatric Senior Registrar, University College London Hospital, London

Dame Sue Bailey
Consultant Child and Adolescent Forensic Psychiatrist, Chair of the Children and Young People's Mental Health Coalition, Vice Chair of the Centre for Mental Health, Chair of the Academy of Medical Royal Colleges, Academy of Medical Royal Colleges London

Karen Broadhurst
Professor of Social Work and Socio-Legal Studies, Department of Sociology, Lancaster University

Mar Cabezas
Philosopher and Lecturer, Complutense University, Madrid, Spain

Pamela Cox
Professor of Sociology, University of Essex

Maddy Coy
Lecturer, Center for Gender, Sexualities and Women's Studies Research, University of Florida, USA

Enys Delmage
Consultant in Adolescent Forensic Psychiatry, St Andrew's Healthcare, Northampton

Domenico Di Ceglie
Lifetime Honorary Consultant Child and Adolescent Psychiatrist, Tavistock Centre, London. Founder (1989) and Former Director of the Gender Identity Development Service, Tavistock Centre. Honorary Senior Lecturer, Department of Clinical, Educational and Health Psychology, University College London. Docente, Scuola di Specializzazione in Psicologia Clinica, La Sapienza University, Rome. Honorary Doctor of Education (Honoris Causa), University of East London

Angela J. M. Donkin
Deputy Director, Department of Epidemiology and Public Health, UCL Institute of Health Equity, London

Fran Feeley
Social Worker, Video Interaction Practitioner and Frontline Practice Tutor, London

Gunter Graf
Study Director, St Virgil Salzburg, Salzburg, Austria

Judith Harwin
Professor in Socio-Legal Studies, School of Law, Co-Director, Centre for Child and Family Justice Research, Lancaster University

Deborah Hodes
Consultant Community Paediatrician, University College London Hospital, London

Sarah Jonas
Consultant Child and Adolescent Psychiatrist, SWIFT Specialist Family Services, East Sussex

Hilary Kennedy
Honorary Senior Lecturer, University College London

Sophie Kershaw
Consultant Social Worker at the Tavistock Clinic, Co-Director FDAC National Unit, Tavistock Clinic, London

Lorraine Khan
Associate Director, Children and Young People Programme, Centre for Mental Health, London

The Honourable Mr Justice MacDonald
Judge in the Family Division of the High Court of Justice for England and Wales, Royal Courts of Justice, London

Claire Mason
Social Worker and Senior Research Associate, Department of Sociology, Lancaster University

Camilla Parker
Legal and Policy Consultant (Mental Health, Disability and Human Rights), Just Equality, London

Jenny Pearce
Professor of Young People and Public Policy, Founder of the International Centre: Researching Child Sexual Exploitation, Violence and Trafficking, University of Bedfordshire; Visiting Professor, Goldsmiths College, London; Chair of three London boroughs' shared Local Safeguarding Children Board

Mary Ryan
Lawyer and Independent Researcher and Consultant, RyanTunnardBrown, Coram Community Campus, London

Gottfried Schweiger
Philosopher and Senior Scientist, Centre for Ethics and Poverty Research, Salzburg, Austria

Richard Scorer
Solicitor and Head of Abuse Law, Slater & Gordon, Manchester

Mike Shaw
Consultant Child and Adolescent Psychiatrist at the Tavistock Clinic, Co-Director FDAC National Unit, Tavistock Clinic, London

Hannele Variend
Consultant in General Adult Psychiatry, Derbyshire Healthcare NHS Foundation Trust, London

Sheena Webb
Consultant Clinical Psychologist at the Tavistock Clinic, Manager of the London FDAC, Coram Community Campus, London

Foreword

Michael Marmot

At a meeting in the US, I showed data on inequalities in the conditions that affect children's growth and development and their subsequent health. Somewhat histrionically, I said: 'These are your children. Concern for their well-being should be above politics. Republican, Democrat; I couldn't care less. Is there a politician in the land who would say that they do not care about children?' A voice called out: 'You'd be surprised.' It was, I must add, before the current administration.

I have been arguing that the level of health of a population, and the degree of health equity, are markers of how well a society is doing in meeting the needs of its citizens. How a society treats its children is surely another marker of a well-functioning society. To continue with the data I showed my American audience (updated), UNICEF in its Report Card 14 reports child poverty in rich (Organisation for Economic Co-operation and Development) countries, where poverty is defined as household income less than 60 per cent of the median. In Finland, Iceland, Norway, Denmark and South Korea, child poverty is between 9 and 11 per cent. In the US it is 29 per cent, not far below Mexico at 32 per cent.

Why should nearly the richest country in the world have such shockingly high levels of child poverty? Answer: because it chooses to.

To translate 'chooses to', UNICEF Report Card 14 shows child poverty before and after taxes and transfers (Innocenti, 2017). The Nordic countries achieve their low levels of child poverty by using the fiscal system – taxes, tax credits and benefits. In Finland, for example, taxes and transfers reduce child poverty by two thirds. In the US, child poverty is only reduced by 18 per cent. I said to my American audience: 'You live in a democracy, this must be the level of child poverty you want, otherwise you'd elect a government that did something different.'

Sick joke, considering that Barack Obama was in the White House at the time, and the current occupant has signed a tax bill that, over the next decade, will be sharply regressive. My audience looked uncomfortable. As well they might. The point is that society can take the decision to reduce child poverty to the 10 per cent level in Nordic countries, the 20 per cent level in the UK, or the 29 per cent level in the US. It is a societal choice with profound implications for the conditions in which children are born, grow and develop. Children's development, in turn, is causally related to health and health inequalities through the life course. The minister of finance may well have a bigger influence on child development and health inequalities than the minister of health.

Using the tax and benefit system to reduce child poverty would be important. All of us concerned with child health and development should have our voices heard as we argue for it. It is a matter of social justice. But that is not all that should, and could, be done. The present volume starts from a justice perspective and looks at other ways that the effect of social disadvantage on children can be mitigated through medical care, social services and the courts.

I take particular pleasure in this approach. I chaired the World Health Organization Commission on Social Determinants of Health (WHO, 2008). On the cover of our report we wrote: 'Social Injustice Is Killing on a Grand Scale.' We put empowerment at the heart of what we were trying to achieve and said that it had three dimensions: material, psychosocial and political. Material: if you cannot afford to feed your children you cannot be empowered. Psychosocial: having control over your life. Political: having voice. Empowerment can act at the level of the individual, the community or, indeed, whole countries.

These are themes that are explored, in depth, in this volume – theoretically and practically. Following the philosopher Michael Sandel (2010), I have suggested three approaches to social justice (Marmot, 2015). The first, utilitarian, approach is maximising utility. One good feature of this approach is that it does not judge that justice is done simply by maximising opportunity. I call it a good feature because maximising opportunity is too often empty rhetoric. A fair distribution of resources – a prominent theme of this volume – is necessary but not sufficient. We know that in Britain social mobility has declined. Opportunity is given to them that have. Further, social mobility in Britain and the US is less than in many European countries. The reasons have much to do with income inequality (Wilkinson and Pickett, 2009). The more unequal incomes in this generation are, the less chance the next generation has of climbing the ladder out of poverty and relative deprivation (www.brookings.edu/blog/social-mobility-memos/2015/05/19/the-great-utility-of-the-great-gatsby-curve/).

By focusing on utility, an outcome, this approach to justice goes beyond some bland equality of opportunity words. My reservation is that it may be blind to distributions. Given that my central focus is inequality, that is a significant limitation.

The second approach to social justice, is maximising freedom. The approach taken by many authors in this volume resonates. Respect for the rights of the child and seeking to support the development of autonomy are entirely consistent with maximising freedom. There is, too, an emphasis on capabilities – itself an 'outcome'. In the Amartya Sen formulation, justice has to do with what people can be and do. A fair distribution of resources is a means to that end. I am very much taken with the legal notion expounded here that the child is a rights-bearing individual who becomes increasingly autonomous on the developmental journey towards adulthood.

Here, I would also place protection of the vulnerable in society. A developing child cannot enjoy freedoms that his rights enshrine if he or she is subject to abuse and damage. Protecting children at risk is providing them with the possibility of flourishing.

Sandel's third approach to social justice is rewarding virtue. Sandel counsels me that I do not give enough space and attention to it. Rewarding virtue is, of course, how much of our society is set up to function. My limitation with it is that we seem to reward 'virtues' such as greed and exploitation more than we do altruism and care for others.

A particular appeal of the present volume is its action perspective. We know the problems well: a damaged child is at greater risk, as he or she grows, of drug and alcohol abuse, mental illness, teenage pregnancy, becoming a perpetrator and victim of domestic violence and repeating the cycle of deprivation, poor social conditions and abuse that damage the next generation. The present authors have three clear messages: this cycle is not inevitable, we can intervene; doing so will take action by the justice system, medical and health practitioners, and social services; such intervention is a moral imperative.

I have alluded to many of the chapters. Here I quote from that of the Honourable Mr Justice MacDonald:

Shulman, citing amongst others John Locke and William Blackstone, notes that the idea that it is society, through the agency of the State, that entrusts parents with custody of the child and that, accordingly, society in the guise of the State may intervene where parents fail to meet their legal duty to take proper care of the child for the benefit of the child and, thus, for the benefit of society is deeply rooted in legal tradition and social conscience.

The duty of the State to assist parents and intervene where necessary in the development of their children is not only a duty discharged for the benefit of the individual child and his or her development but also a function of the need to maintain the integrity and development of society. The rules set in place by society to govern these social transactions comprise the laws administered by the family justice system, which laws may be enlarged or constrained as the wisdom or policy of the times may dictate.

If we take seriously the rights of the child – and social justice demands that we do – then society has a responsibility to do what it can to honour those rights. To settle an old score: there *is* such a thing as society. It is seen at its best in the chapters of this volume.

References

Innocenti (2017) *Building the Future: Children and the Sustainable Development Goals in Rich Countries*. Florence: UNICEF Office of Research, Innocenti.

Marmot, M. (2015) *The Health Gap*. London: Bloomsbury.

Sandel, M. J. (2010) *Justice: What's the Right Thing to Do?* New York: Farrar, Straus and Giroux.

WHO (2008) Closing the gap in a generation: health equity through action on the social determinants of health. Final Report of the Commission on Social Determinants of Health. Geneva: World Health Organization.

Wilkinson, R. G. and Pickett, K. (2009) *The Spirit Level: Why More Equal Societies Almost Always Do Better*. London: Allen Lane.

A Developmental Perspective on Justice

Mike Shaw and Sue Bailey

The Book's Themes

This book explores the values, ideas and structures that promote justice for children and families, and it does so from a developmental perspective. This is because children come into the world completely helpless and only very gradually develop the capacity to look after themselves. For at least a quarter of their natural lifespan they depend on families and communities to meet their needs, protect their interests and nurture their potential.

When children grow up in well-functioning families, parents are sufficiently available and sensitive to recognise their children's needs. Children in such families are able to draw on, as much as their evolving capacities require, their parents' superior physical, intellectual and emotional strength and problem-solving ability. Children do best when they have secure relationships with their parents and open lines of communication. It also helps if children are reasonably outgoing, bright and have a capacity for symbolic thinking. Play and humour are examples of symbolic thinking that make difficult experiences more manageable, thereby creating opportunities for learning. Equally, well-functioning neighbourhoods, schools and other agencies provide further layers of stimulation and support. It follows that children who grow up in well-functioning families and communities are more likely to make the best of their potential.

But all too often things don't go well, and the structures that are supposed to support children's development fail, or worse, inflict harm. Children's health, life chances and life expectancy can be seriously damaged when parents neglect or abuse their children. Similarly, children are much less likely to make the best of their potential when they grow up in communities blighted by poverty, prejudice and poor schools, or where children are victimised and exploited by peers, gangs, criminal organisations, tyrannical governments or war.

We will argue that justice for children and families requires the state to ensure checks and balances that favour:

1. Fairness: a fair distribution of resources and burdens within communities, so that every child and family gets the best possible chance to develop their potential.
2. Protection: resources for families, neighbourhoods, schools and other agencies to help them protect and encourage their children, alongside the means to intervene when these layers of protection fail.
3. Autonomy: encouraging children's voice and participation in decision-making at a level commensurate with their maturity.

We ask to what extent contemporary society meets or falls short of these expectations?

We aim to stimulate interdisciplinary interest, debate and cooperation, and have drawn contributions from practitioners and scholars of philosophy, history, social science, law, social work, psychology, paediatrics, psychiatry, psychotherapy and public health.

We challenged our authors to respond to the book's themes with short chapters on emerging ideas and evidence, with an emphasis on important questions, solvable problems and solutions worth investing in.

We hope this book will influence the practitioners, researchers and policymakers who go on to shape the future of justice for children and families.

The Contents of This Book

The book has five parts: a short Overview, which is followed by the three main themes of Fairness, Protection and Autonomy, and finally a brief Synthesis and Response.

Part I Overview

Following a Foreword by Professor Sir Michael Marmot, Professor of Epidemiology at University College London, and President of the World Medical Association, this part of the book includes the present introductory Chapter 1, 'A Developmental Perspective on Justice' in which the editors set out the themes and structure of the book, and Chapter 2, 'Foundations of Family Law', in which the Honourable Mr Justice MacDonald of the Family Division of the High Court of Justice for England and Wales explores all the themes of the book in a wonderfully well-rounded and lucid account of the evolution of the law on children and families.

Part II Fairness

Fairness shapes our perception of misfortune and our capacity to process it. While misfortune can make us feel singled out and punished, these feelings are easier to tolerate when they are just feelings and not objectively true. For instance, where children miss out on life's opportunities, the disappointment is easier to tolerate if the process has been open and fair. But more often than not, children miss out on life's opportunities because of poverty, parental negligence or discrimination, all of which are objectively unfair.

Unfairness leaves a bitter taste. The 1954 film *On the Waterfront* is set in a poor, tight-knit dockyard community controlled by dishonest union bosses. Terry Malloy (memorably played by Marlon Brando) is a gifted young boxer who feels his career has been choked by betrayal, coercion and corruption. In a classic scene, he tells his brother: 'You don't understand. I coulda had class. I coulda been a contender. I coulda been somebody, instead of a bum, which is what I am.'

The part on fairness begins with Chapter 3, 'The Social Determinants of Child Health', where Dr Angela J. M. Donkin, Deputy Director at the University College London Institute of Health Equity, demonstrates how inequalities in the distribution of wealth, power and resources lead to crucial differences in health behaviour, health outcomes and mortality. She goes on to make powerful and well-evidenced policy recommendations for both reducing inequality and mitigating its impact.

In Chapter 4, 'Philosophical Ethics and Children', Drs Mar Cabezas and Gunter Graf, philosophers from the Centre for Ethics and Poverty Research, argue that philosophy has largely ignored children and childhood. They go on to identify some promising starting points for constructing a child-sensitive ethics, which they call *well-being* and *well-becoming*. In a companion chapter, 'Child Poverty, Well-Being and Social Justice' (Chapter 5), Drs Gottfried Schweiger and Gunter Graf develop *well-being* and *well-becoming* further. They use a 'capability approach', derived from the works of the economist and philosopher Amartya Sen, to explore the damaging effects of poverty on children's health, education, self-respect and inclusion.

In Chapter 6, 'Children and Relational Citizenship: A History', historian and sociologist Professor Pamela Cox from the University of Essex argues that children are 'relational citizens', whose rights as citizens are bound up with the responsibilities of adults to protect them and to meet their needs. She asserts that we are increasingly living in an 'empowerment state', in which 'active citizens are invited, cajoled and sometimes coerced to take on a range of responsibilities for themselves, for the care of others and for the well-being of their communities', and goes on to explore the opportunities and contradictions thrown up by this world view.

In the final chapter in this section, Chapter 7, Dr Maggie Atkinson, Children's Commissioner for England 2010–15, reflects on 'The United Nations Convention on the Rights of the Child (UNCRC)'. She not only provides a lively account of the charter, but also uses powerful examples to illustrate the ways in which contemporary society falls short of treating children as 'citizens now, not citizens in waiting'.

Part III Protection

Morality is about 'doing the right thing'. Sometimes it is difficult to do the right thing, especially where it involves making sacrifices, confronting powerful vested interests or protecting the rights of ostracised minorities. We believe: first, that there is a moral argument for the state to support families and communities to bring up children to fulfil their potential; second, that where families and communities have problems the state should support families and communities to overcome their problems so that they can raise their children safely; and third, that permanently removing children from their parents should be a last resort. In the United States these principles are enshrined in federal law in the Adoption Assistance and Child Welfare Act 1980, and states risk losing their federal funding if they can't demonstrate 'reasonable efforts' to keep children in their families. There is no equivalent statutory framework in the United Kingdom; however, the Family Drug and Alcohol Court (see Chapter 9) stands out as the only family court to guarantee 'reasonable efforts'.

In Chapter 8, 'Birth Mothers Returning to Court: Can a Developmental Trauma Lens Inform Practice with Women at Risk of Repeat Removal of Infants and Children?', Professor Karen Broadhurst and Ms Claire Mason from Lancaster University present their own recent findings that one in four women who have children removed by the court return to court and have further children removed, and that among the youngest women, the rate is one in three. With Dr Sheena Webb of the Tavistock Clinic, they go on to explore 'developmental trauma', which is an emerging diagnostic framework that links complex intrapsychic and interpersonal difficulties in adult life with sustained neglect and abuse as a child. They argue that 'developmental trauma' provides a way of understanding the aetiology and complex symptomatology of this subpopulation, and signposts potential avenues for intervention.

In Chapter 9, 'The Family Drug and Alcohol Court: A Problem-Solving Approach to Family Justice', Professor Judith Harwin of Lancaster University, Ms Mary Ryan of RyanTunnardBrown and Ms Sophie Kershaw of the Tavistock Clinic describe the principles of problem-solving justice and show how they apply to the Family Drug and Alcohol Court (FDAC). They go on to present the evidence that FDAC provides not only a more humane experience of justice that is valued by parents and professionals alike, but also more durable outcomes for children and families. In a companion chapter, 'Why Video Interaction Guidance in the Family Drug and Alcohol Court?' (Chapter 10), Dr Hilary Kennedy of University College London, Ms Fran Feeley of Frontline and Ms Sophie Kershaw of the Tavistock Clinic describe Video Interaction Guidance (VIG) and its adaptation as an assessment and treatment tool within FDAC. VIG uses short video clips of 'better than usual' parent–child interaction that allows parents to see when they are responding in an 'attuned' way to their children's emotional needs, and encourages them to build on these examples. The authors present case illustrations and discuss the theoretical origins and emerging evidence and applications for this powerful new therapy.

In Chapter 11, 'A Life Course Approach to Promoting Healthy Behaviour', Dr Lorraine Khan from the Centre for Mental Health argues that 'severe and persistent behavioural difficulties are our most common, costly and overlooked childhood mental health problem'. She shows that despite a wealth of evidence for how we can reduce the chances of behavioural problems arising, and intervene early when they do occur, current policy and provision favours waiting for the problems to reach the youth justice system and courts.

In Chapter 12, 'Female Genital Mutilation', paediatricians Drs Najette Ayadi O'Donnell and Deborah Hodes from University College London Hospitals analyse the economic and cultural context in which female genital mutilation (FGM) occurs. They argue that 'change in attitude can and should come from within communities'. While communities need to be clear that FGM is illegal and will not be tolerated, it is necessary to educate and challenge the attitudes of women and men alike, and to raise the status of women.

Finally in this part, in Chapter 13, 'Litigation for Failure to Remove', Mr Richard Scorer, Solicitor and National Manager for Serious Injury at Slater & Gordon, describes how 'failure to remove' litigation involves a child seeking monetary damages from a local authority social services department for failure to protect that child from abuse. The abuse will usually have occurred within the child's birth family but in some cases the wider community. The basis of the claim will be that social workers negligently failed to protect the child from abuse which they knew or ought to have known was occurring. He argues that such litigation supports the aims of family justice, first, by compensating children and second, by helping to monitor and uphold the quality of service provided by social work professionals. However, he goes on to describe difficulties with what he argues is excessive attention to the technical calculation of compensation at the expense of justice, and insufficient opportunity for society to learn from the failings and mistakes which these cases reveal.

Part IV Autonomy

Die Gedanken Sind Frei ('Thoughts are free')

Die Gedanken Sind Frei, my thoughts freely flower
Die Gedanken Sind Frei, my thoughts give me power
No scholar can map them no hunter can trap them
No man can deny Die Gedanken Sind Frei
No man can deny Die Gedanken Sind Frei

I think as I please and this gives me pleasure
My conscience decrease this right I must treasure

My thoughts will not cater to duke or dictator
No man can deny Die Gedanken Sind Frei
No man can deny Die Gedanken Sind Frei

And if tyrants take me and throw me in prison
My thoughts will burst free like blossoms in season
Foundations will crumble and structures will tumble
And free men will cry Die Gedanken Sind Frei
And free men will cry Die Gedanken Sind Frei[1]

This is Arthur Kevess' translation of the traditional German folksong about the power, pleasure and far-reaching possibilities of autonomy. Pete Seeger's (1966) rendering of the song spoke to Dr Mike Shaw when he was a child, and it still does. In Chapter 14, 'Towards a Theory for the Development of Autonomy', Dr Shaw draws on his career as a child psychiatrist to argue that actively promoting the development of healthy autonomy is important for all children, but especially for children with complex needs, children who have been abused or neglected or children growing up in communities blighted by problems such as poverty, prejudice or war.

In recent years, children and young people's vulnerability to sexual abuse and exploitation has been highlighted by the accessibility of pornography on the internet, the sexual victimisation of young people on social media and a number of high-profile criminal trials. In Chapter 15, 'Child Sexual Exploitation and Consent to Sexual Activity: A Developmental and Context-Driven Approach', Professor Jenny Pearce OBE, Director of The International Centre: Researching Child Sexual Exploitation, Violence and Trafficking at University of Bedfordshire and Dr Maddy Coy of the Child and Woman Abuse Studies Unit at London Metropolitan University argue that abusive and exploitative sexual activity is often overlooked because of 'three flawed assumptions' about 'consent' to sexual activity: 'first that the child's capacity to consent can be determined solely by their age; second that the child's capacity to consent is independent of the social context within which that child is functioning; and finally, that the onus is on giving, rather than getting consent'. They go on to explore the implications for practice and policy.

In Chapter 16, 'Treatment without Consent', Ms Camilla Parker, mental health, disability and human rights lawyer at Just Equality, argues that 'consent to treatment, particularly in relation to mental health care, is an area of law in which the dynamics between the role of the state, the rights of the child and the rights and responsibilities of parents is both complex and uncertain'. The Human Rights Act (HRA) 1998 has led to a significant change. Whereas in the past the courts considered that parents could override their child's refusal of medical treatment, guidance now advises against relying on parental consent where the child has the competence, or the young person has the capacity, to make such decisions for him or herself. However, the HRA 1998 has not removed the tension between autonomy and protection. Like adults, children and young people aged under 18 can be treated for mental disorder without their consent if they are detained under the Mental Health Act (MHA) 1983. Moreover, unlike adults, the courts can authorise the medical treatment of under-18-year-olds, thereby overriding the refusal of a competent child or capacitous young person. The author argues that even in cases of life-saving treatment, where the court has a 'heavy duty' to take reasonable action to prevent an under-18-year-old's death, children and young people's views are central to determining what is in their best interests. Where such wishes are overridden, clear reasons for doing so should be given.

In Chapter 17, 'Autonomy and Decision-Making in Children and Adolescents with Gender Dysphoria', Dr Domenico Di Ceglie, child and adolescent psychiatrist at the Tavistock Clinic, University College London and Sapienza University, describes how 'adolescents who have a persistent experience of incongruity between mind and body find puberty painful and… are often at high risk of suicide attempts'. He goes on to argue for a 'staged approach to management' that 'provides a containing framework for these unbearable states of mind' and 'gives the young person and the family a sense of orientation and provides a space for reflection about the next intervention and the decision to be made'.

Finally in this part, autonomy provides not only the freedom to take risks, make mistakes and learn, but also the obligation to take responsibility for the decisions made. In Chapter 18, 'Criminal Responsibility', Dr Enys Delmage, adolescent forensic psychiatrist at St Andrews Healthcare, and Dr Hannele Variend, adult psychiatrist at Derbyshire Health Care NHS Foundation Trust, contrast the rights and responsibilities of children under UK civil and criminal law. They argue that the idea of developing competence and or capacity in civil law is commensurate with our understanding of the development of the brain. The criminal law in England, Wales and Northern Ireland sets criminal responsibility at the age of 10 years, which is not only very low in comparison to most other jurisdictions, but also out of keeping with neuroscientific knowledge.

Part V Synthesis and Response

The book concludes with two responses to the parts above. The first is by Dr Sarah Jonas, consultant child and adolescent psychiatrist at the SWIFT Specialist Family Services, Sussex Partnership NHS Trust, entitled 'How Reading This Book Can Contribute to Public Health Strategies for Children and Families' (Chapter 19). Here she picks out the importance of maternal physical and mental health in pregnancy, 'enabling children to have the best possible start' and 'policy targeting the social determinants of health'. She thinks there are huge gains to be made from preventing of adverse childhood experiences (ACEs) and a 'developmental trauma lens' to mitigate the effect of ACEs. She advocates the benefits of emerging approaches such as the Family Drug and Alcohol Court and Video Interaction Guidance. Furthermore, she thinks policymakers would benefit from exploring Amartya Sen's ideas on health and justice, the development of autonomy and changes in children's roles as relational citizens. She also discusses some of the barriers to action, such as the need for further research, the long time frames required to demonstrate the benefits of intervention and the need for coordination and munificence between the health, child protection and family and criminal justice systems, where spending in one part of the system might lead to savings in another.

The book finishes with a powerful chapter by Dr Gwen Adshead, forensic psychotherapist and Honorary Professor of Psychiatry at Gresham College, London, called 'Looking Three Ways: Reflections on a Developmental Perspective on Justice' (Chapter 20). Here she casts a wise eye over first, justice as respect for individual rights, liberty and due process, where she comments 'children who lack attachment security may not be well placed to exercise their "rights" because they lack attachment figures to help them to do so; or the insecurity of their attachment systems means that they struggle to develop a coherent narrative of moral identity'. Second, she considers justice as protection of the vulnerable in society, where she observes '[i]nterference with the vulnerable is the leitmotiv of most human violence, whether as bullying, exploitation or physical attack; and this interference is driven by denigratory attitudes towards dependence, neediness and lack of power'. Finally, she explores justice as the promotion of the good life, in which she reviews the research on adverse childhood experiences and argues that reducing childhood adversity is in our enlightened self-interest because 'I have met the adult incarnations of these young men and women exposed to adversity who have become what Shakespeare called "ruined pieces of nature"; full of promise like every child, but who have been damaged because they missed out on all opportunities for rescue, repair and redemption.'

Concluding Comments

There is a lot more that this book could have included, such as chapters on education, refugees, social mobility and children's relationship with the internet and social media, or chapters written by children and parents. However, this book will have succeeded if it gets the discussion going, and inspires, or perhaps maddens, others into participating in a debate about the values, ideas and structures that promote justice for children and families.

Note

1   'Die Gedanken Sind Frei', written by Arthur Kevess, published by Harmony Music Limited, Roundhouse, 212 Regents Park Road Entrance, London NW1 8AW.

References

Seeger, P. (1966) Die Gedanken Sind Frei. From *Dangerous Songs*, Columbia Records. Available at: www.youtube.com/watch?v=dbwQXVcbkU0

Foundations of Family Law[*]

The Honourable Mr Justice MacDonald

A consideration of the role of the family justice system and, by extension, the state in ensuring that the developmental needs of children are met where a parent struggles or fails in that obligation must begin by asking on what basis, and why, is the state entitled to interfere at all in this arena.

While the superficial answers are that the basis on which the state interferes is the law of the land (primarily embodied in the Children Act 1989), and that the reason the state interferes is to protect the child's best interests, these answers do not suffice on their own. What is the foundation of the law and why have those foundations been laid? By what fundamental right, and for what cause beyond the interests of the individual child, does the law, as administered by the family justice system, allow the state into the homes of autonomous adults to prescribe for a time the manner in which they are to raise their children to adulthood or, in extreme cases, to remove those children from them.

The answer to these questions not only illuminates the reasoned basis on which the family justice system intervenes in family life as a means of safeguarding and promoting a child's physical, emotional and educational development. It also highlights the central rationale for the family justice system continuing to seek to ensure, and to be resourced to ensure, that those families that require it are supported to meet the developmental needs of their children. The answer further serves as the context for an examination of the cardinal principles which ensure that the developing child is also safeguarded within the confines of the operation of the family justice system as a rights-bearing individual who becomes increasingly autonomous on the developmental journey towards adulthood.

Parental Responsibility and Welfare

The following definition of 'welfare' within the context of the law relating to children was promulgated by Boys J in the New Zealand case of *Walker* v. *Walker* v. *Harrison*:

> 'Welfare' is an all-encompassing word. It includes material welfare, both in the sense of adequacy of resources to provide a pleasant home and a comfortable standard of living and in the sense of adequacy of care to ensure that good health and due personal pride are maintained. However, while material considerations have their place, they are secondary matters. More important are the stability and security, the loving and understanding care and guidance, the warm and compassionate relationships, that are essential for the full development of the child's own character, personality and talents.

As early as 1838 the court in the US case of *The Etna* noted that the power of the parent:

> is not a power granted to the parent for his benefit, but allowed to him for the benefit of the child, and it ceases when the faculties of the child have acquired that degree of maturity, that it may be

safely entrusted to its own resources. When, therefore, the parent abuses his power, or neglects to fulfil the obligation from which it results, he forfeits his rights.

As Shulman (2014, p. 2) points out by reference to *The Etna*, parental authority is thus a contingent authority because it is inseparably connected with the parental obligation to meet the needs of the developing child and arises out of that obligation. This is an uncontroversial proposition that is reflected in our modern domestic law. The Law Commission (1988), in its report *Family Law Review of Child Law, Guardianship and Custody*, concluded that parents' rights insofar as they concern their children are only derived from their duties as parents and exist only to secure the welfare of their children. Within this context, the Department of Health's *An Introduction to the Children Act* (1989) further made clear that the concept of parental responsibility 'emphasises that the duty to care for the child and to raise him to moral, physical and emotional health is the fundamental task of parenthood and the only jurisdiction for the authority it confers'.

The domestic law is thus clear that the concept of parental responsibility describes a level of adult authority over the developing child, exercised for the benefit of the child and not the adult and circumscribed in its extent and application by the child's best interests and the child's rights under the European Convention on Human Rights and Fundamental Freedoms, interpreted in accordance with the United Nations Convention on the Rights of the Child (UNCRC). Thus, in *Re D (A Child)* Lord Justice Ryder reiterated that the concept of parental responsibility describes an adult's responsibility to secure the welfare of their child, which is to be exercised for the benefit of the child not the adult. The status conferred by parental responsibility relates to welfare and not the mere existence of paternity or parenthood. Biology does not beget parental rights (Shulman, 2014, p. 7).

But who *grants* to the parent the contingent authority or responsibility deriving from the duty to safeguard the child's welfare? Does it arrive with the child at the point of birth by operation of natural law or is it bequeathed upon the parent by society as a whole? Further, if, by reason of its abuse or neglect, a parent forfeits his or her authority, either in part or completely, by what right, beyond mere operation of law, do those to whom it must be surrendered claim it?

Parenting and Society

The concept of children's rights recognises that upon the birth of the child, that child becomes part of the human family, benefiting from all the rights attendant on his or her equal status in human society. The corollary of this position is that human society benefits from the addition of the child as a member of that society. However, such benefit is dependent upon the child developing to his or her full potential physically, emotionally and educationally under the protection of the human rights conferred upon him or her. The development of children and the development of society are intrinsically and indeed inseparably linked. In a very real sense, the health of our society is dependent upon the physical, emotional and educational health of our children. Specifically, the sound development of the child in all aspects is indispensable to the good order and the just protection of society (*Brooks* v. *Brooks*).

Thus, in the Lockean tradition, what is due to the child from his or her parents is defined, in a general sense, by basic developmental needs and, more particularly, by the developmental needs of the child destined from birth to be a member of the community at large (Shulman, 2014, p. 7). Within this context, the parents' responsibility for ensuring the development of the child must be discharged in order to ensure the child is able to assume his or her place in a liberal, democratic society such that that liberal and democratic society can flourish to the benefit of each and all of its members, including the child.

The foregoing principles illuminate both the *source* of the contingent authority or responsibility for the child conferred upon the parent and the reason why the state is entitled to interfere with that authority or responsibility where a parent fails to discharge it. Parenting is a fiduciary duty owed not only to the child in terms of welfare but also to the wider community of which that child is a member. Parents hold children in trust for the ultimate benefit of the child *and* society. Accordingly, society is entitled to intervene if and when a parent breaches that trust. Shulman, citing among others John Locke and William Blackstone, notes that the idea that it is society, through the agency of the state, that entrusts parents with custody of the child and that, accordingly, society in the guise of the state may intervene where parents fail to meet their legal duty to take proper care of the child for the benefit of the child and, thus, for the benefit of society is deeply rooted in legal tradition and social conscience (Shulman, 2014, p. 3).

Accordingly, the contingent authority or responsibility that the parent has over the child's development does not arise from any biological imperative or fundamental right to parent. Rather, it is bequeathed to the parent by the community of which they and the child are members. If by reason of abuse or neglect a parent forfeits his or her authority or responsibility, those to whom the parents' contingent authority or responsibility must be surrendered claim it as representatives of a society in which the expectation is that each member of the community will act in accordance with the good of all the other members of that community including, but not limited to, the child in question. The duty of the state to assist parents and intervene where necessary in the development of their children is not only a duty discharged for the benefit of the individual child and his or her development but also a function of the need to maintain the integrity and development of society. The rules set in place by society to govern these social transactions comprise the laws administered by the family justice system, which laws may be enlarged or constrained as the wisdom or policy of the times may dictate.

Family Justice and Child Development

Within the foregoing context, childhood is not a single, fixed and universal experience between birth and majority but rather one in which, at different stages of their lives, children require different degrees of protection, provision, prevention and participation (Van Beuren, 2007). A system of family justice based solely on identifying who is a child and who is not would be objectionable as it would fail to account for the continuing development of the child towards autonomous adulthood. A system of family justice that took an overly paternalistic approach to the child would be likewise objectionable as contravening the principle that parental authority is not a power granted to the parents (or in this context, the state) for their benefit but rather for the benefit of the child. Having established the fundamental principles on which the state may intervene through the medium of the family justice system to ensure the physical, emotional and educational development of the child for the benefit of the child and society, how then do we locate children within this paradigm so as to ensure their rights and welfare are enhanced and not prejudiced by the operation of the systems deployed to safeguard the child, and society more widely? The key to achieving this is the proper recognition of child development and, specifically, the concept of 'evolving capacity'.

The concept of 'evolving capacity' is embodied in Art. 5 of the UNCRC and refers to the process of maturation and learning whereby children progressively acquire knowledge, competencies and understanding, including an understanding of their rights and how these can best be realised (Committee on the Rights of the Child General Comment No. 7). The concept of 'evolving capacity' establishes that as children acquire enhanced competencies, there is a reduced need for direction and a greater capacity to take responsibility for decisions affecting their lives. It seeks a balance between recognising children as active agents of their own lives, entitled to be listened to, respected and granted increasing autonomy in the exercise of rights, while also being entitled to protection in accordance with their relative immaturity and youth (Lansdown, 2005, pp. 3 and viii).

A parent's aspirations for their children, the expectations and demands placed on children and the cultural, economic and social environments in which children grow up, as well as their own unique life experiences, all impact on the ranges and level of capacities that children acquire and exercise (Lansdown, 2005). The process of development is dynamic and influenced by a wide range of factors, including attachment (Bowlby, 1969; Howe et al., 1999), cognitive development (Piaget and Inhelder, 1969), resilience (Fonagy et al., 1994) and, not least, the nature of the proceedings in which a child may be involved (Fortin, 2005, pp. 254, 257–67). It must be recognised that there is enormous variation between children in the process of evolving capacity, arising from multiple genetic and environmental influences (Jones, 2003; Fortin, 2005, pp. 72–4, 253–4). Further, the adult tendency to underestimate the extent to which the capacity of the child has evolved must be held in mind when considering a child's evolving capacity (Lansdown, 2005, p. ix). Likewise, it must be acknowledged that there may not necessarily be an exponential link between increasing knowledge, experience and cognitive capacity and an evolving capacity to make rational, 'mature' decisions. Accordingly, when applying the principle of 'evolving capacity' it must be applied by reference to the individual subject child.

The principle of 'evolving capacity' is well recognised within our domestic law. In the seminal case of *Gillick* v. *West Norfolk and Wisbech Area Health Authority* Lord Scarman articulated the principle as follows:

> The principle of the law… is that parental rights are derived from parental duty and exist only so long as they are needed for the protection of the person and property of the child… parental rights yield to the child's right to make his own decisions when he reaches a sufficient understanding and intelligence to be capable of making up his own mind on the matter requiring decision.

Lord Scarman's judgment in *Gillick* demonstrates that the principle of 'evolving capacity' requires that as between children, parents and the state, the child's rights and welfare move from being an exercise of parental responsibility (or state intervention) to an exercise in participation and, finally, to an exercise of self-determination. The child retains the same rights underpinning his or her welfare throughout this developmental process but becomes increasingly autonomous in the application and enforcement of those rights as his or her capacity evolves.

A key element in the process described in the foregoing paragraph is that of the participation of the child in accordance with his or her age, development and understanding. The child's right to participate articulates with the greatest clarity the status of all children as equal members of human society able to hold and exercise rights. Within the context of the child's involvement in the family justice system, it is a requirement of natural justice that a person is able to participate in matters which impact upon them.

The opportunity for children to participate fully and directly in the formulation of their own destiny is a cardinal right, enshrined in Art. 12 of the UNCRC. The child's right to participate also provides a discrete example of the operation of the principle of 'evolving capacity'.

The operation (as distinct from the existence) of the child's right to participate is calibrated to the child's level of development. Art. 12 of the UNCRC requires that the views of the child be given due weight 'in accordance with the age and maturity of the child'. Within the domestic context, the Children Act 1989 s 1(3)(a) requires that the child's wishes and feelings be considered in light of his or her 'age and understanding'. The wording of both Art. 12 of the UNCRC and s 1(3)(a) are designed to move the focus from the question of which decisions children are not competent to make to the question of how children can participate and which elements of decisions they are able to make (Van Beuren, 1998).

Within this context, the operation of the child's right to participate demands that consideration be given to the developmental context in which it takes place. In particular, regard must be had to the chronological and developmental range covered by 'childhood' and the fact that chronological age and developmental age will not necessarily coincide. Thus, in accordance with the principles outlined above, for a child of a given age, the implementation of his or her right to participate must once again be considered within the context of a number of key aspects of developmental psychology and theories of attachment, cognitive development and resilience as well as the child's chronological age.

When it comes to the right to participate, children cannot be 'treated as a homogenous group in relation to whether and how they wish to participate in decision making' (Day-Scalter and Piper, 2001, p. 427). Rather, close regard must be paid to their level development having regard to the principle of evolving capacity in order to maximise the opportunity for the child to contribute to decisions being taken in respect of him or her. It should also be remembered that the child's evolving capacity should not lead to the assumption that the child will always have a settled view on a given topic and may be, as are many adults, entirely undecided on a given issue.

Conclusion

An examination of the family justice system from a developmental perspective demonstrates that the role of that system is not limited to safeguarding and promoting the development of the child but, more widely, extends to safeguarding and promoting the development of society as a whole. Within this context, the justification for a fair distribution of society's resources and burdens so that every child be he 'born to labour' or 'the heir to a dukedom' (Hanway, 1766 [2009], p. 7) may, where necessary, be assisted by way of support or intervention is manifest, both from the perspective of the welfare of the individual child and as a matter of self-interest on the part of the community.

However, it must also be remembered that a child in respect of whose welfare society intervenes through the utility of the justice system does not thereby become simply the property of the state, any more than the child is the property of his or her parents prior to such intervention. Rather, the developing child is and remains a rights-bearing individual within the society that seeks to confer protection and support on him or her. Within this context, the approach to children's 'evolving capacity' and participation in matters concerning their own welfare taken in *Gillick* was rightly described as a domestic 'landmark in children's rights' (Hale et al., 2008). Lord Scarman's careful formulation mirrored the rights-based approach to participation articulated in Arts 5 and 12 of the UNCRC. There remain, though, challenges.

To take but one example, the Court of Appeal in *Re R (A Minor) (Wardship: Medical Treatment)* and *Re W (A Minor) (Medical Treatment: Court's Jurisdiction)* took a significant step away from the purity of Lord Scarman's formulation in *Gillick* in holding that a parent retains a veto in respect of the child's decision to refuse medical treatment, notwithstanding that child having the understanding and intelligence to be capable of making up his or her own mind on the matter requiring decision, where the parent considers that the child is not acting, or is refusing to act in his or her own best interests. While the courts have started along the road back towards an unvarnished application of Lord Scarman's judgment (*Re Roddy (A Child) (Identification: Restriction on Publication)* [2003]; *Mabon v. Mabon and Others* [2005]; *R (on the application of Axon) v. Secretary of State for Health and Another* [2006]), with rights-based principles such as that enunciated in *Gillick* seemingly hard for some to swallow, it may be some time before rights-based ideas such as a presumption that children are capable of exercising rights and responsibilities unless proven otherwise become palatable (Rodham, 1974). Particular reforms may assist with further progress. As Van Buren (1998) comments, a *statutory* presumption of capacity rather than incapacity for children would shift the burden of proof onto those denying a child's capacity to exercise rights. Adopting such a reform would also align the position of all children with that of persons over 16 under the Mental Capacity Act 2005, s 1(2).

As Baroness Hale observed in *Re D (A Child)*, children are quite capable of being moral actors in their own right. Society should avoid the undue paternalism that characterises the argument that parents have, by default, the right to raise their children as they see fit without interference by the state (Guggenheim, 2005) and, equally importantly, should assure to the child his or her rights as an equal member of the human family when the state does intervene. In order to do so, it is vital that those responsible for the operation of the family justice system pay proper regard to the child's development and, in particular, to his or her evolving capacity to operate as a moral actor for his or her own system of ends (Freeman, 1983).

Note

*   The views expressed in this chapter represent the personal views of the author and not those of the judiciary as a whole.

References

Bowlby, J. (1969) *Attachment and Loss, Volume 1 Attachment*. London: Hogarth Press.

Brooks v. Brooks, 35 Barb at 87–88.

Committee on the Rights of the Child General Comment No. 7. *Implementing Child Rights in Early Childhood*, HRI/GEN/1/Rev.8, p. 439, para 17.

Day-Scalter, S. and Piper, C. (2001) Social exclusion and the welfare of the child. *Journal of Law and Society*, 409, 427.

Department of Health (1989) *An Introduction to the Children Act*. London: HMSO, para 1.4.

Fonagy, P., Steele, M., Steele, H. et al. (1994) Theory and practice of resilience. *Journal of Child Psychology and Psychiatry*, 35(2), 231–57.

Fortin, J. (2005) *Children's Rights and the Developing Law*, 2nd edn. Cambridge: Cambridge University Press.

Freeman, M. (1983) *The Rights and Wrongs of Children*. London: Frances Pinter, p. 57.

Gillick v. West Norfolk and Wisbech Area Health Authority [1986] AC 112.

Guggenheim, M. (2005) *What's Wrong with Children's Rights*. Cambridge, MA: Harvard University Press, ch. 2.

Hale, B., Pearl, D., Cooke, E. and Monk, D. (2008) *The Family, Law and Society: Cases and Materials*, 6th edn. Oxford: Oxford University Press.

Hanway, J. (1766 [2009]) *An Earnest Appeal for Mercy to the Children of the Poor*. Whitefish, MT: Kessinger Publishing.

Howe, D., Brandon, M., Hinings, D. and Schofield, G. (1999) *Attachment Theory: Child Maltreatment and Family Support*. London: Macmillan Press.

Jones, D. (2003) *Communicating with Vulnerable Children*. London: Gaskell, p. 9.

Lansdown, G. (2005) *The Evolving Capacities of the Child*. London: UNICEF/Save the Children.

Law Commission (1988) Family Law Review of Child Law, Guardianship and Custody 172, para 2.4.

Mabon v. *Mabon and Others* [2005] EWCA Civ 634, [2005] Fam 366, [2005] 2 FLR 1011.

Piaget, J. and Inhelder, B. (1969) *The Psychology of the Child*. London: Routledge and Kegan Paul.

R (on the application of Axon) v. *Secretary of State for Health and Another* [2006] EWHC 37 (Admin), [2006] QB 539, [2006] 1 FCR 175, paras 56 and 95.

Re Roddy (A Child) (Identification: Restriction on Publication) [2003] EWHC 2997 (Fam), [2004] 1 FCR 30, [2004] 2 FLR 949, [2004] EMLR 8.

Re D (A Child) [2014] EWCA Civ 315.

Re D (A Child) [2006] UKHL 51, [2007] 1 AC 619.

Re R (A Minor) (Wardship: Medical Treatment) [1992] Fam 11 at 23.

Re W (A Minor) (Medical Treatment: Court's Jurisdiction) [1993] Fam 64 at 75.

Rodham, H. (1974) Children under the law. *Harvard Educational Review*, 9, 22.

Shulman, J. (2014) *The Constitutional Parent*. New Haven, CT: Yale University Press.

The Etna 8 F. Cas. 803, 804 (D. Me. 1838).

Van Beuren, G. (1998) *The International Law on the Rights of the Child*. Leiden: Martinus Nijhoff Publishers, p. 137.

Van Beuren, G. (2007) *Child Rights in Europe*. Strasbourg: Council of Europe Publishing, p. 38.

Walker v. *Walker* v. *Harrison* [1981] NZ Recent Law 257.

Chapter

3

The Social Determinants of Child Health

Angela J. M. Donkin

In England, those living in the most affluent local area can expect to have good health for 17 years longer than those in the most deprived local area (The Marmot Review Team, 2010). A wide body of evidence has shown that health inequalities like this do not arise by chance. Health inequalities cannot be attributed simply to genetic make-up, 'bad', unhealthy behaviour, or difficulties in access to medical care, important as those factors may be. The conditions of people's daily life shape their health behaviours and health outcomes, and an unequal distribution of money, power and resources in turn shape the conditions of daily life (The Marmot Review Team, 2010). *Fair Society, Healthy Lives* (The Marmot Review Team, 2010) set out the evidence regarding the drivers of health inequalities in England, and proposed six high-level policy objectives to inform action. These are called the 'social determinants of health' and include:

1. Give every child the best start in life.
2. Enable all children, young people and adults to maximise their capabilities and have control over their lives.
3. Create fair employment and good work for all.
4. Ensure a healthy standard of living for all.
5. Create and develop healthy and sustainable places and communities.
6. Strengthen the role and impact of ill health prevention.

Out of these recommendations, to essentially reduce inequalities in adult health, giving every child the best start in life is seen to be a priority policy, driven by two key facts – inequalities are evident at early ages, and inequalities accumulate. Therefore, reducing inequalities in the early years can have the greatest effect on life chances. In an 'Equal Start' we delve more into the drivers of inequalities in the early years specifically, and identify 21 outcomes to create lasting changes to children's future life chances (Pordes-Bowers et al., 2012). These outcomes cluster into three key groups: improvements in children's cognitive, social and emotional and physical development; improvements in parenting; and improvements in parents' lives. The focus of this work was not purely on child health, although this would be an outcome, but also on other developmental outcomes, recognising that future health would be driven by such factors as their education, ability to control emotions and income, as much as their health in childhood: improving child health is necessary but not sufficient to ensure optimal health outcomes in later life.

This chapter takes a slightly different slant, and focuses solely on identifying the social determinants of child health and mortality, and not on the wider set of outcomes required to minimise inequalities in later life, although there will be some crossover. My approach is to identify the most common causes of mortality and poor health, and to look at the social determinants associated with these.

Birthweight

Let's start at the beginning with infant mortality, which contributes the most to mortality rates in childhood. Deaths among babies who are born weighing less than 2,500 g (less than 5½ lbs) account for about three-quarters of neonatal deaths and two-thirds of infant deaths (Office for National Statistics, 2014). In addition, low birthweight continues to have an impact into childhood and later life, with increased risk of long-term disability and impaired development (Reichman, 2005). Infants born weighing less than 2,500 g are more likely than heavier infants to experience delayed motor and social development (Hediger et al., 2002). Lower birthweight also increases a child's likelihood of having a school-age learning disability, being enrolled in special education classes, having a lower IQ and dropping out of high school (Reichman, 2005). The risk for many of these outcomes increases substantially as birthweight decreases, with very low birthweight babies (less than 1,500 g) being most at risk. There is also some evidence to suggest that there is a higher risk of obesity in later life for those born with a low birthweight (Rogers, 2003). Reducing the prevalence of low birthweight should therefore be a priority and action should help to reduce inequalities given that low birthweight babies are more common in mothers with lower socio-economic status (SES) (Dibben et al., 2006; Oakley et al., 2009).

The main risk factors for low and very low birthweight include multiple births (more than one foetus carried to term), maternal smoking, low maternal weight gain or low pre-pregnancy weight, maternal or foetal stress, infections and violence towards the pregnant woman (Ricketts et al., 2005). In addition, in the UK over 5 per cent of mothers of babies born in 2010 were under 20 years old and low birthweight rates are higher among teenage mothers, possibly because of competition for nutrients between the foetus and its mother who is also growing and developing (Baker et al., 2009) or because teenage diets are poor (Bates et al., 2012). Teenage pregnancies remain approximately twice as high for women living in the most deprived areas compared with the least deprived (Health and Social Care Information Centre, 2013).

Poor health behaviours have been associated with increased prevalence of low birthweight babies in less advantaged socio-economic groups. There are two main pathways by which living in low socio-economic circumstances can be associated with poor health behaviours. The first, relevant to diet for instance, is that incomes can be too low to afford a decent diet; the second, relevant to substance abuse, smoking and domestic violence, is that low incomes and unemployment or poor-quality work increase stress. Depression and stress can lead to negative maternal behaviours, domestic violence, poor prenatal care and substance abuse; antenatal maternal stress and poor maternal mental health have been found to impact on foetal development (Talge et al., 2007) with maternal depression contributing to low birthweight (Gutman et al., 2009; Jennings et al., 1991). Given that 34 per cent of families with children are unable to afford a minimum acceptable standard of living (Padley et al., 2014), the effects of low income on nutritional adequacy, stress and poor health behaviours should not be underestimated, and efforts to address low birthweight may be ineffective without efforts to reduce poverty or mitigate its negative effects.

Cancer

After the first year of life, the most common causes of death are cancer, other non-communicable diseases and external causes including injuries. So far, the prevalence of most childhood cancers has not been linked to social determinants.

Some children inherit DNA changes from a parent that increase their risk of certain types of cancer, but most childhood cancers are the result of DNA changes that happen early in the child's life, sometimes even before birth. Sometimes the causes of gene changes in certain adult cancers are known (such as cancer-causing chemicals in cigarette smoke), but the reasons for DNA changes that cause most childhood cancers are not known. A few environmental factors, such as radiation exposure, have been linked with some types of childhood cancers. Some studies have also suggested that some parental exposures (such as smoking) might increase a child's risk of certain cancers, but more studies are needed to explore these possible links.

However, while there may be little evidence of social determinant *causes* of cancer, there is some evidence of socio-economic differences in *survival*. For example, a study of Norwegian children found that mortality was reduced by about 15 per cent for children with highly educated mothers and children without siblings. These effects were most pronounced for cancers predicted to encompass intense, long-lasting treatments resulting in chronic health problems. Neither earnings nor the marital status of parents affected children's survival. The authors hypothesise that fewer time constraints and various non-economic rewards of parents from their education appear to have an impact on childhood cancer survival (Syse et al., 2011).

In terms of non-communicable diseases, I will focus on three issues: obesity, mental health and oral health.

Obesity

Analysis of data from the Health Survey for England for two–15-year-olds shows that obesity is approximately twice as likely in the poorest compared to the richest households, and by the Index of Multiple Deviation (IMD) that obesity prevalence was highest in the most deprived and lowest in the least deprived areas (Ryley, 2013). Similarly, analysis of National Child Measurement Programme data for four–five-year-olds showed obesity and overweight prevalence varied from 18 per cent in the least deprived areas to 25 per cent in the most deprived ones (Lifestyle Statistics Team, 2013), findings that are based on measurements of over 90 eligible children (Figure 3.1).

As previously stated in the low birthweight discussion, there is evidence to suggest that factors associated with low SES start to impact on the nutrition of the foetus in the womb. Socio-economic adversity or teenage pregnancy during the prenatal period is associated with an increased risk of having a low birthweight baby (Dibben et al., 2006; Oakley et al., 2009); however, low income women are also more likely to enter pregnancy being obese than their peers (Moody, 2013) which, in turn, increases the risk of having a baby above the healthy weight range. Birthweight outside either end of the ideal birthweight range is associated with an increased risk of childhood obesity (Rogers, 2003).

Another contribution to inequalities in obesity could be inequalities in breastfeeding (which can also protect babies from infection and help prevent sudden infant death syndrome in early life). Breastfeeding is less common in more disadvantaged socio-economic

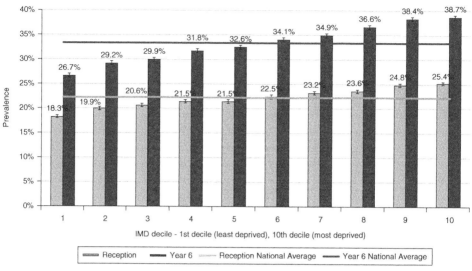

Note: All percentages are rounded to one decimal place.

Figure 3.1 Obesity rates by deprivation decile at Reception and Year Six, 2012/13.
Source: Lifestyle Statistics Team (2013).

groups (McAndrew et al., 2012). Breastfeeding, relative to formula feeding,   is associated with   a   decreased   risk   of   later   obesity (Arenz et al., 2004; Owen et al., 2005). Furthermore, maternal depression, which is more prevalent in low income households, can have a negative impact on the ability of mothers to breastfeed successfully (Gutman et al., 2009; Jennings et al., 1991).

While the factors above contribute to a propensity to obesity at a young age, the figures suggest that obesity levels rise dramatically during primary school years and, in particular, the social gradient becomes more marked, with overweight children more likely to become obese if they are in a more deprived area. As Figure 3.1 illustrates, 38.7 per cent of children in the most deprived areas are overweight or obese by Year 6. People living on low incomes tend to have worse diets (Roberts et al., 2013), and there is some evidence to suggest that this gap is widening. For example, purchases of fruit and vegetables have declined since 2007, and that decline has been most marked in low income households (Defra, 2012). The rapid recent growth of food banks also suggests that the number of people facing food insecurity and nutritional vulnerability is growing, with 1,084,604 people – including 396,997 children – receiving three days' food from the Trussell Trust's network of foodbanks in 2014/ 15, compared with 913,138 in the 2013/14 financial year, an increase of 19 per cent (The Trussell Trust, 2014).

A key point here is that good food, foods that are nutrient-dense per calorie, are more expensive (Maillot et al., 2008). Therefore, people on low incomes will find it harder to buy the type of healthy diet for their children that we know we need to maintain a healthy weight – lean meat, fish and fruits and vegetables are relatively expensive forms of calories. The research has indeed shown that for any given level of energy intake, a lower consumption of fruits and vegetables was associated with lower diet cost (Drewnowski et al., 2007) and that at each level of energy intake, higher dietary energy density was associated with lower diet costs (Drewnowski et al., 2004). In addition, in deprived areas there also tends to be a proliferation of fast-food outlets which serve large portions of unhealthy food which can lead to high levels of temptation.

Mental Health

Moving onto mental health, a key statistic is that children in the poorest households are three times more likely to have a mental illness than children in the best-off households (Department of Health, 1999). Even at an early age these differences are evident; for example, in one study at three years of age, 2 per cent of children from families in the highest income group had socio-emotional difficulties compared with 16 per cent of those from families in the lowest income group (Ermisch, 2008). Also, as children get older there is evidence that the steepness of the gradient in social and emotional problems becomes greater (Power and Matthews, 1997). The effects of poor social and emotional development can be long-lasting. In the EPPE study, for example, children whose parents reported child development problems before the age of three showed lower attainment in mathematics and English at age 11; children who had one behavioural problem had lower skills in self-regulation and fewer positive behaviours (Sylva et al., 2010). There is also growing evidence that children from lower socio-economic backgrounds also have higher rates of mental ill-health and diagnosed mental illness (Bradley and Corwyn, 2002). Based on Melzer's 2000 study of child mental health in Britain, Spencer argues that:

> If all children had the same risk of mental disorder as the highest income groups, then there would be 40.6 per cent fewer mental disorders, 59.3 per cent fewer conduct disorders (anti-social behaviours), 53.7 per cent fewer hyperkinetic disorders (ADHD) and 34.4 per cent fewer emotional disorders. (Spencer, 2008)

Some of these impacts could again occur before birth. For example, foetal alcohol spectrum disorder (FASD) has been identified as a leading known cause of intellectual disability in the Western world (Abel and Sokol, 1986) and is linked to alcohol consumption in pregnancy. People with an FASD can have difficulty in the following areas: learning and remembering, understanding and following directions, shifting attention, controlling emotions and impulsivity, communicating and socialising, practising daily life skills, including feeding, bathing, counting money, telling time and minding personal safety. FASD-related brain damage makes it difficult to deal with routine life situations. It causes people to make bad decisions, repeat the same mistakes, trust the wrong people, and have difficulty understanding the consequences of their actions (National Institute on Alcohol Abuse and Alcoholism, n.d.). Psychosocial stress during pregnancy has also been linked to increased risk for attention deficit hyperactivity disorder, schizophrenia and social abnormalities (Mulder et al., 2002).

Once children are born, the attachments that children form with their parents are important in influencing how they will relate to others (Music, 2010). Children who experience poor treatment at home (physical abuse, physical neglect, psychological unavailability or verbal abuse) are more likely to behave aggressively to peers in nursery school, even if the setting is nurturing and supportive, and this can persist into adolescence (Carlson et al., 2004; Sroufe et al., 2005).

The quality of family relationships can also explain some of the socio-economic gradient in social and emotional outcomes. Financial difficulty and worklessness is associated with higher levels of stress and poor mental health, including depression (Kiernan and Mensah, 2011) and increased social isolation (Gutman et al., 2009), which can, in turn, lead to parents displaying more irrational and volatile behaviour, or being unable to focus on their child's development and needs, both of which can impair the parent–child relationship. Consequently, the development of secure attachment in the child is disrupted as well as the mother's ability to provide positive, responsive parenting and learning opportunities (Maggi et al., 2010).

Children born to mothers with poor mental health, and particularly those children exposed to prolonged or repeated maternal mental ill health, have been found to display delayed language development, greater levels of misconduct, negative social and emotional development, poor physical health and lower levels of attachment. Levels of poor mental health, stress and depression are higher in poorer socio-economic groups (see Pordes-Bowers et al., 2012).

Research has also shown that the presence of adverse childhood experiences (ACEs) can increase the chances of children and young people experiencing mental illness or a low level of mental well-being, including low self-esteem, depression and relationship difficulties. WHO Euro reports that post-traumatic stress disorder has been reported in as many as a quarter of abused children (World Health Organisation, 2013).

An analysis of the 1958 British birth cohort study estimated the impact of childhood adversities on psychopathology (anxiety/affective/mood symptoms and diagnoses) across the life course (Clark et al., 2010). This is one of the few studies that focus on older children. Figure 3.2 summarises some of the results related to adversity in the home.

Figure 3.2 shows varying impacts of different ACEs over time. For example, some ACEs, such as divorce of parents, have a higher impact on mental illness at younger ages, which declines over time. Conversely, the impact of physical or sexual abuse seems to increase with advancing age. The Chief Medical Officer's recent report on mental health has estimated that child abuse is responsible for between a quarter and a third of all adult mental illness (see Howard et al., 2014, p. 228).

It is possible that exposure to ACE during childhood and adolescence increases the likelihood of an individual adopting health-harming behaviours, including substance misuse, alcohol misuse, smoking, sexual risk behaviour, violence and criminality, or behaviours leading to obesity. An English study published in 2014 also found a correlation between number of ACEs and health-harming behaviours. The increased odds ratios associated with four or more ACEs varied from 2.0 for poor diet to 11.34 for incarceration. Heroin or crack cocaine use also showed a significantly increased odds ratio of 10.88 (Bellis et al., 2014).

Adolescents and young people who grow up in disadvantageous conditions face higher risks of external injury, and are more likely to engage in excessive alcohol intake and other risk behaviours. More than half of deaths among adolescents are from external causes; the major modes are transport injuries, intentional and non-intentional injuries including suicide and violent deaths (Wolfe et al., 2014).

Oral Health

Finally, we do need to say something about inequalities in oral health. The 2003 Children's Dental Health Survey (Office for National Statistics, 2003) found that children attending primary schools in socially deprived areas of the UK were reported to have experienced more tooth decay than children in schools in non-deprived areas. In deprived areas, 60 per cent of five-year-old and 70 per cent of eight-year-old pupils have obvious decay in their primary

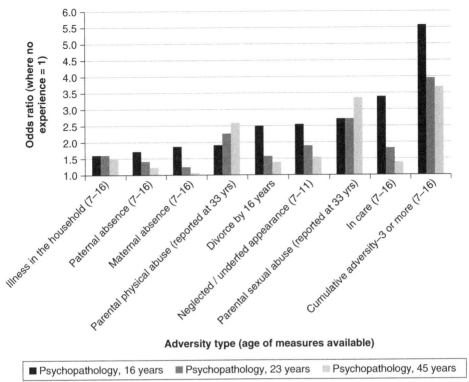

Adversity type (age of measures available)

■ Psychopathology, 16 years ■ Psychopathology, 23 years ▓ Psychopathology, 45 years

Figure 3.2 Varying impacts of different ACEs over time.
Source: using data from Clark et al. (2010).
N.B. this is controlling for sex and SES. There are higher rates for unadjusted rates.

'milk' teeth, compared with 40 per cent of five-year-olds and 55 per cent of eight-year-olds attending schools in non-deprived areas. Among both five- and eight-year-olds the probability of having decay into dentine or obvious decay experience of the primary teeth was about 50 per cent higher in the lowest social group than in the highest.

Policy Options

This chapter provides a broad view of some of the social determinants of poor child health and from this there are some key messages to improve child health, for example, increase breastfeeding, ensure good maternal and child nutrition, reduce smoking and drug and alcohol misuse and ensure children visit dentists regularly. However, all of these are socially graded and if the impact of poverty and education on the ability to buy healthy diets or give up bad behaviours is ignored, then health promotion messaging around these is likely to have limited impact. There are essentially two options for reducing the impact of inequalities – reducing inequalities or mitigating the impact.

Reducing Inequalities

Absolute child poverty is an increasing problem in the UK, with 35 per cent of households with children not having an income high enough to ensure an acceptable standard of living

(Padley et al., 2014). Pressures on families are increasing throughout Europe, and are likely to be exacerbated by ongoing economic problems and reduced public service funding. There are frequent news stories about increasing strain on the National Health Service (NHS) and on Child and Adolescent Mental Health Services (CAMHS). Food poverty and hunger are growing problems in the UK, with over a million households using foodbanks (The Trussell Trust, 2014).

A key policy priority should be to ensure a minimum income for healthy living. In *Fair Society, Healthy Lives* we set out the importance of setting a minimum income for healthy living for addressing inequalities (The Marmot Review Team, 2010). The minimum income for healthy living includes the costs relating to purchasing those things that are needed to ensure adequate levels of nutrition, physical activity, housing, psychosocial interaction, clothing, transport, heating and hygiene (Morris et al., 2000). The University of York have developed a Minimum Income Standard which has a similar focus, but which also includes sufficient resources to participate in society and maintain human dignity, consuming those goods and services regarded as essential in modern-day Britain.

The level of income that a family has is a function of their wages, the available social protection and the costs of the goods and services that they buy. Any attempts to increase incomes should also consider these in the round. A significant challenge is that over half of British children in poverty now live in households where someone is working (MacInnes et al., 2013), and we therefore need to seek ways of improving the incomes of working-poor households. A living wage, based upon how much it costs to live a healthy life, should be available to those earning less than that amount as a first step; however, this is still very low and efforts should be made to ensure that all households across the income distribution earn enough through work. Many councils have adopted the living wage; in addition, ensuring that contracts are awarded to those adopting the living wage is another method of promoting this, as well as the use of local business advisors. For example, Islington Council was one of the first authorities to receive London Living Wage accreditation through Citizens UK, in March 2012. They pay all directly employed staff the living wage and agreed a schedule to ensure all council contracts will meet the living wage criteria by 2014 (Islington Council, 2012). The council is also working with a range of organisations in the borough, including schools, public sector providers and private businesses, to encourage and support them to pay the living wage (Islington Council, 2012).

Social protection (the benefit system) should support those who are unemployed and who do not earn enough to support a family. Ensuring that social protection is sufficient to support a family to live a healthy life is a role for central government. Supportive family policy can help protect children from the damaging effects of poverty and inequality. Countries that spend more on social protection for families have lower child mortality rates (World Health Organisation, 2014). Identifying where money is insufficient and intervening with discretionary grants is a role for local authorities. Local authorities should ensure that they have effective safety nets, and efforts could be made to curb rises in the prices of goods and services and housing at a local level. For example, many local authorities across the country, such as Coventry and Hammersmith and Fulham, chose to absorb the 10 per cent reduction in Council Tax Benefit that was made when the benefit was passed to councils to administer. This relieves some of the pressure on incomes of many households facing financial difficulties.

Mitigating Actions

Inequalities accumulate and so it makes much sense to reduce them as early as possible. Inequalities in the womb and in family life can lead to inequalities in children's health and educational outcomes which then translate to health and economic inequalities later in life.

We need to get better at early identification and treatment of maternal depression, alcohol and drug misuse in pregnancy and we need to provide good quality support to improve parenting skills by communicating 'what works' to all parents, with interventions available to those who might be most at risk.

There are insufficient policies designed to improve social determinants of health, in part because while the public health sector understands the issues, the levers rest with other disciplines and government departments. Anxious to do something, public health officials revert to policies to modify health behaviours. However, these are often set to fail because people with social disadvantages may not have the self-esteem, personal agency, financial resources or positive mental health required to make lasting lifestyle changes. Improving negative health behaviours such as smoking and alcohol consumption requires a nuanced and evidenced approach to health policy. We need to tackle stress alongside asking people to change their behaviours, by, for instance, providing debt or housing advice and solving social problems. Then we need to make healthy choices the easy ones to make – for instance, by implementing policies such as financial subsidies on fruit and vegetables and taxes on less healthy foods, plain packaging of tobacco and minimum price per unit of alcohol (Wolfe et al., 2014). We need to ensure that decent housing is affordable, adequately insulated and free from damp. And all these policies to improve social determinants must be targeted proportionately across the social gradient to reduce health inequalities. We need to recognise that it is not just the difference between the richest and poorest but that there is a social gradient, and ignoring those in the middle, who have worse outcomes than the wealthiest, will miss much of the problem.

I will conclude with two points. The first is that approximately a quarter of all deaths under the age of one could potentially be avoided if all births had the same level of risk as those to women with the lowest level of deprivation (The Marmot Review Team, 2010). And the second is that while we have focused here on determinants of child health, we do believe that practitioners should not lose sight of the determinants of adult health that arise in childhood. For optimal adult health, we need to address not only child health, but also wider development outcomes, because these will impact on economic security in later life. The Equal Start framework developed by the Institute of Health Equity lists the wider set of outcomes that children's services should be seeking to improve and maximise children's life chances (Pordes-Bowers et al., 2012) and *Measuring What Matters* sets out how to measure these outcomes (Roberts and Donkin, 2013; Roberts et al., 2013).

References

Abel, E. L. and Sokol, R. J. (1986) Fetal alcohol syndrome is now leading cause of mental retardation. *Lancet*, 2, 1222.

Arenz, S., Ruckerl, R., Koletzko, B. and Von Kries, R. (2004) Breast-feeding and childhood obesity: a systematic review.

International Journal of Obesity and Related Metabolism Disorders, 28, 1247–56.

Baker, P. N., Wheeler, S. J., Sanders, T. A., Thomas, J. E., Hutchinson, C. J., Clarke, K., Berry, J. L., Jones, R. L., Seed, P. T. and Poston, L. (2009) A prospective study of micronutrient status in adolescent pregnancy. *American Journal of Clinical Nutrition*, 89, 1114–24.

Bates, B., Lennox, A., Prentice, A., Bates, C. and Swan, G. (2012) National Diet and Nutrition Survey. Headline results from Years 1, 2 and 3 (combined of the Rolling Programme 2008/2009–2010/11).

Bellis, M. A., Hughes, K., Leckenby, N., Perkins, C. and Lowey, H. (2014) National household survey of adverse childhood experiences and their relationship with resilience to health-harming behaviors in England. *BMC Medicine*, 12, 72.

Bradley, R. H. and Corwyn, R. F. (2002) Socioeconomic status and child development. *Annual Review of Psychology*, 53, 371–99.

Carlson, E. A., Sroufe, L. A. and Egeland, B. (2004) The construction of experience: a longitudinal study of representation and behavior. *Child Development*, 75, 66–83.

Clark, C., Caldwell, T., Power, C. and Stansfeld, S. A. (2010) Does the influence of childhood adversity on psychopathology persist across the lifecourse? A 45-year prospective epidemiologic study. *Annals of Epidemiology*, 20, 385–94.

Department for Environment, Food and Rural Affairs (Defra) (2012) *Family Food 2011*. London: Defra.

Department of Health (1999) *Saving Lives: Our Healthier Nation*. London: The Stationery Office.

Dibben, C., Sigala, M. and Macfarlane, A. (2006) Area deprivation, individual factors and low birth weight in England: is there evidence of an 'area effect'? *Journal of Epidemiology and Community Health*, 60, 1053–9.

Drewnowski, A., Darmon, N. and Briend, A. (2004) Replacing fats and sweets with vegetables and fruits – a question of cost. *American Journal of Public Health*, 94(9), 1555–9.

Drewnowski, A., Monsivais, P., Maillot, M. and Darmon, N. (2007) Low-energy-density diets are associated with higher diet quality and higher diet costs in French adults. *Journal of American Dietary Association*, 107(6), 1028–32. doi: 10.1016/j.jada.2007.03.013.

Ermisch, J. (2008) Origins of social immobility and inequality: parenting and early child development. *National Institute Economic Review*, 5, 62–71.

Gutman, L. M., Brown, J. and Akerman, R. (2009) *Nurturing Parenting Capability: The Early Years*. Research report 30. London: Centre for Research on the Wider Benefits of Learning, Institute of Education.

Health and Social Care Information Centre (2013) Hospital episode statistics. NHS maternity statistics, 2012–13. HSCIC, London.

Hediger, M. L., Overpeck, M. D., Ruan, W. J. and Troendle, J. F. (2002) Birthweight and gestational age effects on motor and social development. *Pediatric and Prenatal Epidemiology*, 16, 33–46.

Howard, L., Shaw, J., Oram, S., Khalifeh, H. and Flynn, S. (2014) Violence and mental health. In *Annual Report of the Chief Medical Officer 2013, Public Mental Health Priorities: Investing in the Evidence*. Crown Copyright. Available at: www.gov.uk/government/publications/chief-medical-officer-cmo-annual-report-public-mental-health

Islington Council (2012) How Islington is implementing the London Living Wage. Islington Council, London. Available at: www.islington.gov.uk/publicrecords/library/Finance/Information/Factsheets/2012–2013/(2012-07-11)-london-living-wage-case-study.pdf (accessed 7 April 2014).

Jennings, K. D., Stagg, V. and Connors, R. E. (1991) Social networks and mothers' interactions with their preschool children. *Child Development*, 62, 966–78.

Kiernan, K. E. and Mensah, F. K. (2011) Poverty, family resources and children's early educational attainment: the mediating role of parenting. *British Educational Research Journal*, 37, 317–36.

Lifestyle Statistics Team (2013) National Child Measurement Programme: England, 2012/13 school year. HSCIC, London.

MacInnes, T., Aldridge, H., Bushe, S., Kenway, P. and Tinson, A. (2013) *Monitoring Poverty and Social Exclusion 2013*. York: Joseph Rowntree Foundation.

Maggi, S., Irwin, L. J., Siddiqi, A. and Hertzman, C. (2010) The social determinants of early child development: an overview. *Journal of Paediatrics and Child Health*, 46(11), 627–35.

Maillot, M., Ferguson, E. L., Drewnowski, A. and Darmon, N. (2008) Nutrient profiling can help identify foods of good nutritional quality for their price: a validation study with linear programming. *Journal of Nutrition*, 138(6), 1107–13.

McAndrew, F., Thompson, J., Fellows, L., Large, A., Speed, M. and Renfrew, M. J. (2012) *Infant Feeding Survey 2010*. Dundee: Health and Social Care Information Centre.

Moody, A. (2013) Adult anthropometric measures over weight and obesity. In *Health Survey for England 2012. Health, Social Care and Lifestyles*. London: HSCIC.

Morris, J. N., Donkin, A. J. M., Wonderling, D., Wilkinson, P. and Dowler, E. A. (2000) A minimum income for healthy living. *Journal of Epidemiology and Community Health*, 54, 885–9.

Mulder, E. J., Robles De Medina, P. G., Huizink, A. C., Van Den Bergh, B. R., Buitelaar, J. K. and Visser, G. H. (2002) Prenatal maternal stress: effects on pregnancy and the (unborn) child. *Early Human Development*, 70, 3–14.

Music, G. (2010) *Nurturing Natures: Attachment and Children's Emotional, Sociocultural and Brain Development*. Hove and New York: Psychology Press.

National Institute on Alcohol Abuse and Alcoholism (n.d.) Fetal alcohol exposure. Available at: https://niaaa.nih.gov/alcohol-health/fetal-alcohol-exposure (accessed 26 March 2018).

Oakley, L., Maconochie, N., Doyle, P., Dattani, N. and Moser, K. (2009) Multivariate analysis of infant death in England and Wales in 2005–06, with focus on socio-economic status and deprivation. *Health Statistics Quarterly*, 42, 22–39.

Office for National Statistics (2003) *Children's Dental Health Survey*. London: The Stationery Office.

Office for National Statistics (2014) Vital statistics: population and health reference tables, 2014. Available at: www.ons.gov.uk/ons/publications/re-reference-tables.html?edition=tcm%3A77-353343 (accessed 31 July 2015).

Owen, C. G., Martin, R. M., Whincup, P. H., Smith, G. D. and Cook, D. G. (2005) Effect of infant feeding on the risk of obesity across the life course: a quantitative review of published evidence. *Pediatrics*, 115, 1367–77.

Padley, M., Valadez, L. and Hirsch, D. (2014) Households below a minimum income standard: 2008/9 to 2012/13. JRF Programme Paper – Minimum Income Standards, Joseph Rowntree Foundation, York.

Pordes-Bowers, A., Strelitz, J., Allen, J. and Donkin, A. (2012) *An Equal Start: Improving Outcomes in Children's Centres*. London: UCL Institute of Health Equity.

Power, C. and Matthews, S. (1997) Origins of health inequalities in a national population sample. *Lancet*, 350, 1584–9.

Reichman, N. (2005) Low birth weight and school readiness. In 'School readiness: Closing racial and ethnic gaps', *The Future of Children*, 15(1), 91–116. Available at: http://futureofchildren.org/publications/journals/article/index.xml?journalid=38&articleid=118&sectionid=775

Ricketts, S. A., Murray, E. K. and Schwalberg, R. (2005) Reducing low birthweight by resolving risks: results from Colorado's Prenatal Plus Program. *American Journal Public Health*, 57(11), 1952–7.

Roberts, A., Cavill, N., Hancock, C. and Rutter, H. (2013) *Social and Economic Inequalities in Diet and Physical Activity*. London: Public Health England.

Roberts, J. and Donkin, A. (2013) *Measuring What Matters: A Guide for Children's Centres*. London: Institute of Health Equity.

Rogers, I. (2003) The influence of birth weight and intrauterine environment on adiposity and fat distribution in later life. *International Journal of Obesity and Related Metabolic Disorders*, 27, 755–77.

Ryley, A. (2013) Children's BMI, overweight and obesity. In *Health Survey for England 2012. Health, Social Care and Lifestyles.* London: HSCIC.

Spencer, N. (2008) *Health Consequences of Poverty for Children*. London: End Child Poverty.

Sroufe, L. A., Egeland, B., Carlson, E. A. and Collins, W. A. (2005) *The Development of the Person: The Minnesota Study of Risk and Adaptation from Birth to Adulthood.* New York: Guilford Press.

Sylva, K., Melhuish, E., Sammons, P., Siraj-Blatchford, I. and Taggart, B. (2010) *Early Childhood Matters. Evidence from the Effective Pre-school and Primary Education Project.* London: Routledge.

Syse, A., Lyngstad, T. and Kravdal, O. (2011) Is mortality after childhood cancer dependent on social or economic resources of parents? A population-based study. *International Journal of Cancer*, 130(8), 1870–8.

Talge, N. M., Neal, C. and Glover, V. (2007) Antenatal maternal stress and long-term effects on child neurodevelopment: how and why? *Journal of Child Psychology and Psychiatry*, 48, 245–61.

The Marmot Review Team (2010) *Fair Society, Healthy Lives: Strategic Review of Health Inequalities in England Post-2010.* London: Marmot Review Team.

The Trussell Trust (2014) Foodbank use tops 1 million says Trussell Trust. Available at: www.trusselltrust.org/resources/documents/Press/Trussell-Trust-foodbank-use-tops-one-million.pdf (accessed 2 September 2015).

Wolfe, I., Macfarlane, A., Donkin, A., Marmot, M. and Viber, R. (2014) *Why Children Die: Death in Infants, Children and Young People in the UK. Part A.* London: RCPCH and NCD.

World Health Organisation (2013) *European Report on Preventing Child Maltreatment.* Copenhagen, Denmark: WHO.

World Health Organisation Regional Office for Europe (2014) *Review of Social Determinants and the Health Divide in the WHO European Region: Final Report.* Copenhagen, Denmark: WHO.

Chapter

4

Philosophical Ethics and Children*

Mar Cabezas and Gunter Graf

In this chapter, we will first address the question of how philosophy has traditionally explored childhood and show that this topic has been relatively neglected throughout Western philosophical traditions. Second, we will focus on some comparatively recent conceptualisations on children and their moral status, concluding that their vulnerability in combination with their ability to develop and unfold their potentials provide a basis for building a normative theory in favour of children's appropriate recognition as subjects of moral thinking in which the concepts of well-being and well-becoming have a major role to play.

A Brief History of Philosophical Thinking about Children

Ethics is certainly one of the main fields of philosophy and as such it accounts for a vast literature on a variety of topics. However, children have not figured prominently in these discussions for a long time, especially if one looks at what has been done in other fields such as moral psychology or sociology. Children are often introduced only as 'borderline cases' when differences in the moral status of human beings and others species are discussed or when philosophers analyse the controversial issues about the beginning of life, human agency and human nature. In these cases, generalisations and comparisons with other beings (adults and non-human animals) are often made without paying specific attention to substantial differences and differences in degree. As a result, the visibility of the particular moral status and challenges connected to children and childhood is still underdeveloped.

While philosophers have successfully addressed questions about gender, racial and ethnic discrimination, the absence of the specific recognition of children as vulnerable beings seems to have been a persistent feature. As a result, moral problems concerning childhood, such as child poverty, vulnerability, neglect, agency and decision-making, asymmetric relations, peer violence, abuses, sexual trafficking, exploitation, etc., have not played a central role in ethical theories.

Surely, one might think that there are cases in our philosophical past where children played a central role. One could be thinking of Rousseau's *Emile* (1979) or Locke's *Some thoughts concerning education* (1996), or even of Plato's *Republica* (2008). However, the interest was focused on education and/or on how a society should be organised, concretely on how to become an excellent adult, how to flourish, etc., instead of on children as morally relevant beings. In other words, the concern was not related to the value of children *qua* children, but to human *arête*. Some classic paradigmatic examples of this oblivion could be the Aristotelian idea that a son was a father's possession – and that nothing unfair could be done to what is yours – or the Roman *patria potestas*, both focused on adults' rights over children. Another example of the lack of genuine concern about children can be found in the social reformers from the mid-nineteenth century. They were certainly concerned about poor, abandoned or orphaned children. However, the central question at that time was not the immediate well-being of children, nor the damage suffered by them, but the belief that children in those situations could end up being potential criminals in the future. In this sense, the main issue was still adulthood (Cantón and Cortés, 1997).

In the classic nature versus nurture debate young children appear as 'guinea pigs', as a way of observing what is innate for human nature and what is a product of culture and socialisation. From ancient philosophy and the Hellenist Schools of thought, such as Stoicism (Cicero, 2010, Fin III, 16) and Epicurism (Epicurus, 1926, pp. 128–9), to contemporary debates on educative systems, the discussion is centred on what goods are necessary for human beings, what makes human beings happy and what is rescindable. Children are mentioned when arguments against or in favour of human natural egoism, goodness, evilness or sociability are defended, but usually as part of an experiment seeing in them the core of the adult they will become: 'All the ancient philosophers, in particular those of our school, turn to cradles (*ad incunabula accedunt*) because it is in childhood [*in pueritia*] that they think we can most easily recognize the will of nature [*naturae voluntatem cognoscere*]' (Brunschwig, 1986, p. 113).

Indeed, you might be surprised to find that animal rights were recognised and defended in the nineteenth century before the well-being of children was even an issue in public debates.[1] Furthermore, it was not until the mid-twentieth century, thanks to Kempe's work, that a National Centre of Child Abuse and Neglect was created and that the legal situation started changing, obliging paediatrics to report that kind of cases.

At the same time, it is worth remembering that an interest in bioethics was simultaneously emerging during the twentieth century with Potter's (1971) and Helleger's work as a reaction, among other causes, to the abuses against participants' rights in scientific research. This led, first, to the creation – during the same year – of the Joseph and Rose Kennedy Institute for the Study of Human Reproduction and Bioethics; second, and over the following decades, to a tremendous development of medical ethics, applied ethics and gender studies, technology and genetic ethics debates; and, lately, also to a fruitful development of animal ethics and ecoethics. Nevertheless, the specific ethical problems concerning children did not find the same kind of attention.

In bioethics, they are typically brought into the discussion in relation to complex cases and dilemmas concerning reproduction and the beginning of life; such is the case of anencephalic babies (Singer, 1996) and their state of consciousness. In discussions about eugenics, human cloning, genetic engineering and reproduction, the debate is focused on the moral status of embryos and the foetus so that the discussion rarely delves into childhood itself and the potential moral damage throughout this crucial phase of life. Moreover, the debates end up addressing questions about human nature and the abstract concept of humanity, instead of focusing on 'real' children or newborns. The debates commonly revolve around whether there is an intrinsic value of natural beings versus genetically manipulated ones, whether human beings have the right to have a non-manipulated genetic patrimony (Habermas, 2003), the cost and/or wrongness for the species of artificially choosing some traits, and how manipulations would affect the future of human beings and our responsibilities towards future – adult – generations. However, the question of how all these decisions at the beginning of life would affect the living conditions of children is hardly ever addressed.

In relation to abortion, the matter is mainly devoted to when human life begins. Likewise, if the pregnant woman is a minor, then the question becomes whether she is morally autonomous in making her own decisions. Hence, bioethics normally leaps from newborns to mature adolescents.

Children also appeared mainly in a passing way in philosophical thought experiments, as a footnote or as a good example in making a point on whatever was the main issue. They are often mentioned, but seldom the centre of attention; for example, they appear in fictional moral dilemmas such as the implications of killing your baby or saving 20 lives. Likewise, children are mentioned in hypothetical controversial cases such as the *sinking boat* examples where an adult has to decide whether he would save his pet or an unknown woman's baby, just to mention some of the most recurrent examples in exercises of moral imagination. Here, children are almost seen as a tool to exercise moral reasoning and, in debates concerning animal rights, as means to challenge our moral beliefs, concretely against speciesism. Sometimes they are seen as means to persuade us to defend animals rights and/or animal liberation. Just to provide an illustration, there is the famous example of comparing slapping a horse and slapping a human baby as a way to challenge moral thresholds (Singer, 1993). These vast generalisations and analogies obstruct the perceptibility of children, given the fact that the spotlight is set on non-human animals. In fact, philosophy started asking questions about vegetative life, the inherent value of nature and ecosystems – with approaches such as the deep ecology – even before developing specific accounts on children.

You could claim that children played a key role in moral psychology with authors such as Piaget (1997) and Kohlberg (1984), whose theories had a huge impact in practical philosophy. Of course, these theories centred their attention on childhood and morality, but neither in their moral problems per se, nor from a philosophical perspective. Besides, they led to a new wave of feminism and critical scrutiny on their biased interpretation in relation to women (Gilligan, 1993), but not on children.

All this has surely contributed not only to a lack of specific approaches on childhood from a philosophical and ethical point of view, but also to tacit assumptions and idealisations about childhood itself, which does not help explore the complexity involved in the problems concerning children.

Children as Subjects of Philosophy: Insights from Current Debates

As we argued in the first section, philosophy has neglected children widely in its history and even today many theories in ethics, political philosophy and other branches of philosophy do not deal adequately with the specific challenges children pose for normative reasoning and continue treating them in a rather undifferentiated way. However, in recent decades there have been many valuable contributions on the moral status of children, shedding light on many of the complex issues involved, and there is now a vivid and ongoing ethical debate getting more and more attention in the scientific community (e.g. Aiken and LaFollette, 1980; Archard and Macleod, 2002; Archard, 2004; Bagattini and Macleod, 2014). The philosophers involved go beyond a narrow focus on questions regarding the beginning of life, the demarcation of the human species from other animals in terms of ethical value, or the conceptualisation of children primarily as 'adults-to-be' and reflect the wider social and political context children are part of and the particular functions of childhood not only as a developmental phase but also as a life stage with its own value. In this section, we will briefly look at some aspects of these debates, focusing particularly on the nature of children as vulnerable and developing beings on their way to becoming autonomous agents. In doing so, we will not look at them as 'borderline cases' or analyse the morally relevant differences between different species, but we will rather begin by identifying some promising starting points for constructing a child-sensitive ethics. Or to put it differently, we will assume (without arguing for it) that children *have* a moral status and that they are in fact of equal moral worth as all other members of a community or society. But since they possess specific characteristics which make them special for ethical reasoning (Brennan and Noggle, 1997), it is crucial to make them explicit and to address the implications they have.

The first characteristic we want to stress is every child's vulnerability (Mullin, 2014; Gheaus, 2017). In fact, children are, for a considerable time, completely dependent on others and would not even be able to survive on their own. The feature of vulnerability, albeit relevant for all human beings, applies to children to a larger extent and is closely connected to the formative role of childhood for the whole life, as well as the lack of relevant competences for leading a self-determined and autonomous life. Harm in childhood is very likely to cause major damage and children are also in a weak position to secure their own well-being and to defend themselves against negative influences. Of course, these assumptions have to be adapted to different developmental stages and as children grow up, their vulnerabilities decrease and the differences to adults disappear more and more. Nevertheless, it is reasonable to acknowledge that these vulnerabilities in their different degrees significantly contribute to their special status that has to be grasped by ethical thinking.

Children are vulnerable in different aspects, and in a first systematisation one can distinguish between physical, mental and social vulnerabilities (Graf and Schweiger, 2015). Physical ones are directly related to the child's body which is, especially in the early years, very sensitive and which can be seriously injured – or even cause death – by interferences (e.g. shaking heavily) that generally do not generate any harm for adults. These harms affect the child's current situation, but they certainly can have long-lasting consequences, which are often extremely difficult or even impossible to compensate. A second form of vulnerability concerns the mental dimension. For instance, many psychological studies show that childhood is a highly sensitive and, in many aspects, unique phase when it comes to the development of the self and one's personality. There are, for example, clear relations between early attachment security and the levels of emotional health, self-esteem, agency and self-confidence, etc. experienced later on (Thompson, 2007). It is important to separate the physical and mental aspects of children's vulnerability on an analytical level. However, they are highly interconnected and have to be taken together in any applied analysis of child abuse and neglect. The third form of vulnerability we want to mention is the social one. Childhood cannot only be interpreted in relation to biological, psychological and medical knowledge. It is a social category as well that can be framed in many different ways (James and Prout, 2005). The dependence children experience from adults is not only a matter of their 'nature', but always connected to the legal, political and economic system of a society. In many ways, children are powerless and ethical thinking has to reflect to what degree and in which ways this is justifiable or if it constitutes a form of oppression that should be abandoned.

In the previous section we mentioned the tendency of many philosophers to look at children primarily as 'adults-to-be' and criticised this as being too narrow since it neglects the particular interests and needs of children. However, an ethical approach towards children must include considerations of their future and valuable traits a society should try to foster in its members. And it is here, where a second important feature of an ethics of childhood enters: children are developing beings on their way to becoming autonomous agents (Noggle, 2002). Three things are important here. First, childhood is a very dynamic phase and it is difficult to make generalisations about it. What is important for a toddler is very different to what a teenager needs and an ethically adequate treatment has to take these differences into account. Second, the fact that the concept of autonomy with all its legal and political consequences only applies to adults must not be interpreted in a way that conceptualises children as passive beings. They are, on the contrary, active agents from a very early age. Their agency gradually develops, they are capable of participating in their social world and can employ ethical categories (Mayall, 2002). However, their vulnerabilities, lack of relevant skills and experience implies that their agency does not automatically lead to a right of self-determination, which is usually a part of autonomy. Third, autonomy, as we understand it here and which we see as one important goal childhood should prepare one for, has strong moral features and must not be identified with an unconditional freedom of choice of an individual who is detached from a community or social commitments. Rather, it refers to a person's ability to develop, follow and revise a life plan, which is consistent with the interests of other members of the community and includes a person's commitment to contributing to the common good.

A promising way to specify these thoughts and to formulate more clearly what children deserve from an ethical point of view is to connect the discussion to the *well-being* and *well-becoming* of children. These concepts have been developed for some time in different disciplines, with a focus on empirical knowledge, questions of measurement and policy issues (McAuley and Rose, 2010; Ben-Arieh et al., 2014). However, recently moral philosophers have taken up these insights and shown that they can play a valuable role in addressing different normative issues and provide an empirically informed basis for the entitlements of children (Bagattini and Macleod, 2014; Graf and Schweiger, 2015). To give a full definition of *well-being* and *well-becoming* from an ethical perspective is beyond what we can achieve in this chapter. However, let us briefly mention some important aspects. *Well-being* relates to the actual state of a child. It expresses what is important for a child in its current situation. *Well-becoming*, on the other hand, focuses on the transition from one state to another. It therefore points to the fact that childhood is also a phase where developments happen and where many skills, competencies and capabilities for a later phase in one's life must be learned. Both the concept of *well-being* and of *well-becoming* typically are discussed as multidimensional ones. They capture different aspects of children's lives (e.g. material, physical and mental and emotional aspects) and integrate objective and subjective dimensions. In other words, it is important for the *well-being* and *well-becoming* of children that they are subjectively happy, but such feelings have to be backed up by many more features of their lives, which are known to contribute to children's flourishing.

A focus on the *well-being* and *well-becoming* of children allows one to consider what is typical and important for different life phases of children and various forms of vulnerability as well as agency. Ethical claims therefore get closer to their 'realities' than has been the case for many years. There is still a lot of work to do and, as is generally the case with any ethical inquiry, it is unlikely that there is a clear-cut end to be found. However, philosophy is certainly on its way to giving a theoretical foundation for one of the most important ethical challenges of our time: to make sure that our world becomes a better place for children.

Notes

* This research was funded by the Austrian Science Fund (FWF): P 26480-G15.

1 While in New York a law against cruelty to animals existed and the American Society for the Prevention of Cruelty to Animals (ASPCA) was already established, no law against child abuse was enacted until the famous Mary Ellen Wilson case in 1874. Thanks to this case, a new law was made and the American Society for the Prevention of Cruelty to Children was instituted, in analogy to the ASPCA (Watkins, 1990). The case can also be consulted in the *New York Times* archives, 28 April 1874, http://query.nytimes.com/mem/archive-free/pdf?res=9D03EFD61039EF34BC4A52DFB266838F669FDE

References

Aiken, W. and LaFollette, H. (eds) (1980) *Whose Child? Children's Rights, Parental Authority, and State Power*. Littlefield Quality Paperbacks 358. Totowa, NJ: Littlefield.

Archard, D. (2004) *Children: Rights and Childhood*, 2nd edn. London and New York: Routledge.

Archard, D. and Macleod, C. M. (eds) (2002) *The Moral and Political Status of Children*, 1st edn. Oxford and New York: Oxford University Press.

Bagattini, A. and Macleod, C. M. (eds) (2014) *The Nature of Children's Well-Being: Theory and Practice*, 1st edn. New York: Springer.

Ben-Arieh, A., Casas, F., Frønes, I. and Korbin, J. E. (eds) (2014) *Handbook of Child Well-Being: Theory, Indicators, Measures and Policies*, 1st edn. Dordrecht and New York: Springer.

Brennan, S. and Noggle, R. (1997) The moral status of children: children's rights, parent's rights, and family justice. *Social Theory and Practice*, 23(1), 1–26.

Brunschwig, J. (1986) The cradle argument in epicureanism and stoicism. In M. Schofield and G. Striker (eds), *The Norms of Nature*. Cambridge: Cambridge University Press, pp. 113–44.

Cantón Duarte, J. and Cortés Arboleda, Ma. R. (1997) *Malos tratos y abuso sexual infantil: causas, consecuencias e intervención*. Madrid: Siglo XXI.

Cicero, M. T. (2010) *De Finibus Bonorum et Malorum*. Cambridge: Cambridge University Press.

Epicurus (1926) Letter to Menoeceus. In *Epicurus: The Extant Remains*, ed. C.

Bailey. Oxford: Oxford University Press, pp. 83–93.

Gheaus, A. (2017) Children's vulnerability and legitimate authority over children. *Journal of Applied Philosophy*, doi:10.1111/japp.12262.

Gilligan, C. (1993) *In a Different Voice: Psychological Theory and Women's Development*. Cambridge, MA: Harvard University Press.

Graf, G. and Schweiger, G. (eds) (2015) *The Well-Being of Children: Philosophical and Social Scientific Approaches*, 1st edn. Berlin: De Gruyter.

Habermas, J. (2003) *The Future of Human Nature*. Cambridge: Polity.

James, A. and Prout, A. (eds) (2005) *Constructing and Reconstructing Childhood: Contemporary Issues in the Sociological Study of Childhood*, 2nd edn. London and Washington, DC: Falmer Press.

Kohlberg, L. (1984) *The Psychology of Moral Development: The Nature and Validity of Moral Stages*, 1st edn. Essays on Moral Development, v. 2. San Francisco, CA: Harper and Row.

Locke, J. (1996) *Some Thoughts Concerning Education and of the Conduct of the Understanding: And of the Conduct of the Understanding*. Indianapolis, IN: Hackett.

Mayall, B. (2002) *Towards a Sociology for Childhood: Thinking from Children's Lives*. Buckingham and Philadelphia, PA: Open University Press.

McAuley, C. and Rose, W. (eds) (2010) *Child Well-Being: Understanding Children's*

Lives, 1st edn. London and Philadelphia, PA: Jessica Kingsley Publishers.

Mullin, A. (2014) Children, vulnerability, and emotional harm. In C. Mackenzie, W. Rogers and S. Dodds (eds), *Vulnerability*, 1st edn. New York: Oxford University Press, pp. 266–87.

Noggle, R. (2002) Special agents: children's autonomy and parental authority. In D. Archard and C. M. Macleod (eds), *The Moral and Political Status of Children*, 1st edn. Oxford and New York: Oxford University Press, pp. 97–117.

Piaget, J. (1997) *The Moral Judgment of the Child*. New York: Free Press Paperbacks.

Plato (2008) *Republic*. Translation and notes by Robin Waterfield. Oxford: Oxford University Press.

Potter, V. R. (1971) *Bioethics: Bridge to the Future*. Englewood Cliffs, NJ: Prentice Hall.

Rousseau, J. (1979) *Emile or On Education*. Introduction, translation and notes by Allan Bloom, 1st edn. New York: Basic Books.

Singer, P. (1993) *Practical Ethics*, 2nd edn. Cambridge and New York: Cambridge University Press.

Singer, P. (1996) *Rethinking Life and Death: The Collapse of Our Traditional Ethics*. New York: St Martin's Griffin.

Thompson, R. A. (2007) The development of the person: social understanding, relationships, conscience, self. In W. Damon and R. M. Lerner (eds), *Handbook of Child Psychology. Volume Three: Social, Emotional, and Personality Development*, 6th edn. Hoboken, NJ: John Wiley and Sons, pp. 24–98.

Watkins, S. A. (1990) The Mary Ellen myth: correcting child welfare history. *Social Work*, 35(6), 500–3.

Child Poverty, Well-Being and Social Justice*

Gottfried Schweiger and Gunter Graf

The extent and depth of child poverty is one of the most serious problems of today. Despite the absence of consensus on how it should be conceptualised and measured, all existing studies are clear in stating that the figures are alarmingly high. This is both the case for an absolute understanding of poverty as it is generally used for the global scale and poorer countries, as for a relative concept of child poverty, which is used to capture and assess child poverty in richer countries (UNICEF IRC, 2013). For example, according to the National Center for Children in Poverty in the US, more than 16 million (22 per cent) children under the age of 18 lived in poor families in 2011 (Addy et al., 2013). On a global scale, the World Bank recently reported that more than 400 million children live in severe poverty (Olinto et al., 2013). These figures, as disturbing as they are, can only provide the starting point in examining the normative dimension and injustice of child poverty from a philosophical perspective.

Our considerations in this chapter point towards a more inclusive social policy for children in poverty, which should be guided by the goal of social justice for all children and which should give them the opportunity to live a life in *well-being* and *well-becoming*. By concentrating explicitly on the normative aspect of child poverty and connecting it to its influence on the well-being and well-becoming of children, we also put forward the view that empirical and explanatory knowledge alone, as produced by the social sciences, is neither enough to fully understand child poverty nor can it alone guide practice and politics. In fact, such empirical research is often interspersed by normative assumptions and goals seldom made explicit, which is, or so we will argue, a serious neglect for any theory of poverty.

Social Policy, Justice and the Well-Being of Children

Justice can be conceptualised within different theories and traditions. In the analysis we give in this chapter, we will focus on the so-called 'capability approach', which originated from the works of the economist and philosopher Amartya Sen (1999, 2009). It is influential in a variety of academic disciplines such as the social sciences, development studies, poverty research and philosophy. In addition, it has had a considerable impact on different policy issues. For instance, the United Nations draw on it in their Human Development Index and it informed the work of The Equality and Human Rights Commission in Britain (Deneulin and Shahani, 2009; Burchardt and Vizard, 2011). In regard to justice, the philosopher Martha Nussbaum has further developed it into a partial theory of justice.

One of the central claims of the approach is that evaluations of societal arrangements, quality-of-life assessments and judgements about social justice, development or poverty should primarily focus on people's 'capabilities' and 'functionings'. Functionings are the activities and states that make up a person's life; they are the different 'beings' and 'doings' of which living consists. And since human existence consists of many different doings and beings, the category of functionings is a broad one. Being healthy and educated, having a shelter, taking part in the life of the community are examples of functionings, as are being undernourished, killing animals or feeling emotional distress.

But for the capability approach, it is not enough to look only at the functionings realised by a person in order to compare his or her situation to those of others, but especially at the 'capabilities' one person has. Capabilities are defined as those functionings a person actually has access to and reflects the person's freedom to realise different achievements. To give an example, eating is a functioning while the real opportunity to eat is the respective capability. Resources and goods are very important for a person to enjoy these real freedoms or capabilities. However, there are many factors that determine what someone can do with his or her resources and how he or she can 'convert' them into valuable outcomes. A person's abilities and skills, as well as the political, social and economic context she or he finds herself or himself in, all contribute to this relation between a good and the achievement of certain beings and doings. These different factors, which are relevant for a person's ability to use his or her resources for his or her aims, are usually called 'conversion factors'. We see, then, that material goods do play a fundamental role in the approach. However, they are only considered a means to live a life one has reason to value. What matters in the end is, in the perspective of the capability approach, what each and every person is effectively able to do and to be, not what he or she possesses (Sen, 1999; Nussbaum, 2011). The capability approach has proven to be a useful framework for the evaluation of poverty, including child poverty, and to guide the implementation of justice for children living in poverty. It focuses on questions about what children can really do and achieve in their lives and what the society, the state and its institutions owe to children in terms of capabilities and functionings.

According to the capability approach, a minimal condition for social justice is that a certain threshold of functionings and capabilities is guaranteed for every member of society, and that human flourishing is not the privilege of a small elite but a real option for everyone. The human potential to self-realisation and to unfolding particular powers, which waste away if not fostered and stimulated, ground basic claims of justice which clearly influence the way a society should be arranged. Every person should be seen as an end, not simply as the agent or supporter of the ends of others. Where this threshold has to be set is a question that cannot be determined independently of context and deliberation processes. However, the guiding idea used in the capability approach is that it denotes a level 'beneath which it is held that truly human functioning is not available to citizens' (Nussbaum, 2006, p. 71).

Despite some recent discussions of the topic of social justice for children, it is still under-recognised in the capability approach and most considerations are concerned with fully developed and reasonable adults. We want to try to adapt the central assumptions and claims to the specific status of children in order to give a first brief sketch of what justice for children from a capability perspective could mean. We see the 'well-being' and 'well-becoming' (see definitions in Chapter 4) of children as the normative benchmark and goal of social justice, which means that every child has a claim to grow up in well-being and to have those opportunities for well-becoming and to develop into an autonomous member of society. Such a focus on well-being and well-becoming does justice to the claims of children qua children and to the phase of childhood as one of crucial development. But well-being and well-becoming are not to be understood as states of mere subjective satisfaction. They are multidimensional and encompass a whole range of different capabilities and functionings. A fully developed theory of social justice for children would have to clarify those capabilities and functionings in detail and also discuss their distribution. It would have to look closely at the available theories of child well-being and well-becoming in different disciplines and to flesh out the content of these concepts (Aldgate, 2010; Axford, 2012; Ben-Arieh et al., 2014). Our aims are more modest here. We do not think that for a critique of child poverty as unjust and harmful such a fully elaborated theory is necessary. Rather, it suffices to select some fundamental and relatively uncontroversial dimensions of the well-being and well-becoming of children and to investigate how they are influenced by child poverty. In this way, basic injustices that relate to child poverty can be identified without having a fully developed theory of justice, well-being and well-becoming. We will make clear here that we see health, education, self-respect and inclusion as four fundamental dimensions of well-being and well-becoming. But let us first highlight four crucial issues regarding justice for children.

First, we must note that children are of equal moral worth as all other members of the community and that they deserve the same moral consideration as adults. Their interests and moral claims must not be dismissed simply due to the fact that they are children, still on their way to becoming fully autonomous members of society (Nussbaum, 2006; Brennan and Noggle, 1997). Rather, their status of dependency and immaturity – which, in turn, reduces their own influence regarding access to valuable material and immaterial resources – should actually grant them priority status from a social justice perspective.

Second, empirically speaking, we know that the development of capabilities is a dynamic and complex process starting from a very early age. Therefore, it is necessary as a matter of social justice to engage with human development and to specify age-appropriate sufficiency thresholds for all relevant capabilities. This, of course, involves many empirical investigations and we will not be able to deal with this question in detail here, but it is clear that it is of central importance for the capability approach's understanding of justice for children.

Third, considerations about justice for children have to account for both their current and future well-being, which is sometimes labelled 'well-becoming'. This means that, on the one hand, childhood should be seen as an intrinsically valuable part of human existence, which draws its normative value not only from the benefits it provides for the development of full rational autonomy (Macleod, 2010; Brighouse, 2002). On the other hand, a developmental perspective cannot be ignored either, since childhood is a decisive stage in the formation of many characteristics we value in adulthood.

Fourth, the characteristics of some conversion factors, as we introduced earlier, are typically different in the case of children (Biggeri et al., 2011). The conversion of resources depends heavily on the decisions and actions of others, particularly of those in charge of the child's upbringing. These actions and decisions, however, are also influenced by the entitlements of their caregivers to certain goods, services and rights. A child's age, too, represents a conversion factor, related to individual competencies and social and legal norms that determine, to a certain point, what a child can do and be with the resources to which he or she has access.

Now, there are many functionings and capabilities which are relevant for the well-being and well-becoming of children. For the purpose of this chapter, though, we want to focus on four of them, which are of particular relevance for social justice for children and which must be secured to a sufficiency level for all children of any given society: health, education, self-respect and inclusion. There is a long and unresolved discussion within the capability approach about how a set or list of central capabilities and functionings can be chosen and justified, and we do not claim to have a new solution to this problem. Rather, we argue that there are good reasons to think of four capabilities and functionings as central and as important in any such list or set: health, education, self-respect and inclusion. Certainly, there are other important capabilities and functionings for the well-being and well-becoming of children as well (Biggeri and Mehrotra, 2011), but our claim that child poverty is unjust and harmful for those children can already be supported comprehensively by focusing on these four. Therefore, our arguments in this chapter can be understood as being a part of a bigger project to examine the injustice of child poverty and should not be seen as exhaustive (Graf and Schweiger, 2015).

The reason to select health, education, self-respect and inclusion is twofold: first, all of them represent particularly fundamental aspects of human existence, and there is broad agreement in the capability approach that they are *intrinsically valuable* elements of a good human life (Sen, 1999); second, they are also *instrumentally valuable*, which means that they have a key function in relation to many other dimensions of life, starting in childhood and lasting until old age. They tend to promote the evolvement of other capabilities if adequately cultivated, but may have an extremely corrosive effect if endangered (Biggeri et al., 2011; Wolff and De Shalit, 2007). These interactions and possible synergies deserve particular attention when justice for children is at stake.

The Injustice of Child Poverty

Children in poverty are not able to reach the sufficiency level required and to which they are entitled. They are denied adequate access to at least the basic capabilities and functionings that constitute the minimum threshold in a just society and which must be available before we can speak of a life in well-being. Rather, child poverty is a source of ill-being and ill-development. Therefore, the injustice of child poverty is related to two different areas of concern: the actual well-being of the child and the well-becoming of the child, that is, the effects of child poverty later in life. Both are important in any consideration of the evaluation of child poverty. We will now examine child poverty and its relation to those four basic capabilities of health, education, self-respect and inclusion, and we will particularly look at the life-course effects of child poverty on them.

Health is most definitely a basic capability and a fundamental prerequisite to realise many, if not most, other capabilities and functionings in life (Venkatapuram, 2011). The literature on the relation of health and poverty has grown over recent years and is now conclusive on the negative effects of poverty and socio-economic inequalities on both children and adults (Braveman et al., 2011). In developing countries, problems linked to poverty such as under- and malnutrition, poor hygiene, lack of access to health care and clean water lead to the early death of millions of children each year (Liu et al., 2012). Similarly, in rich countries, children growing up in poverty are not only more likely to have health problems during childhood, but also suffer ill-health in their later lives and die younger than their non-poor peers (Conroy et al., 2010). The pathways are multifactorial and influenced by environmental factors, housing conditions, behavioural patterns, inadequate nutrition, restricted access to health care and to information. Poverty seems to be influential even before birth, with some evidence of negative health outcomes for children resulting from chronic stress due to poverty and financial strains during pregnancy (Dunkel Schetter and Glynn, 2010). Ill health also translates into other problems which affect well-being and has a significant impact on education, inclusion and self-respect as well.

The second capability we have defined as important regarding justice for children is education, which is, again, also a prerequisite for many other capabilities and functionings and for the realisation of real freedoms in life (Walker and Unterhalter, 2010). Education is the basis for reasonable decision-making processes and for the ability to choose and to participate in a whole range of social, cultural, political and economic activities. It is reasonable to speak of knowledge as power; and education is needed to acquire that power and to critically reflect the choices and actions of oneself and others. The influence of poverty on education and on later outcomes in life is well studied: children growing up in poverty have lower academic achievements, face more problems in acquiring skills and knowledge in reading, writing and mathematics; they have more behavioural problems in schools and are more likely to drop out of school and training (Duncan and Murnane, 2011). They are given lower grades than their non-poor peers, and only a few children from lower socio-economic backgrounds pursue tertiary education (Condron, 2011). Such problems in the area of education weigh heavily and are closely connected to unemployment and to the persistence of poor economic status over the life course. Although most of the literature focuses on the relation between poverty and schooling and academic achievement, a concept of education that does not go beyond these terms would be too narrow, since it leaves out important humanist aspects.

The third basic capability we will examine here is that of self-respect, that is, the ability to have a positive self-relation. This capability describes especially the subjective dimension of well-being and how children view themselves, their experiences and their relationship to others and their environment. As we laid out earlier, we define well-being as the composition of highly interrelated, dynamic subjective and objective dimensions (Camfield et al., 2009; McAuley and Rose, 2010). Many children experience their poverty and the poverty of their families negatively. Poor children are often the targets of bullying; they feel humiliated, ashamed, excluded and sometimes even responsible for their own poverty. This knowledge about the subjective dimensions of poverty and the inclusion of the voices and narrations of children is growing and useful (Ridge, 2009; Crowley and Vulliamy, 2007). It clearly shows that poverty lowers the subjective self-perception of these children, and that such experiences may have long-lasting effects. Poor children have lower expectations for their lives. The incidence of depression, drug abuse, self-aggression and suicide is higher in poor adolescents and adults who grew up in socio-economically disadvantaged conditions (Yoshikawa et al., 2012).

Inclusion or belonging is the fourth and final capability we will look at. We understand inclusion as the ability to engage in activities agreed as standard in a certain community. Likewise, exclusion would mean the involuntary inability to engage in such activities (Millar, 2007). In a broad sense, the concepts of inclusion and exclusion can be understood to cover many aspects of health, education and self-respect as we discuss them here, too, but we would rather employ a narrower understanding. Inclusion and belonging refer more to activities like being able to go on holiday, to have adequate and not stigmatising clothing, toys and school materials, to be able to go to the cinema, to engage in shared activities or clubs or to have other children invited (Ridge, 2002; Main and Bradshaw, 2012). Inclusion is about 'fitting in' without shame and, as children grow older, also being heard and included in decisions about their lives. Children's well-being and their well-becoming is to a great extent dependent on the possibility of being part of the community in which they live and grow up and to engage in activities that are viewed as standard by themselves and by others; the ability to engage in such activities is crucial to friendships. The danger of exclusion, as well as isolation and loneliness, is closely connected to poverty. A main reason for this is the general environment in which most poor children grow up. Living in non-child-friendly settings easily leads to insecurity and frustration. In addition, parents in poverty often are not able to spend sufficient time with their children because this would involve too high a personal and psychological cost (Russell et al., 2008).

Conclusion

We argue that poverty has a negative and severe influence on children's well-being and well-becoming, and that it is therefore unjust, as poor children are not able to reach a sufficient level of basic capabilities and functionings. We have concentrated our argument on four of such basic capabilities – health, education, inclusion and self-respect – and examined the theoretical and empirical evidence supporting our claims. We are aware that this is just a partial examination, but one that is further supported by the growing literature on children's well-being in relation to poverty. Child poverty is a severe injustice from which those children – in the European Union, they make up for 20 per cent of the total infant population – neither necessarily nor naturally suffer, but rather it is the result of systemic failure of respective societies in providing adequately for all of their children. In particular, the publicly acclaimed and politically supported ideology of market-based deserts and merits cannot be called legitimate, as long as children remain victims of such unequal chances and opportunities in their lives. Child poverty is therefore one of the main obstacles standing in the way of a socially just access to all kinds of capabilities and functionings. Unfortunately, the trajectories of the economic crisis, and the welfare reforms triggered by it, point towards an even more unequal distribution of life chances due to child poverty, which, if not tackled, translates into further injustices over the life course.

Note

*   This research was funded by the Austrian Science Fund (FWF): P 26480-G15.

References

Addy, S., Engelhardt, W. and Skinner, C. (2013) *Basic Facts About Low-Income Children: Children Under 18 Years, 2011*. New York: National Center for Children in Poverty. Available at: www.nccp.org/publications/pdf/text_1074.pdf

Aldgate, J. (2010). Child well-being, child development and family life. In W. Rose and C. McAuley (eds), *Child Well-Being: Understanding Children's Lives*. London: Jessica Kingsley, pp. 21–38.

Axford, N. (2012). *Exploring Concepts of Child Well-Being: Implications for Children's Services*. Bristol: Policy.

Ben-Arieh, A., Casas, F., Frønes, I. and Korbin, J. (eds) (2014). *Handbook of Child Well-Being: Theory, Indicators, Measures and Policies*. Dordrecht: Springer.

Biggeri, M., Ballet, J. and Comim, F. (2011) Children's agency and the capability approach: a conceptual framework. In M. Biggeri, J. Ballet and F. Comim (eds), *Children and the Capability Approach*. Basingstoke and New York: Palgrave Macmillan, pp. 22–45.

Biggeri, M. and Mehrotra, S. (2011) Child poverty as capability deprivation: how to choose domains of child well-being and poverty. In M. Biggeri, J. Ballet and F. Comim (eds), *Children and the Capability Approach*, 1st edn. Basingstoke and New York: Palgrave Macmillan, pp. 46–75.

Braveman, P., Egerter, S. and Williams, D. R. (2011) The social determinants of health: coming of age. *Annual Review of Public Health*, 32

(April 21), 381–98. doi:10.1146/
annurev-publhealth-031210-101218.

Brennan, S. and Noggle, R. (1997) The moral
status of children: children's rights, parents'
rights, and family justice. *Social Theory and
Practice*, 23(1), 1–26.

Brighouse, H. (2002) What rights (if any) do
children have? In D. Archard and C. M.
Macleod (eds), *The Moral and Political
Status of Children*, 1st edn. Oxford and
New York: Oxford University Press.

Burchardt, T. and Vizard, P. (2011)
'Operationalizing the capability approach
as a basis for equality and human rights
monitoring in twenty-first-century Britain.
*Journal of Human Development and
Capabilities*, 12(1), 91–119. doi:10.1080/
19452829.2011.541790.

Camfield, L., Woodhead, M. and Streuli, N.
(2009) What's the use of 'well-being' in
contexts of child poverty? Approaches
to research, monitoring and children's
participation. *The International Journal of
Children's Rights*, 17(1) (January 1), 65–109.
doi:10.1163/157181808X357330.

Condron, D. J. (2011) Egalitarianism and
educational excellence: compatible
goals for affluent societies? *Educational
Researcher*, 40(2) (March 29), 47–55.
doi:10.3102/0013189X11401021.

Conroy, K., Sandel, M. and Zuckerman, B.
(2010) Poverty grown up: how childhood
socioeconomic status impacts adult
health. *Journal of Developmental
and Behavioral Pediatrics*, 31(2)
(February), 154–60. doi:10.1097/
DBP.0b013e3181c21a1b.

Crowley, A. and Vulliamy, C. (2007) *Listen Up!
Children and Young People Talk: About
Poverty*. Cardiff: Save the Children.
Available at: www.savethechildren.org.uk/
sites/default/files/docs/wales_lu_pov_1.pdf

Deneulin, S. and Shahani, L. (eds) (2009) *An
Introduction to the Human Development
and Capability Approach: Freedom and
Agency*, 1st edn. London, Sterling, VA
and Ottawa: Earthscan/International
Development Research Centre.

Duncan, G. J. and Murnane, R. J. (eds) (2011)
*Whither Opportunity? Rising Inequality,
Schools, and Children's Life Chances.*

New York and Chicago, IL: Russell Sage
Foundation; Spencer Foundation.

Dunkel Schetter, C. and Glynn, L. M.
(2010) Stress in pregnancy: empirical
evidence and theoretical issues to
guide interdisciplinary researchers.
In R. J. Contrada and A. Baum
(eds), *The Handbook of Stress
Science: Biology, Psychology, and Health*.
New York: Springer, pp. 321–43.

Graf, G. and Schweiger, G. (2015) *A
Philosophical Examination of Social Justice
and Child Poverty*. Basingstoke and
New York: Palgrave Macmillan.

Liu, L., Johnson, H. L., Cousens, S., Perin, J.,
Scott, S., Lawn, J. E., Rudan, I. et al. (2012)
Global, regional, and national causes of
child mortality: an updated systematic
analysis for 2010 with time trends since
2000. *Lancet*, 379(9832) (June 9), 2151–61.
doi:10.1016/S0140-6736(12)60560–1.

Macleod, C. M. (2010) Primary goods,
capabilities and children. In H. Brighouse
and I. Robeyns (eds), *Measuring
Justice: Primary Goods and Capabilities*.
Cambridge and New York: Cambridge
University Press, pp. 174–92.

Main, G. and Bradshaw, J. (2012) A child
material deprivation index. *Child
Indicators Research*, 5(3) (June 9), 503–21.
doi:10.1007/s12187-012-9145-7.

McAuley, C. and Rose, W. (eds) (2010) *Child
Well-being: Understanding Children's Lives*.
London and Philadelphia, PA: Jessica
Kingsley Publishers.

Millar, J. (2007) Social exclusion and social
policy research: defining exclusion. In
D. Abrams, J. Christian and D. Gordon
(eds), *Multidisciplinary Handbook of Social
Exclusion Research*. Chichester: John Wiley
and Sons, pp. 1–16.

Nussbaum, M. C. (2006) *Frontiers of Justice.
Disability, Nationality, and Species
Membership*. Cambridge, MA and
London: The Belknap Press of Harvard
University Press.

Nussbaum, M. C. (2011) *Creating
Capabilities: The Human Development
Approach*, 1st edn. Cambridge, MA
and London: Belknap Press of Harvard
University Press.

Olinto, P., Beegle, K., Sobrado, C. and Uematsu, H. (2013) *The State of the Poor: Where are the Poor, Where is Extreme Poverty Harder to End, and What is the Current Profile of the World's Poor?* Washington, DC: World Bank. Available at: http://siteresources.worldbank.org/ EXTPREMNET/Resources/EP125.pdf

Ridge, T. (2002) *Childhood Poverty and Social Exclusion: From a Child's Perspective.* Bristol: Policy Press.

Ridge, T. (2009) *Living with Poverty: A Review of the Literature on Children's and Families' Experiences of Poverty.* Research Report No 594. London: Department for Work and Pensions. Available at: http://research. dwp.gov.uk/asd/asd5/rports2009-2010/ rrep594.pdf

Russell, M., Harris, B. and Gockel, A. (2008) Parenting in poverty: perspectives of high-risk parents. *Journal of Children and Poverty*, 14(1) (March), 83–98. doi:10.1080/10796120701871322.

Sen, A. (1999) *Development as Freedom.* New York: Anchor Books.

Sen, A. (2009) *The Idea of Justice.* London and New York: Allen Lane.

UNICEF IRC (2013) Child well-being in rich countries: a comparative overview. Innocenti Report Card 11, UNICEF Innocenti Research Centre, Florence. Available at: www.unicef.org/media/files/ RC11-ENG-embargo.pdf

Venkatapuram, S. (2011) *Health Justice.* Cambridge and Malden, MA: Polity Press.

Walker, M. and Unterhalter, E. (eds) (2010) *Amartya Sen's Capability Approach and Social Justice in Education.* Basingstoke: Palgrave Macmillan.

Wolff, J. and De Shalit, A. (2007) *Disadvantage.* Oxford: Oxford University Press.

Yoshikawa, H., Aber, J. L. and Beardslee, W. R. (2012) The effects of poverty on the mental, emotional, and behavioral health of children and youth: implications for prevention. *American Psychologist*, 67(4), 272–84. doi:10.1037/a0028015.

Children and Relational Citizenship

6

A History

Pamela Cox

As dependent subjects, children are partial citizens. Their rights as citizens are inextricably – and rightly – bound up with the responsibilities of adults to protect them and to meet their economic, social and emotional needs. In this sense, 'the child citizen' embodies the notion of relational citizenship – a view of citizenship that emphasises the relational (rather than individual) nature of our personal autonomy.

This chapter traces turning points in the emerging construction of children as relational citizens. It focuses on developments in Britain from the late nineteenth century onwards and explores children's right to protection, welfare and participation, connecting these with the wider expansion of adult citizenship and its own attendant rights and responsibilities. It identifies key shifts across three broad historical periods: the early investment state, the classic welfare state and the empowerment state. It begins with a brief overview of the concept of relational citizenship.

Relational Citizenship

The concept of relational citizenship has developed from human rights-based approaches to community development stressing relationships over autonomy. It differs from normative liberal views of citizenship that have emphasised *individualised* agency, autonomy and access to political, economic and social rights. Instead, it develops within relationships between people and is therefore embedded in relational questions, interests and concerns (Lawy and Biesta, 2006; Pols, 2006).

Relational citizenship extends our thinking about what it means to be a citizen. Knop (2001) argues that it is more than a legal notion as it is based on a concept of the social or relational self and acknowledges that particularities of relationships play a part in constituting the meaning of individuals' lives and identities. In this sense, the notion of relational citizenship has much in common with the notion of 'relational autonomy' as developed by feminist communitarians who view individualism as a product of socialisation and autonomy as a capacity that can only be developed within relationships rather than in isolation (Mackenzie and Stolijar, 2000; Sclater et al., 2009). The concept also connects with the idea of social citizenship that, similarly, highlights the importance of interdependencies. Cockburn (1998, 2012) sees recent developments in social citizenship as offering the best way of balancing child and adult rights. This chapter suggests that we can, in fact, trace a longer history of social and relational citizenship and argues that these concepts have shaped the emergence of children's rights for over a century.

The Right to Protection, Education and Welfare: Early Investment State

The foundations of British children's status as modern relational citizens lie in late nineteenth- and early twentieth-century legislation that removed them from the labour market and gave them new rights to protection, education and welfare. Among the first formal rights to be accorded to children were rights as protected workers. In the eighteenth and nineteenth centuries, the majority of working-class children (and, thereby, the majority of children in the population) were workers. They were generally employed in unskilled positions within domestic service, spinning, weaving, laundering, tailoring, street selling, farm work, mining, fishing and more. Many left their own homes around the age of 12 to take up live-in apprenticeships in skilled trades. Child labour had underpinned the early industrial revolution with its new demand for vast numbers of low-cost workers. In turn, working-class families became increasingly dependent on child wages.

From the early nineteenth century on, legislation was introduced to limit children's working hours (at least in certain kinds of workplaces, notably factories) and then to require their employers to provide them with access to basic education. These requirements reframed the relationship between employers and their child workers and thereby began to mould a new kind of relational citizenship. When state education itself was first introduced in the 1870s and made compulsory in the 1880s, it marked the beginning of the end of regulated child labour and the start of a new relationship between the state and its child citizens.

The gradual removal of children from workplaces to schools signalled a shift from a strongly professional participation of children with minimal protection in the eighteenth and nineteenth centuries to a strong protection of children with minimal professional participation during the twentieth (Jens, 2004). It also marked a shift in the broader cultural position of working-class children. As Zelizer (1985) argues, as their contributions to family incomes declined, they gradually became economically worthless but emotionally priceless.

By investing in a national education system, the state was investing in children as a national resource. The principal driver here was an economic one. Initial industrialisation had largely depended on unskilled labour but secondary industrialisation required a more highly skilled workforce. Granting children the right to education also needs to be understood, however, in terms of the broader rise of 'the social'. This refers to the idea that society was an identifiable social sphere that could be managed, directed and disciplined, and to the belief that citizens were resources that could be mobilised by state investment. As the final section of this chapter shows, this earlier history is often overlooked by more recent accounts of the rise of the new empowerment state. Many commentators have analysed the place of children in the rise of 'the social' from the late nineteenth century on (James et al., 1998; Hendrick, 2003). Children embodied the nation's future – as future parents, workers and defenders of empire. As Cooter (1992) argues, this helps to explain why so many of the new measures linked to the new interventionist state were enacted 'in the name of the child'. Alongside education reform, other measures included an expansion of the state's obligations to children in relation to infant welfare, child health, school meals, child poor relief and juvenile justice.

Prominent among these measures were new regulations around child protection. In 1889 the state greatly extended its right, emergent since the 1830s, to intervene in relations between parents and children. The Act for the Prevention of Cruelty to, and Protection of, Children allowed police to arrest persons found ill-treating a child and to enter a home if a child was believed to be in danger. It also empowered leading voluntary agencies, such as the National Society for the Prevention of Cruelty to Children, to initiate cases and present evidence. The Act marked a further turning point in the framing of children's rights by creating a new form of relational citizenship between them and the adults responsible for their care. It did so by undermining the traditional authority of fathers as heads of their household and by challenging prevailing models of adult male citizenship predicated upon the powers they could exercise (if they chose) over their wives and children. Over time, men's individual autonomy within the private family would be forced to give way to a more relational one through the expansion of, for example, women's rights as wives to own property and initiative divorce, and their rights as mothers to claim custody of their children.

Changes in child protection initiated by the 1889 Act were further cemented by the 1908 Children Act which codified an emerging consensus around how best to deal with children at risk and children in trouble (Cox, 2012a, p. 6). They should not be allowed to remain unsupervised in unsafe families and those most at risk should be removed from the family altogether and either boarded out to registered foster parents or sent to a children's home or to a juvenile justice facility. The new juvenile courts set up by the Act should take on some responsibility for dealing with those in need of care and protection, alongside those who had committed an offence. Children should no longer be sent to adult prisons and, if sent to a workhouse, should continue to be separated from adult inmates. Children's rescue and reform was to be carried out in children's spaces – many of which were funded and managed by the voluntary sector and many of which divided children by type: boys from girls, innocent from corrupted, Protestants from Catholics from Jews. Those children removed from their homes should be engaged in constructive training and not subject to punishment for its own sake. On leaving these reform institutions, many boys were placed directly in the military or merchant navy (until the end of the First World War) while the majority of girls were placed in domestic service (until the end of the Second World War). Significantly, the post-release reoffending rates for these young people were much lower than those released from youth custodial institutions today (Godfrey et al., 2017).

The 1908 Children Act signified a broader reconfiguration of the child as a distinct political body (Cox, 2012a, p. 6). Like the earlier measures introducing the right to state education and the right to protection from neglect, it sought to harness children's potential for community, nation and empire. The framework it created was extended by the 1933 Children Act, which broadened the powers of juvenile courts and introduced supervision orders for children at risk. Together with the campaigning efforts of another large voluntary agency, Save the Children, the 1908 Act also informed international dialogues around child rights. In 1924, the League of Nations issued its Declaration of the Rights of the Child, a charter of five non-binding 'guiding principles' to be used to shape the protection and care of children by League members around the world (Milne, 2008).

Children, Parents and Citizenship: Classic Post-War Welfare State

This discussion has thus far shown how the early expansion of children's citizenship rights was bound up with the expansion of responsibilities of different groups of adults to protect, educate and train them. Children's experience of citizenship was relational in that it depended on the ability, willingness and resources of these adults to fulfil these new responsibilities.

In other words, children's ability to enjoy their rights was – and remains – closely linked to relevant adults' ability to access supporting resources.

Discussions of child rights and the classic welfare state generally celebrate the passing of the 1944 Education Act that raised the school leaving age to 15 and introduced free secondary education for all. Historical accounts of key developments in family law in this period single out the 1946 Curtis Committee and its radical overhaul of child protection (following a child death in foster care), and the 1948 Children Act that followed and greatly expanded local authority control of children's services. Just as significant, however, for children's status as citizens were measures that enhanced the welfare rights of their parents and expanded a range of state services from education and the new National Health Service, to new social housing programmes and new income maintenance schemes. Incomes of all families, but especially the poorest, were raised by the 1945 Family Allowance Act which introduced child benefit, and the 1946 National Insurance Act which expanded coverage of the existing scheme and the 1948 National Assistance Act which provided a further financial safety net for the most vulnerable. These redistributive measures had their limits but, together, they helped to lift thousands of poor families out of poverty and, in doing so, clearly enhanced the life chances of children within those families. They arguably represented a further early form of relational citizenship in that some levels of benefit were calculated on the basis of parental status and parental relational responsibilities. Further, the material benefits received were shared within families.

This expansion of adult citizenship rights was particularly significant for mothers. Family allowances, for example, augmented working families' wages and increased the disposable income of many households, albeit in a modest way. Access to state health care, free at the point of use for the first time, greatly improved levels of child, maternal and family health. These measures built on earlier ones introduced by the early investment state at the turn of the twentieth century and are described by some historians as helping to create a new model of 'maternal citizenship' (Lewis, 1980; Allen, 2005). In short, if the state sought to enact policies 'in the name of the child', it needed to engage with the mothers of those children as those who – de facto – held greater responsibilities for domestic and family well-being. The infant welfare movement, akin to the child protection movement, succeeded in lobbying to secure interventions that had a significant impact on the emergent relational citizenship rights of infants. These included the 1907 Notification of Births Act which required a local health officer to be informed of a birth within six weeks so that a health visitor could attend the family, and the landmark 1918 Maternity and Child Welfare Act which greatly expanded state maternity services and the existing network of infant welfare clinics (although never to the level they would reach in other parts of Europe). Again, these new rights were relational, accorded to women on the basis of their relational responsibilities.

The concept of maternal citizenship continues to be much debated today (for an overview, see Allen, 2005). For some, it is deeply problematic because it defined women's citizenship in terms of their circumscribed role as mothers dependent on a male breadwinner (rather than as workers or taxpayers in their own right), because it excluded fathers from the realms of childcare and because it exposed mothers to heavy-handed external scrutiny. Others point to measurable improvements delivered by 'maternalist' measures, including significant falls in infant mortality rates by the 1920s and the empowering of mothers through their contact with support services. Today, the question of how the state meets the needs of marginal mothers remains a pressing one, particularly within the realm of family law and the challenge it faces in reducing high levels of recurrent care proceedings involving the serial removal of more than one child from the same birth mother (see Broadhurst et al., Chapter 8 in this volume; Cox, 2012b; Cox et al., 2017).

Children and Citizenship in the Empowerment State

The final section of this discussion considers aspects of how aspects of children's status as relational citizens have changed in an era marked by a retreat from the redistributive classic welfare state and the rise of what some term the empowerment state. Such a state continues to make social investments in citizens as a resource (as pioneered in the early investment state a century ago) but targets these much more directly on those deemed to present particular social risks. Here, citizens are expected and encouraged to become much more 'active' in creating and improving their own life chances (Cruickshank, 1999; Newman and Tonkens, 2011). Active citizens are invited, cajoled and sometimes coerced to take on a range of responsibilities for themselves, for the care of others and for the well-being of their communities.

The rise of the empowerment state divides commentators (for an overview, see Newman and Tonkens, 2011). Some see the concept of 'active citizenship' as an extension of a punitive and divisive welfare strategy which seeks to make marginal groups responsible while withdrawing redistributive public investment in the broader material resources they need to realise their potential. Others see it as marking an important new chapter in policymaking that seeks to empower marginal individuals and communities by encouraging them to identify their capacities, capabilities and strengths. According to the latter view, only active citizens can be participating citizens. It follows from this that, for supporters of this view, models of participatory citizenship must include children and the adults around them obliged to meet their various needs.

Empowerment and participation approaches now characterise many child- and family-related policy areas (Roche, 2005; Cockburn, 2007, 2012). The Troubled Families initiative works with marginal families at an intensive and highly personal level to identify their foundations for relational change, while the new AssetPlus framework used within youth justice programmes uses a more strengths-based approach intended to build up existing close relationships in a young person's network. In mainstream public law family proceedings, new pre-proceedings meetings provide a space for parents and carers to work with professionals to try to create their own solutions to safeguard the children in their care. Experimental problem-solving courts (such as the Family Drug and Alcohol Court – see Harwin et al., Chapter 9 in this volume – and mental health courts) take this further by using therapeutic jurisprudence to challenge those appearing before them to make significant changes in their personal lives and, crucially, to walk with them through those changes. Of course, all these initiatives face challenges and failures but, taken together, they push the boundaries of relational citizenship in positive ways by insisting that children's ability to enjoy their rights as citizens rests heavily on the ability of the adults in their lives to meet their needs and by recognising that those adults often need to be empowered to be able to do this.

One of the many challenges generated by the empowerment state is the blurring of relationships at the service-provider level. The final theme addressed here considers some of the contradictions this creates in efforts to promote participatory citizenship.

The empowering state still invests heavily in children. It now manages that investment, however, in quite distinct ways. Public services have been transformed by 'new public management' techniques, notably the introduction of market-type mechanisms in a perpetual quest to drive out inefficiencies and drive up quality. In the past, much less attention was paid to the quality of provision of child-related and other services. The focus of the early investment state, for example, was on securing public access to education or child protection while that of the classic welfare state was on expanding and regulating such services. Many argue that citizens of the empowerment state are now primarily defined as consumers exercising choices rather than rights (Rose, 1999). Following this line of argument, we might regard children as indirect 'consumers' – or at least, 'users' – of services from education and leisure to child protection and safeguarding. This is a contentious development but it has been an important factor in the opening up of significant new dialogues between all kinds of service providers and their child clients. Children's views as service users are now routinely sought – arguably for the first time in the history examined here. Training courses abound in ways of listening to children and encouraging their participation in the development of services affecting them (see for example, Children's Society, 2001; Clark and Moss, 2001; Bruce, 2014; Roose and De Bies, 2008). Participatory citizenship is now a much-discussed model in the field of child rights and focuses on 'citizenship-in-practice', or the collective framing of new needs and interventions (Cockburn, 2012; Lawy and Biesta, 2006).

Such developments could be argued to expand the notion of relational citizenship in that they deepen relationships between citizens, stakeholders and service providers. However, the changing profile of service providers in the empowerment state demands some attention here. New public management models have encouraged the rapid development of mixed economies of provision involving private and third sector partners working in partnership with public sector agencies. These arrangements can be complex but that complexity is often concealed with the result that the client may not always be aware of a private provider's full profile. For example, global corporate giant G4S runs eight children's homes in England as part of its vast portfolio of security and justice services while its counterpart, Sodexo, is a lead partner in many local authority youth justice services. Meanwhile, many expert reports compiled for family law proceedings are produced by psychologists contracted to a small number of private consulting firms. In these situations, with whom does the relational citizen have a relationship? How do service users – including children – participate in a meaningful way to really shape services delivered through these opaque market-type mechanisms?

Conclusions

The foregoing discussion has suggested that children's status as citizens was first defined through the early social investment and classic welfare states and the interventions they enacted 'in the name of the child' *but also* through the interventions they enacted in the name of maternal citizenship and a redistributive polity. In other words, these interventions were partly shaped by a belief that the improvement of children's life chances rested on the improvement of the life chances of their parents, families and communities. Today, the empowerment state has taken this belief to new levels but pulls in contradictory directions. Active citizens are encouraged to participate in realising their own potential and in shaping services to assist that process. However, many continue to lack the material resources needed to do this in a meaningful way. Further, the empowerment state places new emphasis on the quality of its child- and family-related services and places new value on user experiences as 'consumers' of those services. In doing so, it encourages children to participate and speak up. However, the complexity of that mixed economy service provision can threaten to drown out these newfound voices.

References

Allen, A. T. (2005) *Feminism and Motherhood in Western Europe, 1890–1970: The Maternal Dilemma*. Basingstoke: Palgrave.

Bruce, M. (2014) The voice of the child in child protection: whose voice? *Social Sciences*, 3, 514–26.

Children's Society (2001) *Young People's Charter of Participation*. London: Children's Society.

Clark, A. and Moss, P. (2001) *Listening to Young Children: The Mosaic Approach*. London: National Children's Bureau.

Cockburn, T. (1998) Children and citizenship in Britain: a case for a socially interdependent model of citizenship. *Childhood*, 5(1), 99–117.

Cockburn, T. (2007) Partners in power: a radically pluralistic form of participative democracy for children and young people. *Children and Society*, 21(6), 446–57.

Cockburn, T. (2012) *Rethinking Children's Citizenship*. Basingstoke: Palgrave Macmillan.

Cooter, R. (ed.) (1992) *In the Name of the Child: Health and Welfare, 1880–1940*. London: Routledge.

Cox, P. (2012a) *Bad Girls in Britain: Gender, Justice and Welfare, 1900–1950*. Basingstoke: Palgrave Macmillan.

Cox, P. (2012b) Marginal mothers, reproductive autonomy and repeat losses to care. *Journal of Law and Society*, 39(4), 541–61.

Cox, P., Barratt, C., Blumenfeld, F., Rahemtulla, Z., Taggart, D. and Turton, J. (2017) Reducing recurrent care proceedings: initial evidence from new interventions. *Journal of Social Welfare and Family Law*, 39(3), 332–49.

Cruickshank, B. (1999) *The Will to Empower: Democratic Citizens and Other Subjects*. Ithaca, NY: Cornell University Press.

Godfrey, B., Cox, P., Shore, H. and Alker, Z. (2017) *Young Criminal Lives: Life Courses and Life Chances from 1850*. Oxford: Oxford University Press.

Hendrick, H. (2003) *Child Welfare: Historical Dimensions, Contemporary Debate*. Bristol: Policy Press.

James, A., Jenks, C. and Prout, A. (eds) (1998) *Theorizing Childhood*. Cambridge: Polity.

Jens, M. (2004) Children as citizens: towards a contemporary notion of child participation. *Childhood*, 11(1), 27–44.

Knop, K. (2001) Relational nationality: on gender and nationality in international law. In T. A. Aleinikoff and D. Klusmeyer (eds), *Citizenship Today: Global Perspectives and Practices*. Washington, DC: Carnegie Endowment for International Peace, 89–126.

Lawy, R. and Biesta, G. (2006) Citizenship-as-practice: the educational implication of an inclusive and relational understanding of citizenship. *British Journal of Educational Studies*, 54(1), 34–50.

Lewis, J. (1980) *The Politics of Motherhood: Child and Maternal Welfare in England, 1900–39*. London: Croom-Helm.

Mackenzie, C. and Stoljar, N. (eds) (2000) *Relational Autonomy: Feminist Perspectives on Autonomy, Agency, and the Social Self*. Oxford: Oxford University Press.

Milne, B. (2008) From chattels to citizens? Eighty years of Eglantyne Jebb's legacy to children and beyond. In J. Williams and A. Invernizzi (eds), *Children and Citizenship*. London: SAGE.

Newman, J. and Tonkens, E. (2011) *Participation, Responsibility and Choice: Summoning the Active Citizen in Western European Welfare States*. Amsterdam: Amsterdam University Press.

Pols, J. (2006) Washing the citizen: washing, cleanliness and citizenship in mental health care. *Culture, Medicine and Psychiatry*, 30(1), 77–104.

Roche, J. (2005) Children, citizenship and human rights. *Journal of Social Sciences*, 9, 43–55.

Roose, R. and De Bies, M. (2008) Children's rights: a challenge for social work. *International Social Work*, 51(1), 37–46.

Rose, N. (1999) *Powers of Freedom: Reframing Political Thought*. Cambridge: Cambridge University Press.

Sclater, S. D., Ebtehaj, F., Jackson, E. and Richards, M. (eds) (2009) *Regulating Autonomy: Sex, Reproduction and the Family*. Oxford: Hart.

Zelizer, V. (1985) *Pricing the Priceless Child: The Changing Social Value of Children*. New York: Basic Books.

The United Nations Convention on the Rights of the Child (UNCRC)

Maggie Atkinson

I wrote this chapter as I stepped down as Children's Commissioner for England in 2015. I express my own views throughout the chapter, though they remain in accord with those of the current postholder and are picked up and reflected in the work of the Office of the Children's Commissioner (OCC). Much of the supporting material I refer to is based on, and references, work undertaken by the Office during my term.

The Office's work has been ongoing since 2005, under three incumbents each serving a term limited by law. The role was established by Part 1 of the 2004 Children Act. Its powers and duties are described in Schedule 2 and the role was strengthened and its primary function changed to the promotion and protection of the rights of the child by Part 5 and Schedule 6 of the 2014 Children and Families Act.

This chapter is informed by my having been steeped in the rights of the child for at least the last five years of my term in office, and on reflection, for my entire 40 years of working with and in the interests of children and young people. As a teacher, like teachers in every type and character of school, I taught children with experience of both public and private law and the family justice system. As a local authority Director of Children's Services, I made decisions about the circumstances in which some children should be brought up by the state rather than their birth families; what foster carers could and should do; what residential care should strive to achieve, and what care-leavers should be supported to do, in vital areas of life such as – to quote only one example from the many that apply– taking up careers in the armed services. To be a corporate parent for somebody else's child in this way is a serious undertaking, not just a legal requirement or nicety.

In this chapter, I explore what children's rights mean, with a particular concentration on the context of family justice. I explore society's comfort or discomfort in accepting that children's rights are both real, and upheld by a binding international treaty, the United Nations Convention on the Rights of the Child (UNCRC) to which the UK became a State Party in 1991. I exemplify what some of these rights look like when they are upheld, and what difficulties arise for children when they are denied, ignored or simply unrecognised by adults. I challenge us all to ensure children both understand them, and are supported to achieve them. For children encountering the family justice system should surely be helped by professionals, who have the power they lack: the power to ensure their rights are fulfilled.

The UNCRC: What It Means and Why It Matters

The UNCRC is the world's most signed and ratified international Human Rights Instrument. It consists of a preamble, which states the UN's aspirations for children worldwide but is not justiciable, and 54 Articles. Most of these are also not justiciable, but some match elements of legislation in State Parties, including the UK. The Convention is not incorporated in UK law, but the courts, and debates in Parliament, regularly raise how far it is fulfilled. State Parties including the UK are called to account by the UN Committee on the Rights of the Child – in the UK's case, this took place in 2016. The four UK Children's Commissioners' websites all have links to the UN Committee's Concluding Observations, many of which were as critical in 2017 as they were in 2008, on children's well-being: issues such as ongoing austerity, punitive criminal justice, access to services, equality of treatment and regard.

The UN Convention's Articles taken together address all aspects of childhood, making children Rights Holders. The Articles imply the work adults must do to ensure the Convention is brought to life. Forty-two Articles are about what children should experience as rights-holders, and how adults as duty-bearers should promote, protect and ensure them. The final 12 stress how governments and civil society should ensure the rights are fulfilled. Some Articles are supported by detailed General Comments, expanding on and exemplifying what fulfilment of that particular Article looks like.

The Convention is summarised in short, plain English documents by charities such as Unicef and Save the Children, and organisations like the British Institute for Human Rights. I use the language of such summaries below in examining some Articles.

Such summaries are useful introductions to the Convention, and are widely used with children and young people. However, to understand the Convention in all its many dimensions, I recommend you read in full the many documents available, to understand their meanings for policymaking, legal precedent setting, and practice in teaching, social work, medicine, local government, criminal and family justice, economic, civil and cultural life. The UNICEF website, which contains links to and explanations of the Articles of the Convention, is also a source for the General Comments.

Commentaries on the Convention can also be found both on the United Nations' website where the Convention and its General Articles are published, though navigating the site can be a challenge. There are also commentaries by eminent lawyers in the UK context (Lady Hale, in *Re ZH (Tanzania)* v. *SSHD* [2011]; MacDonald, 2011).

The Convention's Articles are clustered into themed groups. One vital cluster embraces the Convention's General Principles of Implementation. These apply to all children and in all situations, whichever other Articles on particular themes or issues might also apply. The General Principle Articles are as follows, with my commentaries in italics:

- Article 1: Everybody under the age of 18 holds all the rights in the Convention. *In reality, in England, if a child is disabled or has care system experience, the rights apply until an individual is 25, following a number of Acts of Parliament.*
- Article 2: The Convention applies to every child without discrimination of any kind, whatever their ethnicity, gender, religion, language, abilities or any other status, whatever they think or say, whatever type of family they come from. *Though this Article does not explicitly mention children with experience of family justice, the principle of non-discrimination has profound resonances. The fact is that children are discriminated against by dint of their being children and lacking agency, whether discrimination is deliberate, or arises through lack of forethought. This means that adults regularly either actively defy or simply ignore the Convention. That they may not know of its existence, or how it applies in their circumstances or practice, is also a long-standing concern. It does not pay policymakers to publicise a Convention that could challenge them, after all.*
- Article 3: The best interests of the child must be a primary consideration in all decisions and actions that affect children. *Like the 1989 Children Act Paramountcy*

Principle, this is easy to say, but as children and young people in the family justice system regularly report, it is all too often placed in the 'too hard' box. The former Children's Rights Director for England Sir Roger Morgan, whose team and work were absorbed by the Office of the Children's Commissioner for England in 2014, championed the need for vulnerable children's interests to be paramount in all decisions made about their lives, particularly those in care, or otherwise living and learning away from home. All his reports are also on the Commissioner's website, alongside the work published by each of the three Commissioners who have undertaken the role since 2005. All four UK Children's Commissioners' websites contain reports and reviews which illustrate the issues children face in getting their voices both heard and taken seriously.

- Article 6: Every child has the right to life. Governments must do all they can to ensure children survive and develop to their full potential. *The preamble to the Convention, which is not justiciable, refers to rights held by the unborn child. The Convention itself, which is justiciable, is clear the Articles apply from birth to age 18 years.*

- Article 12: Every child has the right to express their views, feelings and wishes in all matters affecting them, and to have their views taken seriously and considered. Children have the same right during court and administrative processes that affect them. *For the purposes of this chapter, and in daily practice across the system, this is the most important right in the Convention. Its implications for practice, especially finding the time to let children have their say, should challenge family courts' work. The Article sets a benchmark for practice that ensures children are heard, that their views matter, and that whether they get what they want or not, adults explain the decision-making processes and the reasons why a particular decision is reached.*

One cluster of Articles refers directly to and should impact on practice throughout: family justice. The words are simple to write and quote. Alongside the General Principles Articles, they place the voice and interests of the child, not those of adults in a situation, at the centre of practice, as prime concerns even when those adults are vociferous. The Articles' simplicity of expression, and our broad acceptance of them as principles, is belied by how difficult we find it to honour what they say.

- Article 18: Both parents share responsibility for bringing up their children and should always consider what is best for the child. Governments must support parents by creating child care services and giving parents the help they need to raise their children. *'Shared responsibility' does not mean apportioning percentages of parental contact or shared parenting. Both can bedevil court proceedings, and deeply upset and potentially damage children and young people if parents' separation is acrimonious (see OCC: A Child Rights Impact Assessment (CRIA) on Parts 1 to 3 of the Children and Families Bill 2013 (OCC, 2013), available at www.childrenscommissioner.gov.uk). This Article, put simply, means what it says: the issue is that parenting is a shared responsibility. Not lightly do affected children accuse acrimoniously separating or divorcing parents of 'passing me like a parcel' or treating them like unregarded tokens in an adult game. Under the age of 18, contact is a child's, not an adult's, right (OCC, 2011, 2015; Clifton, 2014).*

- Article 19: Governments must do all they can to ensure children are protected from all forms of violence, abuse, neglect and bad treatment by their parents or anyone else who looks after them. *If children are to be safe, it is not their responsibility to ensure their safety. It is society's. In particular, there is a weight placed on governments. That we are presented with scandals when a child dies because they were not safeguarded shows that we struggle, both politically and professionally, to learn what we must so that it does not happen again, rather than simply promising it will not. Children in the family justice system, especially in public law, may have suffered neglect and abuse before they were 'rescued' so the system could find a safer adoptive or foster family or other care. That we do not always manage to achieve such 'rescue' is our abiding challenge. It is made still more pointed because we have shelves heavy with reports, informed by the voices of children, critiquing the system and giving their direct advice on improving it (The All-Party Parliamentary Group for Looked After Children and Care Leavers, 2013, 2014; Centre for Social Justice, 2015).*

- Article 39: Children who experience neglect, abuse, exploitation, torture or who are victims of war, must receive special support to help them recover their health, dignity, self-respect and social life. *Achieving such rehabilitation is not the role of the child. It is the role of policymakers, in local and national government, to set the parameters and devise the system. It is the role of all professionals, across all disciplines, to be part of the team for that child. It is a duty on those making decisions on how scarce resources are used to pay for this work.*

Tragedies like those of Maria Coldwell, Victoria Climbie, Khyra Ishaq, Peter Connelly, Daniel Pelka, Keanu Williams and so many other others are deeply and abidingly shocking. They remain worrying for society, and an influence on professional practice, long after a case moves off the front page. Many of these totemic cases have led to legislation seeking to right the wrongs identified when they are investigated. To quote some specific examples of rights-based work on children's behalf, the OCC's statutory work, like much of the troubling material arising from such cases brought to the media and through the courts since at least 2013, have brought to public attention – where they should remain – children and young people whose voices have gone unheard, particularly as victims of sexual exploitation and abuse by their peers in gangs, or by older abusers either alone or in groups. The reports for the OCC's Inquiry into Child Sexual Exploitation in Gangs and Groups (Berelowitz et al., 2012, 2013; Coy et al., 2013) speak fearlessly for these children and young people. They challenge us all to listen first, not when it is too late; and crucially, to act on what we hear.

Article 34 of the Convention explicitly states the right of the child to be actively protected from all forms of sexual abuse and exploitation, that protection being provided by adults who are placed by the Convention in the role of Duty Bearers. It matters deeply that we understand and enact what the Convention requires of us, and that we take the time to read and understand it in detail if our work is done with children and young people.

- Article 20: If a child cannot be looked after by their family, the government must give them special protection and assistance. This includes providing alternative care that is continuous, and respects the child's culture, language and religion. *The implications for all practice are clear: how a child is placed into alternative care, what care looks like, how the system support foster carers, how adoptive families are chosen and then supported in the very long term, matter both to the child, and the adults in their lives: birth families, and those who care for them in alternative circumstances. The state's most serious intervention in the life of a child is to remove them from the people who brought them into the world but cannot provide the care they need. That the care system saves many lives is not at issue. That for too many – a minority of the care population, but in each case a vulnerable child – we fail to do as we would for our own child, is a perennial shame (OCC, 2011, 2015). We seem either unable to hear what they are saying, or working in a system that does not let us do so.*

- Article 25: If a child has been placed away from home (in care, hospital or prison, for example), they have the right to a regular review of their treatment, the way they are cared for and their wider circumstances. *Readers should remember that Articles 3 (Best Interests), 6 (right to life and to development) and 12 (right to a voice that is heard, taken seriously and acted on in decision-making and practice by professionals) also apply, meaning that children and young people should be treated as partners who are experts by experience in the conditions that affect them and influence their lives. If they are care leavers or former prisoners, the Convention's provisions do not cease as they turn 18 but continue to apply until they are 25.*

A young person living in the care of an English local authority spoke to me directly in the closing weeks of my term as Commissioner, acting under the duties I inherited from Sir Roger Morgan under the 2014 Children and Families Act. His case, sadly, was by no means unusual. He explained that his Independent Reviewing Officer (IRO) had tried to make him leave his own Care Review meeting. The young person had exercised his legal right and remained in the meeting. At it, the IRO had then shared confidential information with other professionals at the table, for which the teenager had, ahead of the meeting, explicitly withheld his permission under Article 16 of the Convention, the right to privacy. The IRO proceeded to chair the meeting so that those present knew about, but consciously and explicitly ignored, the CAFCASS- and Advocate-supported presentation the young person had composed as part of his contribution to his own review. Clearer evidence of the contravention of a child's rights and the negation of that child's agency in their own life would be difficult to find. It is, to the system's shame, not an uncommon reported experience in the lives of some of our children and young people.

The care system, lest we forget, in fact saves thousands of children and young people's lives, giving them the start in life they need. For a minority of them – and if every life matters, I would argue that a minority of even one is too many – unacceptable decisions are made, both in and beyond the courts. Unmaking them is difficult, once they have been made. At what cost to the child?

I close with two examples, from a far bigger selection about which the OCC has had to take action. In taking over the Office of the Children's Rights Director (OCRD) role after the 2014 Children and Families Act, I took on the helpline used by children covered by that remit. In Part 6 and Schedule 5 of the Children and Families Act 2014 referring to the work of the Children's Commissioner, the groups concerned are specified, and readers will hear them referred to as 'Children covered by Section 8A' of the Act: those in or leaving care, receiving social care services, or living and learning away from home. The OCC therefore now receives multiple calls a week and there is clearly still a need for a champion for relevant children.

Between April 2014 and leaving office in February 2015, in fulfilling the duties I held for these children, I wrote formally to over half of the 152 Directors of Children's Services in England to challenge their localities' practices, including ensuring that children's placement moves were frozen until I was satisfied by their responses. Every case in which I intervened left me wondering quite how the people concerned would have felt if this child had been their own. I quote below two examples of clear denials of the rights of the child. They are presented here as 'blended' examples illustrating what can happen, not cases of individual or traceable children. I am well aware that cases that eventually came to me were those at the end of the line, on the edge of breakdown; and that there are thousands of children in care whose lives are immeasurably improved by that same system. However, the dreadful exceptions, in each case, concern the life and potential long-term life chances of a child.

1: Young person 'A': aged 17, living in kinship care in an English local authority area. The kinship carer lived where the child's abusive and criminal birth and extended family, whose cumulative behaviours had led to the child being placed in care, also lived. The carer and the local authority had worked together to find and organise an educational placement in a reasonably priced residential school. Despite teething problems early on, the child did well at GCSE and in first year study towards A levels. In the same week as return to school for year 2 of study was due, the child turned 18. Pertinent facts in considering what should happen at that milestone birthday included the dangers of this child returning home; the reasonable cost of the schooling part of her placement and permanence, and the potential for enormous disruption if schooling were disrupted at this vital point. Nonetheless, the authority – this child's corporate parent – deemed it fitting to return this child to live with the kinship carer full time, in a location in the midst of the family from which the child had been removed. The local authority's plan was to place this child, to complete A levels, in the local further education college. This was a setting which extended family members also attended, and which offered almost, but not quite, the A level courses this child was studying. Nobody in the authority seemed to think there was anything wrong with this decision, which had been relayed as a fait accompli to the child only once it had been finalised, without reference to the child, the carer, the residential school, their views, opinions or expertise. My intervention first halted, and then changed the decision. The challenging question I would still pose is twofold. First, what would the Director of Children's Services and staff have thought of this course of events had this been their child? And second, what possessed anybody in the authority to think this was a reasonable decision in the first place?

2: Child 'B': aged 16, close to seventeenth birthday. A long-term foster care experienced young person, bright and articulate, but with a range of both mental and emotional health-related issues, this child mostly managed well, though with some very challenging episodes at times. After an earlier placement failed, the authority in whose care this child lived found what was considered and expected to be a stable place, preparing the child well for and supporting the placement, with an agency foster carer whom the authority knew well and had used before. The child settled, was optimistic, and had not had to change schools for the four A level courses already embarked on. The school understood the child, was Attachment Aware and resourced for some of the difficulties this child faced, and taught 'B' very well. Suddenly and with no warnings communicated to 'B', the carers served on the authority an immediate notice of their intention to quit offering their service. 'B's' social worker's take on the matter was that this young person did not deal well with change and transition. The worker's decision, apparently with no reference elsewhere, then led to no discussions being undertaken with 'B' ahead of the worker arriving with bags, insisting on 'B's' immediate packing of all belongings for an immediate move to a temporary placement 'while we decide what to do with you', a placement about which 'B' had no knowledge, with unknown people, at an address outside the school catchment area, in a rural county with no travelling possibilities for getting to school where 'B's' four A level courses were underway. At the time of this dreadful personal upheaval, 'B' was midway through sitting first-year sixth form exams. My intervention challenged this frankly shameful practice, which entailed an abdication of the social worker's professional duty to support 'B' far better and in a far more rounded way if a move of this magnitude in 'B's' life was so urgently necessary. The social worker had assumed that because 'B' struggles with change, this child should simply be moved, whatever he thought, felt or said. Are you appalled? Good. Do we know how to fix such things? We should. But the jury is still out as to whether we do have that knowledge, and if we do, whether the practice will change for the better.

The system would have a long way to go to reach excellence if such examples were one-off aberrations. Sadly, they are not.

I close by paraphrasing the words of a care-leaver, speaking in an open session in a crowded Parliamentary meeting room, in a meeting of the All-Party Parliamentary Group (APPG) on Children in Care and Care Leavers held as part of its 2014–15 inquiry into care-leavers' life chances. The speakers presenting to MPs, peers and eventually the then-children's minister through the APPG, and those who also addressed the Commons Education Select Committee on the same issues in the same period, were facilitated to present their views by the Who Cares Trust, now renamed Become, the charity which administers the APPG and does a range of other work to bring parliamentarians and children in the care system together.

> You don't get it. This is not administrative work. When you change my social worker or Personal Adviser, when you move me because it's cheaper, when you send somebody I trust away and replace them with somebody else, a piece of my heart goes away each time. I can never get that back.

Conclusions and Reflections

Busy professionals working with children and young people are strongly regulated, governed and have their work framed by a large library of legislation and attendant guidance. It is all too tempting to say there is enough there to safeguard the children and young people with whom they work. My argument here is that the UNCRC gives a fuller – and more fulfilled – sense of what such professionals come into their work to do. It reminds professionals, and importantly it challenges State Parties who sign and ratify it as the UK did in 1991, that children are to be seen and treated as citizens now, not citizens in waiting.

We bring up children and educate them to be constructive contributors to society. They are entitled to learn about and understand their rights, both in law and under the UNCRC, as part of that upbringing and education. This chapter has presented examples of how the UNCRC serves that purpose and might best be understood and used to enrich our understanding of childhood – not as a phase that will pass to enable emergence into rights as an adult at age 18, but as a life stage with entitlements enshrined in an international treaty.

There is nothing for us to fear and much to gain in enabling children and young people to access and exercise their rights. Certainly, such an enabling approach does not diminish, rather it strengthens, the work of professionals who take the trouble to understand and apply the UNCRC.

References

Berelowitz, S., Firmin, C., Edwards, G. and Gulyurtlu, S. (2012) 'I thought I was the only one. The only one in the world.' The Office of the Children's Commissioner's Inquiry into Child Sexual Exploitation in Gangs and Groups, Interim Report.

Available at: www.childrenscommissioner.gov.uk/sites/default/files/publications/I%20thought%20I%20was%20the%20only%20one%20in%20the%20world.pdf

Berelowitz, S., Clifton, J., Firmin, C., Gulyurtlu, S. and Edwards, G. (2013) 'If only someone had listened.' The Office of the Children's Commissioner's Inquiry into Child Sexual Exploitation in Gangs and Groups, Final Report. Available at: www.childrenscommissioner.gov.uk/sites/default/files/publications/If_only_someone_had_listened.pdf

Centre for Social Justice (2015) Finding their feet. Equipping care leavers to reach their potential. Available at: www.centreforsocialjustice.org.uk/library/finding-feet-equipping-care-leavers-reach-potential

Clifton, J. (2014) The child's voice in the child protection system. In M. Blyth and E. Solomon (eds), *Effective Safeguarding for Children and Young People: What Next after Munro?* London: Policy Press.

Coy, M., Kelly, L., Elvines, F., Garner, M. and Kanyeredzi, A. (2013) 'Sex without consent, I suppose that is rape': How young people in England understand sexual consent. A report commissioned for the Office of the Children's Commissioner's Inquiry into Child Sexual Exploitation in Gangs and Groups. Available at: www.childrenscommissioner.gov.uk/sites/default/files/publications/Sex_without_consent_I_suppose_that_is_rape_newprint.pdf

MacDonald, A. (2011) *The Rights of the Child: The Law and Practice.* Bristol: Jordan Publishing.

Office of the Children's Commissioner (OCC) (2011) 'Don't make assumptions.' Children's and young people's views of the child protection system and messages for change. Available at: www.childrenscommissioner.gov.uk/sites/default/files/publications/Dont%20Make%20Assumptions%20Childrens%20views%20of%20the%20protection%20system%20A4%20paper.pdf

Office of the Children's Commissioner (OCC) (2013) A child rights Impact Assessment of Parts 1–3 of the Children and Families Bill 2013. Available at: www.childrenscommissioner.gov.uk/sites/default/files/publications/Children_and_Families_Bill_CRIA.pdf

Office of the Children's Commissioner (OCC) (2015) Why rights matter. The United Nations Convention on the Rights of the Child and the Work of the Children's Commissioner for England (p 2–26). Available at: www.childrenscommissioner.gov.uk/sites/default/files/publications/Why_Rights_matter_WEB.pdf

Re ZH (Tanzania) v. *SSHD* [2011] UKSC 4.

The All-Party Parliamentary Group for Looked After Children and Care Leavers (2013) The Entitlements Inquiry Report with recommendations.

The All-Party Parliamentary Group for Looked After Children and Care Leavers (2014) The Entitlements Inquiry 'One Year On' Report.

Chapter

8   Birth Mothers Returning to Court

Can a Developmental Trauma Lens Inform Practice with Women at Risk of Repeat Removal of Infants and Children?

Karen Broadhurst, Claire Mason and Sheena Webb

In 2015, members of our research group published new evidence about the size of the population of birth mothers who lose not one but multiple children to public care and adoption in England on account of child protection concerns (Broadhurst et al., 2015). This was the first empirical evidence that returning to the family court having lost a child previously through a court order was far from unusual. Based on national records from the Child and Family Court Advisory (n = 43,541 birth mothers) on care proceedings completed between 2007 and 2014, we estimated that at least one in every four women would return to court over a seven-year period and for the youngest women the probability of return increased to one in three. In our discussions, we also made reference to published work in the US (Grant et al., 2011, 2014), in Australia (Taplin and Mattick, 2015) and in Canada (Novac et al., 2006), which although falling short of providing comparable population estimates, indicates that these particular repeat clients are reported in a range of international jurisdictions.

This new empirical evidence prompts searching questions about whether it is possible to prevent women's return to court – which turns on the question of what kind of personal and environmental difficulties are associated with this particular pattern of repeat appearances? What makes presenting risks difficult to modify and how might the aetiology of women's complex difficulties be explained. Above all, the evidence indicates the need to *differentiate* mothers within child welfare services and the family courts.

In this chapter, we argue that the construct of developmental trauma disorder (variously referred to as complex trauma or complex trauma disorder), provides a conceptual framework for understanding the complex difficulties that beset the lives of this population of women and equally may offer avenues forward in terms of intervention. Starting with illustrative interview extracts from women who have lost multiple children to public care and adoption (from the study referenced above: Nuffield Foundation, 2014–2017), we describe the cumulative and developmental nature of women's difficulties, which start with the care they received in childhood. We then consider in detail the research concerning developmental trauma disorder, together with relevant tools and frameworks for professional intervention. The chapter concludes with a recommendation that further research to test the utility of the construct of developmental trauma disorder, both as an explanatory framework and also in regard to practice tools, may be of considerable value for work with high-risk parents in family court proceedings.

The Impact of Cumulative Trauma in Childhood: Insights from Birth Mothers

The following qualitative extracts from *Gemma* and *Lisa* provide a useful starting point for our discussion of developmental trauma disorder. As part of a multi-method approach, semi-structured interviews were completed with 72 women across seven local authorities, which provided space for women to tell their personal stories of the factors they considered causal in the successive removal of their own children. For the purposes of this chapter we provide illustrative extracts to ground our discussion of developmental trauma disorder (DTD) – a full account of our methodology and findings is published elsewhere (Broadhurst et al., 2015). Gemma and Lisa describe childhoods characterised by abuse and neglect. The two women provide qualitative accounts of what they see as the links between childhood adversity and the complex difficulties they experienced in their adult lives:

Gemma

I was sexually abused as a child, and to blank it out I started taking heroin. I never injected it. I just smoked it. Then obviously it takes a hang on you. Found out I was pregnant and I cut down. I was on £300 a day. I can't remember for the life of me how I was getting that much money, but I did. Then I come off, I think I went down to £100 a day when I was pregnant with my first baby. And then her dad ran out on us. I didn't know what I was doing, because the hospitals nowadays – and I think it's a load of crap – they don't make sure that you can bath your child, you can feed your child, and you can dress your child, especially at 17.

I was living in my own property, just down the road from where I am now actually. But that was hard. Empty house and all I've got is this screaming child. I thought oh my god, what am I going to do? Then my heroin went back up to £300 a day. Two o'clock in the morning you get woken up by a screaming child and it's oh my god, just go to sleep. Some mornings I'd turn over. I will be honest, I'd turn over. But she'd scream that loud that I just couldn't sleep, so I had to get up. I just thought, I can't do this. That's when my heroin went up.

Lisa

My dad died when I was 12 and I remember saying to my mum well, what happens now? And she went off the rails; it was like we can't stay in one place and be happy, we have to keep moving all the time. What happened was when I was 15 I got into a relationship with a man really older than me, he was 40. I was in a woman's refuge with my mum but my mum was staying with her boyfriend at his place and left me within the women's refuge with other people. And this lady that was there said I'm going out; do you want to come with me? And I thought well, it's better than just staying in a big house by myself, so I says yeah, I'll come out with you…

I met him and got pregnant straight away. And it happened straight away. I was in a bad place, I had a bad childhood, he was so much older than me, so obviously he was a lot stronger, a lot wiser than I was… I got postnatal depression and I had obviously depression because he used deliberately to mentally torture me… I never understood until I came out of the relationship with him because I did domestic violence classes, but I used to be… well, I still am, I'm very aware of my looks and I don't feel… I feel very different to people and the way I look, and I'm very insecure about my looks and my weight. And that's always been a problem and he was the only first person really to accept me for the way I was.

These are accounts of *cumulative* personal difficulties – for both women, abuse and neglect in childhood predisposed them to difficulties in adolescence and their adult lives. Gemma says, 'I was sexually abused as a child'; Lisa says, 'I had a terrible childhood.' Gemma's pattern of heroin use developed in adolescence to block out the trauma of sexual abuse, but became an unhelpful coping strategy in the face of demands from her first child. When Gemma describes her partner abandoning her and her baby, her sense of isolation is invoked in her description of an 'empty house'. To cope with the abandonment her heroin use increases, a strategy of coping developed in her youth.

Lisa's father is dead and her mother is absent, her adolescence marked by transience with time spent in temporary accommodation and a women's refuge. Like Gemma, she appears alone in the world and her pattern is to fall into the hands of an abusive older man at the age of 15 with whom she becomes entrapped, despite having successive children removed from her care on account of his abuse of her. Gemma is conflicted in her feelings towards him, and unable to fully grasp the extent of the harm he has inflicted on her and her children. An unhelpful belief system makes it difficult for her to leave him because of negative perceptions of self: 'I feel very different to people and the way I look… that's always been a problem… he was the only person really to accept me for the way I was.'

In both cases, there is a developmental sequence to the difficulties and exposure to harm is cumulative. Both Gemma and Lisa unequivocally implicate childhood trauma and neglect in the difficulties they encountered as adults and continued to experience at the time of interview. Both women received help from children and adult services, but the combination of difficulties they presented were difficult to resolve, resulting in both women losing multiple infants and children to public care and adoption. These are almost textbook accounts of what the National Child Traumatic Stress Network (NCTSN) in the US describe as the 'dual problem' of complex trauma. The NCTSN's definition prompts the analyst or practitioner to consider that childhood trauma has an immediate effect but also impacts on long-term outcomes – it renders children vulnerable to secondary harms and victimisation in adolescence and can seriously impact on adult relationships and parenting capacity. To explain this further, we now turn to look in more detail at the literature.

Developmental Trauma

Judith Herman's (1992) work has been influential in challenging received understandings of trauma. She drew a distinction between the symptomatology of time-limited or event-specific trauma captured by the diagnostic category PTSD (post-traumatic stress disorder) and the complex symptomatology of trauma that results from enduring exposure to multiple stressful events and experiences. Since then a wealth of literature has emerged that has sought to find a way to capture and explain the impact of childhood harms that are persistent and sequential and implicate children's caregivers (van der Kolk et al., 2005; Cloitre et al., 2009; Briere and Lanktree, 2012; Kisiel et al., 2014). A number of frameworks have emerged such as 'relational trauma', 'developmental trauma' and 'complex trauma'. These are overlapping concepts that have in common the aim of accounting for the full range of chronic difficulties suffered by victims of repeated interpersonal trauma.

Developmental trauma disorder (DTD) is one such framework and captures the enduring harms in the context of *interpersonal dependence* (van der Kolk et al., 2005) and is perhaps most relevant to this group of mothers. The proposed symptomology is of a pattern of dysregulated emotion, attention or behaviour in response to trauma cues, as well as persistent distortions in self-concept and expectations of caregiving. Harms can involve emotional, sexual and physical abuse, exposure to violence or neglect (D'Andrea et al., 2012). In addition, problems in the caregiver system intersect with material disadvantage (income and housing) and poor social support networks. In circumstances where children are hurt or in danger, parents and other caregivers are usually able to protect children and help them restore a felt sense of safety and control. Where caregivers are unable to offer this protection and this absence is enduring, proponents of DTD argue that children become intolerably distressed such that they experience their environments as intrinsically unsafe (Bransford and Blizard, 2016).

Returning to the extracts above, Gemma begins using heroin to manage the stress resulting from sexual abuse, but this becomes a maladaptive way of regulating (blocking) emotion. For Lisa, it is her unhelpful belief system about self, coupled with her sense of isolation that renders her vulnerable to exploitation from an older man and without the skills and confidence to exit this highly abusive relationship. A developmental approach to understanding these parents' complex difficulties would suggest that Gemma and Lisa evidence impairments in *developmental processes* related to capacity for emotion regulation and effective interpersonal behaviours (e.g. van der Kolk et al., 2005; Anda et al., 2006; Briere et al., 2008). For both women, their vulnerability means that they accumulate further adverse experiences as they enter adulthood. It is important to emphasise that court-ordered child removal (however necessary to protect children) must be considered a further traumatic event for women who come before the family courts. Child removal will most likely trigger or exacerbate maladaptive coping mechanisms, compound unhelpful belief systems and potentially alienate women further from informal and formal helping networks.

Evidence for the Developmental Impact of Early Trauma

There is a substantial evidence base that confirms the negative impact of childhood abuse and neglect upon adult functioning (Felitti et al., 1998; Widom, 1999; Johnson and Lieberman, 2007; Dube et al., 2005; Koenen et al., 2008). However, as Kisiel et al. (2014) have argued, decades of research on abuse has tended to *isolate single types of abuse* (e.g. sexual abuse or domestic violence) and search for adult correlates of abuse such as problems of mental health, substance misuse or self-harm, rather than identify the core psychological disturbances that are associated with childhood adversity. The work of Bessel van der Kolk and colleagues (2005) has been particularly influential in providing empirical evidence for the need for a new diagnostic framework such as DTD, finding, for example, that 82 per cent of traumatised children seen at the National Child Traumatic Stress Network did not meet the diagnostic criteria for PTSD, despite displaying a range of functional difficulties (Spinazzola et al., 2005). Moreover, a consistent pattern of dysfunction could be observed, comprising: (1) a pervasive pattern of dysregulation, (2) problems with attention and concentration, and (3) difficulties getting along with themselves and others. Trickett et al. (2011), following up 84 girls who had been sexually abused, found that compared to matched controls the abused girls had greater cognitive deficits, depression, dissociation, self-harm, sexual problems, health problems and educational disruption. They also noted a tendency for these girls to have accumulated a host of different, seemingly unrelated, psychiatric diagnoses.

The Adverse Childhood Experiences (ACE) Study conducted by the Kaiser Permanente health maintenance organisation and the Centers for Disease Control and Prevention (CDC) in the US is considered a notable landmark in epidemiological research on this topic, given the size of the sample of individuals followed up and the longevity of the study. Participants were first recruited in 1995 and continue to be followed up today ($n = 17,421$ participants).

Published outputs from this study have clearly demonstrated that exposure to multiple traumas in childhood is associated with increased symptom complexity, mental and physical health problems and a range of risky behaviours (Anda et al., 2006; Felitti and Anda, 2010). Further studies, similarly informed by a trauma lens, provide a consistent body of evidence in favour of the hypothesis that exposure to multiple and or cumulative traumas are predictive of symptom complexity (Copeland et al., 2007; Larson et al., 2008; Green et al., 2010; Widom, 1999; Kisiel et al., 2014; Bremness and Polzin, 2014). A comprehensive account of this work is beyond the scope of this chapter; however, it is clear that this wealth of evidence might clearly inform our own project which is to differentiate parents in the family courts who are at risk of becoming repeat clients.

Despite this accumulation of evidence linking a consistent pattern of psychosocial dysfunction to childhood trauma, and growing clinical consensus concerning the practical utility of DTD concepts and applications (van der Kolk et al., 2005; Cloitre et al., 2009; D'Andrea et al., 2012; Ford et al., 2005), this body of work has had insufficient impact on policy and practice and certainly has not found its way into mainstream thinking about parents within the family courts. Major efforts on the part of trauma researchers who pressed for a new diagnosis of DTD to be included in DSM-5 (*The Diagnostic and Statistical Manual of Mental Disorders*, 5th edition) were unsuccessful (Bransford and Blizard, 2016). Thus, the symptoms of DTD are acknowledged in the DSM-5 only as 'associated and descriptive features of PTSD' (van der Kolk et al., 2005, p. 396). Proposals are in place for the inclusion of a diagnosis of Complex PTSD in the International Classification of Diseases Revision (ICD-11) (Cloitre et al., 2013), although this is still built around the presence of PTSD symptoms and therefore may not capture those impacted by more insidious forms of early relational trauma. As it stands however, there is no accepted framework for diagnosis for those who have experienced complex relational trauma.

Arguably, this 'diagnostic gap' results in the mislabelling of symptoms and ineffective treatment. As the sequelae of complex trauma often manifest as troublesome behaviours, many of the parents we see feel that their underlying emotional need is never addressed, while greater and greater sanctions are applied by the system. The lack of ratification in psychiatric nosology means that services are not obliged to recognise or treat the condition, and experts to the court are bound to shoehorn the spectrum of observed symptoms into an officially recognised, but potentially inaccurate, diagnosis. In this context, the construct of DTD may offer a more comprehensive way of working with parents in the family justice system, if this body of work can find its way into mainstream social work and clinical practice.

Developmental Trauma Disorder and High-Risk Parents in the Family Courts

In our large national cohort study at least one in four women who had one or more children removed by the court returned to court with a subsequent child in the next seven years. The construct of DTD provides a way of understanding both the aetiology of complex symptomatology in this subpopulation of women and potential avenues of intervention. Bringing a developmental trauma lens to professional intervention with women (and indeed fathers) in the family court work requires the practitioner to pay far greater attention to parents' social histories, in order to identify individuals who need a more highly skilled therapeutic response. These are parents who have difficulties engaging with, or who do not respond to, social work's traditional casework model. Signposting these parents to services that offer short-term parent education or domestic violence programmes alone (as is the dint of contemporary social work services) will do little to remedy their complex problems.

While professionals working in the field of social care may recognise that the parent has experienced trauma there appears little understanding of how this trauma impacts on their ability to parent. Rather than offering treatments to deal with the underlying issue of DTD the parent is more likely to be signposted to a range of psycho-educative programmes that compartmentalise and deal separately with presenting symptoms; for example, substance misuse or mental health problems or conflictual intimate relationships. However, these presenting issues are interlinked and unless the core problem of DTD underlying these issues is addressed, it is highly likely that problems will simply persist or re-emerge. Informed by DTD, parents' difficulties are better understood as *complex adaptations* to trauma, developed over the life course, that pose a significant challenge to the helping professional. In this context, there is a fundamental mismatch between social work services that typically monitor difficulties and offer short-term practical assistance and the needs of this particular population of parents.

Assessment tools and instruments have been developed to evaluate the various dimensions of complex trauma and their relative degree of severity (described by Briere and Spinnazola, 2005). Regarding intervention, DTD proponents underscore the importance of supporting, proactively, the creation of safe environments and relationships. In turn, a sense of safety fosters improved emotional regulation and self-management skills. Careful assessment of parents' current level of functioning helps tailor intervention and in addition, the practitioner should identify domains of resilience that can provide the foundation for recovery. There is a general consensus that intervention needs to be sequenced and progressive for those with histories of exposure to complex trauma. The work of Ford and colleagues (2005) has been particularly influential. Ford et al. devised an intervention framework comprising three phases: (a) symptom reduction and stabilisation, (b) processing of traumatic memories and emotions, and (c) life integration and rehabilitation after trauma processing.

A developmental lens would also require far greater investment in state responses to problematic adolescents, given that DTD indicates continuity between adolescent and adult difficulties (Larkin et al., 2014). Individuals with a history of repeat exposure to trauma tend to exhibit a pattern of successive disorders across the life course, including regulatory difficulties in infancy, attachment problems at preschool age, conduct disorder at school age and/or combined conduct and emotional disorders during adolescence (Cook et al., 2005). As such, they are more likely to be received into the criminal justice system and other state services than to receive appropriate mental health treatment. A better understanding of the effects of traumatisation might lead to improved psychosocial treatment options for children and adolescents, drawing on a wealth of published resources and clinical tools (see for example, Ghosh-Ippen et al., 2002; Najivatas, 2002). However, this may require a 'flexing' of the current rigid boundaries between social and health care and adult and children's services. In addition, a greater awareness of long-term outcomes of child abuse and neglect may strengthen the practitioner's sensitivity to adolescents presenting with complex difficulties. Young people presenting with complex difficulties arising from DTD all too easily overwhelm services rather than catalyse effective action.

To conclude, high-risk parents who present as repeat clients of the family court will most likely have presented to services as adolescents but have been deemed hard to help. As adults, this group of parents will most likely be diagnosed with a personality disorder, depressive condition, or be treated for drug and alcohol dependence. However, an improved understanding of the developmental antecedents of a parent's difficulties may lead to a more comprehensive approach to help that aims not only for symptom reduction, but also fully recognises the significance of past relational trauma and the impact that has on adult relationships and engagement with services.

References

Anda, R. F., Felitti, V. J., Bremner, J. D., Walker, J. D., Whitfield, C. H., Perry, B. D., Dube, S. R. and Giles, W. H. (2006) The enduring effects of abuse and related adverse experiences in childhood. *European Archives of Psychiatry and Clinical Neuroscience*, 256(3), 174–86.

Bransford, C. L. and Blizard, R. A. (2016) Viewing psychopathology through a trauma lens. *Social Work in Mental Health*, 15(1), 80–98.

Bremness, A. and Polzin, W. (2014) Commentary: developmental trauma disorder: a missed opportunity in DSM V. *Journal of the Canadian Academy of Child and Adolescent Psychiatry*, 23(2), 142–5.

Briere, J., Kaltman, S. and Green, B. L. (2008) Accumulated childhood trauma and symptom complexity. *Journal of Traumatic Stress*, 21(2), 223–6.

Briere, J. N. and Lanktree, C. B. (2012) *Treating Complex Trauma in Adolescents and Young Adults*. London: SAGE.

Briere, J. and Spinazzola, J. (2005) Phenomenology and psychological assessment of complex posttraumatic states. *Journal of Traumatic Stress*, 18(5), 401–12.

Broadhurst, K., Alrouh, B., Yeend, E., Harwin, J., Shaw, M., Pilling, M., Mason, C. and Kershaw, S. (2015) Connecting events in time to identify a hidden population: birth mothers and their children in recurrent care proceedings in England. *British Journal of Social Work*, 45(8), 2241–60.

Cloitre, M., Stolbach, B. C., Herman, J. L., van der Kolk, B., Pynoos, R., Wang, J. and Petkova, E. (2009) A developmental approach to complex PTSD: childhood and adult cumulative trauma as predictors of symptom complexity. *Journal of Traumatic Stress*, 22(5), 399–408.

Cloitre, M., Garvet, D., Brewin, C. R., Bryant, R. A. and Maercker, A. (2013) Evidence for proposed ICD-11 PTSD and complex PTSD: a latent profile analysis. *European Journal of Psychotraumatology*, 4(1).

Cook, A., Spinazzola, J., Ford, J., Lanktree, C., Blaustein, M., Cloitre, M. and van der Kolk, B. (2005) Complex trauma. *Psychiatric Annals*, 35(5), 390–8.

Copeland, W. E., Keeler, G., Angold, A. and Costello, E. J. (2007) Traumatic events and posttraumatic stress in childhood. *Archives of General Psychiatry*, 64(5), 577–84.

D'Andrea, W., Ford, J., Stolbach, B., Spinazzola, J. and van der Kolk, B. A. (2012) Understanding interpersonal trauma in children: why we need a developmentally appropriate trauma diagnosis. *American Journal of Orthopsychiatry*, 82(2), 187–200.

Dube, S. R., Anda, R. F., Whitfield, C. L., Brown, D. W., Felitti, V. J., Dong, M. and Giles, W. H. (2005) Long-term consequences of childhood sexual abuse by gender of victim. *American Journal of Preventive Medicine*, 28(5), 430–8.

Felitti, V. J. and Anda, R. F. (2010) The relationship of adverse childhood experiences to adult medical disease, psychiatric disorders and sexual behavior: implications for healthcare. In R. A. Lanius, E. Vermetten and C. Pain (eds), *The Impact of Early Life Trauma on Health and Disease*. Cambridge: Cambridge University Press, pp. 77–87.

Felitti, V. J., Anda, R. F., Nordenberg, D., Williamson, D. F., Spitz, A. M., Edwards, V., Koss, M. P. and Marks, J. S. (1998) Relationship of childhood abuse and household dysfunction to many of the leading causes of death in adults: the Adverse Childhood Experiences (ACE) study. *American Journal of Preventive Medicine*, 14(4), 245–58.

Ford, J. D., Courtois, C. A., Steele, K., Hart, O. V. D. and Nijenhuis, E. R. (2005) Treatment of complex posttraumatic self-dysregulation. *Journal of Traumatic Stress*, 18(5), 437–47.

Ghosh-Ippen, C., Ford, J., Racusin, R., Acker, M., Bosquet, K., Rogers, C., Ellis, C., Schiffman, J., Ribbe, D., Cone, P., Lukovitz, M. and Edwards, J. (2002) Traumatic Events Screening Inventory – Parent Report Revised. The Child Trauma Research Project of the Early Trauma Network and The National Center for PTSD Dartmouth Child Trauma Research Group, San Francisco, CA.

Grant, T., Graham, J. C., Ernst, C. C., Peavy, K. M. and Brown, N. N. (2014) Improving pregnancy outcomes among high-risk mothers who abuse alcohol and drugs: factors associated with subsequent exposed births. *Children and Youth Services Review*, 46, 11–18.

Grant, T., Huggins, J., Graham, J. C., Ernst, C., Whitney, N. and Wilson, D. (2011) Maternal substance abuse and disrupted parenting: distinguishing mothers who keep their children from those who do not. *Children and Youth Services Review*, 33(11), 2176–85.

Green, J. G., McLaughlin, K. A., Berglund, P. A., Gruber, M. J., Sampson, N. A., Zaslavsky, A. M. and Kessler, R. C. (2010) Childhood adversities and adult psychiatric disorders in the national comorbidity survey replication I: associations with first onset of DSM-IV disorders. *Archives of General Psychiatry*, 67(2), 113–23.

Herman, J. L. (1992) Complex PTSD: a syndrome in survivors of prolonged and repeated trauma. *Journal of Traumatic Stress*, 5(3), 377–91.

Johnson, V. K. and Lieberman, A. F. (2007) Variations in behavior problems of preschoolers exposed to domestic violence: the role of mothers' attunement to children's emotional experiences. *Journal of Family Violence*, 22(5), 297–308.

Kisiel, C. L., Fehrenbach, T., Torgersen, E., Stolbach, B., McClelland, G., Griffin, G. and Burkman, K. (2014) Constellations of interpersonal trauma and symptoms in child welfare: implications for a developmental trauma framework. *Journal of Family Violence*, 29(1), 1–14.

Koenen, K. C., Stellman, S. D., Sommer, J. F. and Stellman, J. M. (2008) Persisting posttraumatic stress disorder symptoms and their relationship to functioning in Vietnam veterans: a 14-year follow-up. *Journal of Traumatic Stress*, 21(1), 49–57.

Larkin, H., Felitti, V. J. and Anda, R. F. (2014) Social work and adverse childhood experiences research: implications for practice and health policy. *Social Work in Public Health*, 29(1), 1–16.

Larson, K., Russ, S. A., Crall, J. J. and Halfon, N. (2008) Influence of multiple social risks on children's health. *Pediatrics*, 121(2), 337–44.

Najivatas, L. M. (2002) *Seeking Safety: A Treatment Manual for PTSD and Substance Misuse*. New York: Guilford Press.

National Child Traumatic Stress Network (NCTS) (n.d.) How to conduct a comprehensive assessment of complex trauma. Available at: www.nctsn.org/trauma-types/complex-trauma/assessment (accessed 6 January 2017).

Novac, S., Paradis, E., Brown, J. and Morton, H. (2006) A visceral grief: young homeless mothers and loss of child custody. Centre for Urban and Community Studies, University of Toronto.

Spinazzola, J., Ford, J. D., Zucker, M., van der Kolk, B. A., Silva, S., Smith, S. F. and Blaustein, M. (2005) Survey evaluates complex trauma exposure, outcome and intervention among children and adolescents. *Psychiatric Annals*, 35(5), 433–9.

Taplin, S. and Mattick, R. P. (2015) The nature and extent of child protection involvement among heroin-using mothers in treatment: high rates of reports, removals at birth and children in care. *Drug and Alcohol Review*, 34(1), 31–7.

Trickett, P. K., Noll, J. G. and Putnam, F. W. (2011) The impact of sexual abuse on female development: lessons from a multigenerational, longitudinal research study. *Development and Psychopathology*, 23, 453–76.

Van der Kolk, B. A., Roth, S., Pelcovitz, D., Sunday, S. and Spinazzola, J. (2005) Disorders of extreme stress: the empirical foundation of a complex adaptation to trauma. *Journal of Traumatic Stress*, 18(5), 389–99.

Widom, C. S. (1999) Posttraumatic stress disorder in abused and neglected children grown up. *American Journal of Psychiatry*, 156(8), 1223–9.

9 The Family Drug and Alcohol Court

A Problem-Solving Approach to Family Justice

Judith Harwin, Mary Ryan and Sophie Kershaw

Children and their parents who are involved in public law care proceedings are one of the most vulnerable groups in society. The parents have frequently experienced multiple hardships which in turn places their children at risk of significant harm. In the search for ways to break this cycle of harm little attention has been paid to the role of the family court as an agent of change. In this chapter, we consider whether a problem-solving court can play a more active role in effecting change. We use the Family Drug and Alcohol Court (FDAC) as a case example. The FDAC is arguably the most radical development in family justice since the Children Act 1989. Set up to address the widespread problem of parental substance misuse in care proceedings, it is the only type of court that combines treatment of parents during care proceedings with adjudication.

The justice model on which FDAC is based actively includes parents in the legal process, providing them with an opportunity to demonstrate their capacity to change. The way in which the court process is delivered includes entirely new features that are not found in ordinary care proceedings, so to what extent has FDAC been able to improve the life chances of children in England by effecting change in their parents? And what impact has FDAC had on the direction of family justice today? We probe these questions by exploring the origins of FDAC, its treatment outcomes and its justice model. We conclude by considering how far this type of court has the potential to help improve children's prospects when their vulnerability springs from problems other than parental substance misuse.

Problem-Solving Courts: Principle and Practice

Problem-solving courts originated in the USA where they were developed to provide an alternative court approach in criminal justice, particularly where substance misuse or mental health problems were involved in the offending behaviour. US Family Drug Treatment Courts were developed to address problems of child neglect and abuse linked to parental substance misuse that are so serious that the child may need permanent removal from the birth mother. They were a later development than criminal drug courts but their growth across the USA has been rapid. However, outside of the US, there are very few family drug treatment courts. England has the largest number and since the first FDAC opened in 2008 more than 10 courts have been established in different parts of the country. Australia set up its first such pilot court in Victoria in 2014 and Lord Justice Gillen's recent 2016 review of civil and family justice has recommended urgent consideration to the setting-up of a pilot FDAC in Northern Ireland (Review of Civil and Family Justice, 2016). It is noteworthy that problem-solving courts are only to be found in adversarial judicial systems.

The main purpose of problem-solving courts is to address the underlying psychosocial problems that contribute to either offending or to child neglect and abuse in order to prevent recurrence of problems and the likelihood of return to either the criminal or family court. The aim in criminal justice is to help motivate offenders to change and in the family courts it is to motivate parents to change. The principles and practices on which problem-solving courts are rooted is a body of knowledge called 'therapeutic jurisprudence' (Winick, 2002) which draws on motivational psychology and solution-focused approaches. In criminal law the process is based on a mixture of incentives and sanctions. In family courts the incentive is the prospect of regaining care of the child. Failure to do so at the end of the care proceedings is considered to be sufficient loss to dispense with the need for any other sanction.

The growth of the problem-solving court approach in the USA has led to the principles of problem-solving justice being identified. These are:

- Enhanced information – specialist assessment and insight into the problems faced by those before the court and improved understanding of the options available to resolve these issues.
- Collaboration – multidisciplinary teams working to bring about change.
- Procedural fairness – treating people with dignity and respect, listening to what they have to say, showing an interest in helping them, ensuring they understand the process and the consequences of their actions, and making decisions on the best available evidence.
- Accountability – holding people accountable for their actions.
- Focus on outcomes – monitoring the outcomes of the justice system (Wolf, 2007).

FDAC: Developing a Problem-Solving Court within Care Proceedings

A primary reason for developing FDAC in England was to try and find a new way of breaking the cycle of harm associated with parental substance misuse and to improve child and parent outcomes. Parental substance misuse is a leading cause of child neglect and abuse and although there has been no recent research into the prevalence of this issue earlier research suggests it is involved in up to 60–70 per cent of all care proceedings (Forrester and Harwin, 2006). The damage it causes to children's health and development is well-substantiated (Cleaver et al., 2011; Forrester and Harwin, 2011; Adamson and Templeton, 2012; Brandon et al., 2012; Brandon et al., 2013; Hatzis et al., 2017) and without intervention the harm is also likely to be long-term (Felitti and Anda, 2010). Judges and practitioners were also concerned at the number of substance misusing mothers who repeatedly lost children through care proceedings.

The FDAC was piloted between January 2008 and April 2012 in the Central London Family Proceedings Court. It was based on the Family Drug Treatment Courts (FDTCs) operating in the USA but was adapted to fit within the English and Welsh legal and welfare systems (Ryan et al., 2006). Local authorities refer cases into FDAC when they issue care proceedings under s.31 of the Children Act 1989, where the main concern of the local authority is that the child is suffering or at risk of suffering significant harm as a result of parental substance misuse. Parents are given the opportunity to opt out if they do not wish their case to be heard in FDAC. This is the first practical expression of parents being encouraged to take responsibility for decision-making in FDAC.

Other distinguishing features of FDAC are in line with problem-solving court models. They are judicial continuity, fortnightly judge-led review hearings without lawyers present, and a specialist multidisciplinary team that advises the court, provides intensive support to parents as well as closely monitoring their progress and coordinates the delivery of community services to parents. The non-lawyer review hearings are an important judge-led forum for problem-solving and motivation of parents. Also central to FDAC is the role of the specialist team in problem-solving with the judge, and with families and practitioners outside of the court room.

In ordinary care proceedings there is no multidisciplinary team working in this way or judge-led review hearings where the judge plays a problem-solving role and seeks to motivate parents to change. Nor do parents in ordinary proceedings engage in conversation with the judge.

Improving the Life Chances of Children by Effecting Change in Their Parents: The Evidence Base for FDAC

The US evidence base tells a strong and consistent story about the better outcomes achieved in FDTCs for mothers and children at the end of the court proceedings. Compared to ordinary court and service delivery, FDTCs achieve higher rates of family reunification which are linked to higher rates of maternal substance misuse cessation. As a result, rates of out-of-home care are lower and in this way financial savings are secured. These are the main findings which come from the large-scale national evaluation of over 2,000 cases and more recent studies of FDTCs in different states (Worcel et al., 2008; Marlow and Carey, 2012). The higher reunification rates are attributed to greater success in engaging FDTC mothers in substance misuse and other types of treatment, lower rates of dropout, higher re-entry rates after dropout, and higher rates of treatment completion. A crucial question is how far these results are sustained after the court process ends. Compared with the extent of information on outcomes at the end of the court proceedings, there is a lack of longer-term evidence on sustainability in FDTC cases in the US. Small studies following up substantiated child maltreatment and re-entry to foster care in FDTC reunification cases is limited and inconclusive.

The research evidence base in England also tells a strong story, demonstrating that FDAC achieves significantly higher rates of substance misuse cessation and family reunification at the end of proceedings compared to ordinary care proceedings. These results are based on a cohort study of FDAC cases entering the London FDAC and comparison cases entering ordinary proceedings in the same court between January 2008 and August 2012 (Harwin et al., 2014a). Later research published in 2016 is important because as well as looking at outcomes at the end of proceedings it has examined the durability of substance misuse cessation and family reunification up to five years after the court proceedings and FDAC intervention ended (Harwin et al., 2016). Such a long-term follow up of cohort cases after proceedings end is unusual.

The 2016 study found four statistically significant results. At the end of the proceedings a significantly higher proportion of FDAC than comparison mothers had ceased to misuse drugs or alcohol (46% v. 30%; $p=0.017$; sample size is 133 FDAC and 96 comparison mothers) and the rate of family reunification was also significantly higher (37% v. 25%; $p=0.047$; sample size is 140 FDAC and 100 comparison families). Five years after the care proceedings and FDAC intervention ended – and based on survival analysis methodology – more than twice as many FDAC reunification mothers were estimated to have sustained cessation (58% v. 24%; p= 0.007; sample size is 44 FDAC and 22 comparison mothers) and to experience no disruption to family stability three years after proceedings ended (51% v. 22%; p= 0.007; sample size is 44 FDAC and 22 comparison mothers). Due to data availability, this analysis was done at three- rather than five-year follow-up. A composite variable was used (no substance misuse, permanent placement change for a child/children, or return to court).

There were two other results concerning the durability of reunification which would merit further investigation on a larger sample. Neither result reached statistical significance but sizeable percentage differences between FDAC and comparison cases were detected. They were: a higher proportion of FDAC reunified children experienced no disruption within three years after proceedings ended (57% v. 39%; p=0.053; sample size is 61 FDAC and 33 comparison children) and a lower proportion of FDAC than comparison reunified children were estimated to return to court within five years after proceedings ended (34% v. 55%; p=0.058; sample size is 71 FDAC and 42 comparison children).

These results suggest that the FDAC approach is helping achieve better medium-term outcomes for reunified children than ordinary court and that it is better able to reduce the single biggest risk for child re-entry to care, which is return to maternal substance misuse. The results also suggest that FDAC offers an important way of reducing dependency on public care resulting in savings to the public purse.

Empowering Parents: The Contribution of the Court

Many reasons are likely to help explain why FDAC brings about better results for parents than ordinary proceedings and larger studies than are currently available are needed to tease out the different factors. However, as with the US studies, a conclusion of the English evaluations in 2014 and 2016 is that the FDAC court process is a crucial agent of change. The FDAC seems better able than normal proceedings to build on parents' potential to change their lifestyle during the proceedings and for that change to be sustained over time. But even when change is not achieved, the court experience is held to be more humane and compassionate than ordinary court.

Parents, and especially mothers, who misuse substances are heavily stigmatised and their misuse is more likely to be seen as a moral failing than a public health issue. The FDAC is built on a presumption that the parent can change and should be encouraged and supported to do so. It offers hope, which is particularly important for substance misusing mothers who are at risk of losing their children in care proceedings. Starting with a presumption that change is possible creates an entirely different climate in the court. The ethos is one of treating parents with respect, honesty and a determination to reverse the powerlessness that typically characterises addictions (Orford, 2013).

Interviews with 28 mothers and nine fathers in the London FDAC in 2009–11 (Harwin et al., 2014) show just how receptive parents are to this approach. As 15 of the mothers had had previous children removed by the court they were able to draw out the differences they experienced between the FDAC and ordinary court.

In FDAC the judge and team made them feel 'normal', they 'treated you like a human being', 'talked about normal things', 'put you at your ease'. Parents valued 'not being judged straight away'. In ordinary care proceedings they felt they had been treated as 'junkies' or 'prostitutes'.

FDAC also made them feel hopeful whereas in ordinary court mothers said that they were made to feel that there was very little chance of being allowed to keep their child. 'Instead of trying to help us', commented one parent about children's services, 'it felt as if they were trying to find the case to put against us'.

Earning the praise of the judge in particular motivated parents because it made them feel 'hopeful' and it confirmed their progress. It tended to be valued much more than praise from other professionals and it boosted confidence.

> No-one praised me before. My solicitor does, but I expect that. When I go to court I come out feeling really happy. My social worker never praises me, or never says it in a way that feels nice. (Parent)

However, as important as hope was honesty, because parents knew where they stood. They felt the process was transparent.

> Instead of fibbing we're encouraged [by the team] to be honest and if we relapse, or lapse even, we're told it wouldn't be the end of it, because they would work with us about that. They were being honest with us and making it easier for us to be honest with them. (Parent)

> The judge today was very definite. I am back in court in two weeks and I could lose my child then. You know where you stand. It is upsetting to be told I might lose her, but I'd rather know – it means I've got a goal to work towards. (Parent)

The non-lawyer review hearings enabled problems to be aired in a 'open and honest' way and positive feedback boosted parents' confidence.

> It is positive for us to see how we are progressing and have progressed, and we like everyone else to see how well we are doing too. (Parent)

The availability and support of the FDAC team was a key ingredient in helping parents take back some control over their lives and sustain it.

> I was all over the place. I was missing appointments because I didn't know what the hell I was doing. When I got introduced to FDAC it was like they were my diary and they were telling me where I had to be. They were my rock and my support. (Parent)

By contrast:

> I've been through an ordinary care case before and normally you wouldn't get any advice. This is what I think I need. In the other court no-one actually works with you. All that the social workers said was 'go to rehab'. (Parent)

Professionals' views were gathered through interviews and focus groups and they too were positive about the ethos of hope and transparency within FDAC and were unanimous in their view that FDAC as a whole (the specialist team and the court process) supported parents in an intensive way that is markedly different from what happens in ordinary care proceedings.

> Clients say they don't feel pushed around, patronised and intimidated like they do in ordinary care proceedings. (Social worker)

Professionals also commented on the advantages of an approach that was focused on helping parents to succeed in overcoming their problems.

> The whole FDAC philosophy is that the approach CAN work – and parents get that message very early on, whereas in other cases parents feel everyone has given up on them. (Lawyer)

Perhaps unsurprisingly given the experiences of honesty and clarity, lawyers, social workers and guardians all noted that there is much less conflict and antagonism in FDAC cases than in ordinary care proceedings.

The collaborative nature of proceedings did not serve to hinder progress of this case in any way, or cause tensions amongst involved parties. If anything, the atmosphere generated at FDAC allowed for more open discussion and exploration about the best way forward. (Social worker)

If parents have all the services they need offered to them, but still cannot control their substance misuse, this helps them accept that they cannot care for their child. (Family lawyer)

The judge's role in problem-solving was demonstrated by court observations carried out between 2008 and 2012 in the pilot FDAC and more recently in 10 FDACs, some newly established, in 2016 (Harwin et al., 2014a; Tunnard et al., 2016).

The overall conclusion of these observations was that the judges were operating in accordance with problem-solving principles and the 2016 study found that new FDACs were achieving fidelity to the evaluated model of the London FDAC. This was an encouraging indicator that FDAC can be successfully rolled out beyond the pilot. The judges were talking to parents and inviting their views; acknowledging family strengths and praising parents; explaining the aims of FDAC and decisions made; urging parents to take responsibility and explaining the consequences of prioritising their own needs over those of their children.

If this happens again it will feed into my decision-making. You have to show you can sustain it for the children... that's the question for me, even though I want them to stay with you for the rest of their childhood. (Judge to parent)

Don't forget what you have heard today. People speak the truth and everyone is very pleased with the progress you are making. (Judge to parent)

The ethos of hope and transparency in FDAC is something FDAC judges appreciate.

It gives parents a real chance to change with appropriate support. Importantly, it is humane. Even parents who do not succeed come away acknowledging that they have had a proper chance. That is why so few cases end in contested final hearings. (Judge)

Building on FDAC: What Has Been the Impact of FDAC on Family Justice?

The evidence to date suggests that the FDAC approach is providing an entirely new way of supporting parents to meet their children's developmental needs. Traditionally, courts have been seen as a last resort: in FDAC they are the vital vehicle of change. The help is directed at parents rather than their children but the child's welfare comes first, whether that means return home or permanency in an alternative family. In this way, FDAC provides the same protection rights as ordinary court but gives opportunities that would not otherwise be available to build new lives.

The FDAC model is taking root and in its relatively short life it has proved remarkably influential among policymakers and service planners. It was endorsed by the Family Justice Review (2011, p. 19, para 100) as 'showing considerable promise' and by the Munro Review of Child Protection (2011, pp. 102–4) for its distinctive multidisciplinary approach and its wider applicability beyond just the court arena. The President of the Family Division (View from the President's Chambers, 2014) has called for FDAC to be rolled out nationally because 'it works' and he has held FDAC up as the template for the family court more generally: 'The family court must become, in much of what it does, a problem-solving court' (View from the President's Chambers, 2016). The President went on to note that by tackling the parents' underlying problems, FDAC is more effective than ordinary proceedings in reducing the risk of return to court.

Debates have begun about the possibility of extending the FDAC approach to other types of problems apart from parental substance misuse. As neglect is the single largest cause of care proceedings nationally, the potential value of extending FDAC to neglect cases that are not triggered by parental substance misuse is considerable. Other problems that are seen as potentially suitable for a problem-solving approach are domestic violence and mental health. These problems are frequently part of the presentation in FDAC cases in any event and FDAC specialist teams often include professionals with expertise in working with domestic violence and adult mental health problems. One established FDAC has also included cases of physical abuse and cases where adolescents are beyond the control of the parents. The challenge here will be identifying ways of measuring change in parents that are robust and in ensuring that parents can access interventions and approaches that show evidence of effectiveness.

The possibilities of extending problem-solving courts to young recurrent mothers caught up in a cycle of frequent re-entry into the court have also been considered (Harwin et al., 2014b). There are several reasons to think that a specialist FDAC-type of court would be particularly beneficial for this group of parents. It would help intercept the negative cycle of ever-swifter returns to court and repeat removal of infants. It would allow the voice of the mother (or young father) to be heard directly, and aim to provide a positive experience of courts that would help these very young parents become problem-solvers. A new pilot is looking at an Early FDAC model working with pregnant mothers who have had one child removed, and early feedback has been positive.

Despite calls for wider roll-out from the President of the Family Division, a sound evidence base and popularity among policymakers, extending FDAC's impact on family justice and sustaining that has proved challenging. The major impact of the Family Justice Review has been to reinforce the idea of the court as a last resort for speedy adjudication and although FDAC has demonstrated it can work within the tighter time limits which now apply to proceedings (S 14 Children and Families Act 2014, amending s.32 Children Act 1989), the message from the evaluation that cases should go into FDAC as early as possible (Harwin et al., 2014a) is contrary to the focus on intensive pre-proceedings work before cases enter court.

Introducing any innovation in times of austerity is particularly difficult and harder still when the approach requires a complete culture change from ordinary court and activity in relation to care proceedings. The continuing barrier to wider roll-out is the need for additional resources to set up the specialist team and the need for a new FDAC to run for at least three years before new sites will be able to get a true sense of outcomes being achieved. Currently, the funding of the specialist team comes primarily from children's services departments with contributions from Public Health in some sites and although there is evidence of longer-term cost benefits of FDAC, there are insufficient immediate cash savings for many local authorities. Wider roll-out will remain a challenge while the burden for financing FDAC remains on hard-pressed local authorities.

Conclusions

The evidence presented in this chapter suggests that FDAC is an example of a court taking a proactive, and effective, approach to support parents to achieve change. It is contributing to more durable medium-term parent and child outcomes and providing a better and more humane experience of justice and value for money that is valued by parents and professionals alike. Moreover, the model is replicable, laying the foundations for future good outcomes in the new FDAC courts that are being established.

There is every reason to invest in FDAC and to continue to research its impacts once the numbers accessing FDAC have grown sufficiently to enable a fuller study of its contribution than is currently possible. At the present time, FDAC is the most promising approach within the court arena to breaking the cycle of intergenerational harm for children affected by parental substance misuse.

References

Adamson, J. and Templeton, L. (2012) *Silent Voices: Supporting Children and Young People Affected by Parental Alcohol Misuse.* London: The Office of the Children's Commissioner.

Brandon, M., Sidebotham, P., Bailey, S., Belderson, P., Hawley, C., Ellis, C. and Megson, M. (2012) New learning from serious case reviews. Department for Education, Research Report DFE-RR226.

Brandon, M., Bailey, S., Belderson, P. and Larsson, B. (2013) Neglect and serious case reviews. University of East Anglia/NSPCC.

Cleaver, H., Unell, I. and Aldgate, J. (2011) *Children's Needs, Parenting Capacity: The Impact of Parental Mental Illness, Problem Alcohol and Drug Use and Domestic Violence on Children's Development*, 2nd edn. London: The Stationery Office.

Family Justice Review (2011) Final report. Available at: www.gov.uk/government/uploads/system/uploads/attachment_data/file/217343/family-justice-review-final-report.pdf

Felitti, V. J. and Anda, R. F. (2010) The relationship of adverse childhood experiences to adult health, well-being, social function, and healthcare. In R. Lanius, E. Vermetten and C. Pain (eds), *The Impact of Early Life Trauma on Health and Disease: The Hidden Epidemic.* Cambridge: Cambridge University Press (www.theannainstitute.org/Lanius.pdf).

Forrester, D. and Harwin, J. (2006) Parental substance misuse and child care social work: findings from the first stage of a study of 100 families. *Child and Family Social Work*, 11(4), 325–35.

Forrester, D. and Harwin, J. (2011) *Parents Who Misuse Drugs and Alcohol.* Chichester: Wiley.

Harwin, J., Alrouh, B., Ryan, M., Tunnard, J. et al. (2014a) Changing lifestyles, keeping children safe: an evaluation of the first Family Drug and Alcohol Court (FDAC) in care proceedings. Brunel University. Available at: http://wp.lancs.ac.uk/cfj-fdac/publications/

Harwin, J., Broadhurst, K., Kershaw, S., Shaw, M., Alrouh, B. and Mason, C. (2014b) Recurrent care proceedings: part 2: young motherhood and the role of the court. *Family Law*, 44, 1439–43.

Harwin, J., Alrouh, B., Ryan, M., McQuarrie, T., Golding, L., Broadhurst, K., Tunnard, J. and Swift, S. (2016) After FDAC: outcomes 5 years later. Final Report. Lancaster University. Available at: http://wp.lancs.ac.uk/cfj-fdac/publications/

Hatzis, D., Dawe, S., Harnett, P. and Barlow, J. (2017) Quality of caregiving in mothers with illicit substance misuse: a systematic review and meta-analysis. *Substance Abuse: Research and Treatment.*

Marlow, D. B. and Carey, S. (2012) Research Update on Family Drug Courts, National Association of Drug Court Professionals NADCP, file:///C:/Users/Judith/Documents/INNOVATION%20FUND%2004.11.15/RESEARCH/Reseach%20Update%20on%20Family%20Drug%20Courts%20-%20NADCP.pdf

Munro, E. (2011) *The Munro Review of Child Protection. Final Report. A Child*

Centred System. London: Department for Education.

Orford, J. (2013) *Power, Powerlessness and Addiction*. Cambridge: Cambridge University Press.

Review of Civil and Family Justice (2016) The Review Group's Draft Report on Family Justice, 4 August.

Ryan, M., Harwin, J. and Chamberlain, C. (2006) Report on the feasibility of establishing a family drug and alcohol court at Wells St Family Proceedings Court. Available at: http://wp.lancs.ac.uk/cfj-fdac/publications/

Tunnard, J., Ryan, M. and Harwin, J. (2016) Problem solving in the court: current practice in England. Available at: http://fdac.org.uk/wp-content/uploads/2016/09/Problem-solving-in-court-current-practice-in-FDACs-in-England-September-2016_BA.pdf

View from the President's Chambers (12) (2014) The process of reform next steps. Available at: www.familylaw.co.uk/news_and_comment/12th-view-from-the-president-s-chamber-the-process-of-reform-next-steps#.WJRaz_mLTIU

View from the President's Chambers (15) (2016) The looming crisis. Available at: www.judiciary.gov.uk/wp-content/uploads/2014/08/pfd-view-15-care-cases-looming-crisis.pdf

Winick, B. J. (2002) Therapeutic jurisprudence and problem solving courts. *Fordham Urban Law Journal*, 30(3), Article 4.

Wolf, R. V. (2007) Principles of problem solving justice. Centre for Court Innovation, New York. Available at: www.courtinnovation.org/topic/problem-solving-justice

Worcel, S., Furrer, C., Green, B., Burrus, S. and Finigan, M. (2008) Effects of family treatment drug courts on substance abuse and child welfare outcomes. *Child Abuse Review*, 17, 427–43.

10

Why Video Interaction Guidance in the Family Drug and Alcohol Court?

Hilary Kennedy, Fran Feeley and Sophie Kershaw

This chapter describes an adaptation of Video Interaction Guidance (VIG) as an assessment and treatment tool in the Family Drug and Alcohol Court (FDAC). In the previous chapter the authors described FDAC as one of the most radical developments in family justice since the Children Act 1989 and the only type of court that combines treatment of parents during care proceedings with adjudication (see Chapter 9 in this volume). The FDAC model continues to develop and innovate and the incorporation of VIG is an example of this. The three authors write from different perspectives in this chapter: Sophie Kershaw, Co-Director of the FDAC National Unit and previously Service Manager of the London FDAC; Hilary Kennedy, lead trainer/supervisor in VIG; and Fran Feeley, Senior Practitioner in FDAC and VIG practitioner (trainee). We describe how VIG was introduced to and then works in FDAC. We will look at the research evidence on the effectiveness of VIG as an intervention and then more recent evidence on its use as an assessment tool. VIG working in FDAC is then illustrated with some case studies. Finally, we will consider how useful VIG has been in the FDAC model and the new directions for VIG in FDAC.

The Start of the Story

The FDAC model is described in detail in Chapter 9. However, very briefly, FDAC works with families in care proceedings. It is a combination of three elements: first, a problem-solving family court; second, a therapeutic team with child, adult and family specialists, linked to a network of treatment agencies that deal with drug and alcohol abuse, domestic abuse, mental health and much more; and third, a 'trial for change', which is an individualised programme of assessment, treatment and support designed to give families the best possible chance to overcome their problems in a timescale compatible with their child/ren's needs.

When FDAC started in 2008, the 'trial for change' focused on parents demonstrating change in their substance misuse. Within a few months of getting going, the partner local authorities asked FDAC to undertake a more holistic assessment and intervention to include parents demonstrating change in their capacity to meet their children's needs. The FDAC team set about finding an approach that would help parents learn new skills in parenting and developing relationships quickly, because timeliness was becoming increasingly important as care proceedings shortened.

Sophie Kershaw became interested in VIG when she first heard Hilary Kennedy speaking at the Association for Child Psychology and Psychiatry headquarters. She was particularly keen on how VIG appeared to fit with FDAC's principles around building relationships and developing insight. She thought that VIG would assist the team to assess and promote parents' insight, reflective capacity, mentalisation and sensitivity and responsiveness to their child and others. She also saw VIG as a chance to give the social workers in her team the opportunity to develop their engagement and intervention skills.

She contacted Hilary and the London FDAC team were all trained and supervised, and now as new workers joining the team they continue to be trained and supervised. This productive collaboration has now lasted over seven years. The strong supervision element of VIG means practitioners can be trained for two days and then get started working with parents and their children immediately.

Using VIG in Assessment

VIG is more usually used as an intervention rather than as part of an assessment and intervention process. The FDAC wanted to adapt VIG as a way of developing the team's skills in assessment and intervention, and to offer parents an opportunity to take part in a process of change while under assessment. They believed that assessment should go alongside intervention forming a 'dynamic assessment' (Feuerstein et al., 1979 [2002]) or, in other words, assessing the capacity to change alongside the current level of functioning.

It could be argued that from the moment a parent connects with FDAC, they are being given a 'supported' chance to change. In this context, which requires very careful transparency, FDAC aims to determine the parent's capacity to learn and change, by starting where they are, looking for the parent's strengths however small and seeing how far they can travel during the VIG assessment/intervention process.

To understand how VIG fits within the FDAC assessment model, the next section will give a short introduction to VIG as an intervention, and the interested reader is directed to the first chapter of the recent book on VIG (Kennedy et al., 2011) and the website www.videointeractionguidance.net.

What is VIG as an Intervention?

VIG is a relationship-based intervention that helps parents become more sensitive and attuned to their child's emotional needs by seeing and interpreting their children's signals and exploring their own successful responses with an 'attuned' professional.

The core theoretical principles for VIG were derived from the acute observations of Colwyn Trevarthen, a psychologist and psychobiologist using ethological methods. He saw how active the tiniest infants are in developing cooperative activities with their parents and studied successful interactions between infants and their primary caregivers, and found that the mother's responsiveness to her baby's initiatives supported and developed 'intersubjectivity' (shared understanding), which he regarded as the basis of all effective communication, interaction and learning. The way intersubjectivity and mediated learning underpin VIG are explored in the VIG book (Cross and Kennedy, 2011; Trevarthen and Aitken, 2001) and are illustrated in Figure 10.2.

In practice, VIG starts by engaging parents in a possible change process and helps them form questions about how to improve their relationship with their child. A filming session is carefully set up to capture the best possible interactions achievable at that time. The VIG practitioner then takes five to 10 minutes of video of the parent interacting with their child. The aim is to capture moments of 'better than usual' interaction on video by prompting or encouraging if necessary. The VIG practitioner then edits the video, selecting a few very short clips of successful interaction that link to the parent's goals for change. These are very likely to be exceptions to the usual pattern and exemplify various principles of attuned

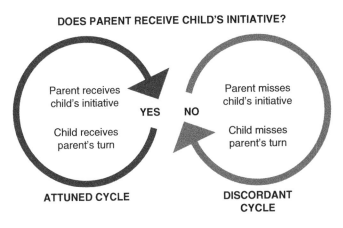

Figure 10.1 'Yes' cycle and 'no' cycle.

contact, especially the parent's reception of their child's initiatives. In the shared review session that follows, the parent and VIG practitioner study the selected micro-moments very carefully working out together what the parent is doing that helps to build an attuned relationship with her child and moves her towards her own goal. Through seeing their own attuned responses to their children, parents can start to observe and then to understand how important these experiences are for their children. The parents are active in their own learning process, first describing what they see themselves and their children doing, and then exploring their thoughts, feelings and their child's developmental needs. They lead their own 'learning journey' by identifying their own strengths and setting new goals at each reflective session. At the same time, they are experiencing an attuned interaction with the VIG practitioner who follows their initiatives. This 'shared review' is filmed and taken to VIG supervision where the trainee and supervisor micro-analyse the moments of optimal contact and discuss plans for further improvements in the quality of interaction in the shared review.

VIG is a compassionate approach where hope is maintained and trust is formed through building respectful therapeutic relationships. VIG practitioners demonstrate their beliefs, from the first meeting, by their own attuned interaction with their clients. They convey that change, even in adverse situations, is always a possibility and that the key to supporting change is an affirmation and appreciation of strengths alongside an empathetic regard for what people are already managing in difficult circumstances. This 'sympathetic' professional relationship is often in stark contrast to others encountered in the child protection system, where parents can easily feel blamed.

The parents are not taught how to interact better with their children, but rather to learn by seeing themselves being attentive to their children's signals, then seeing the impact on their children of returning an attuned response. This learning starts with an emotional response before the cognitive understanding. The VIG practitioner also observes the pleasure on parents' faces as they see themselves succeeding in responding to their child. This is the first step in restoring a sense of pride in themselves as parents, and moving away from the feelings of shame that have predominated.

The aim of VIG is to support the move from 'no' to 'yes' cycle interaction patterns, as illustrated in Figure 10.1. This is something that families find easy to understand and helps them set plans for their own change.

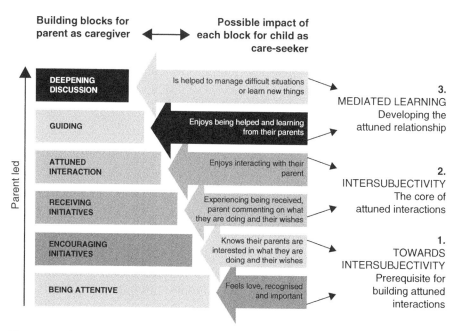

Figure 10.2 The building blocks of VIG.

Often parents involved in FDAC will ignore most of their children's initiatives (signals), and respond in a discordant way to those that are noticed. VIG can immediately focus on the heart of the problem and support the parent to notice their initiatives and then respond in a sensitive, attuned way.

Some children, who have lived with parents who have been unable to focus on them, may have given up trying to communicate with their parents and VIG provides the foundations for parents to restore contact with their children. Babies who have been ignored often arch away or look towards another adult who seems engaging. The parents are encouraged to start 'being attentive' to their child and then 'encourage initiatives' from their child by leaving space and simply saying what they see their child doing, and perhaps thinking or feeling. Parents are supported to find the language for their own and their children's emotions during the shared reviews.

The VIG attuned principles for interaction and guidance are illustrated below as steps. Once the first two steps are mastered, the parent is ready to receive their child's initiative and then to start playing; having fun and guiding their child to learn new skills and manage difficult situations. Many interventions start with helping parents guide or 'teach' their children. VIG focuses on restoring a loving relationship where the parent can follow their child before they help the child follow the parent (Figure 10.2).

The principles for attuned interaction are equally important for the relationship between the VIG practitioner and the parent. In VIG the practitioner is encouraged to establish a trusting relationship by activating the parent, receiving their thoughts and emotions before 'giving advice'. In turn, the VIG supervisor uses the attuned principles to maximise the active enjoyable learning in supervision. There is a parallel process where both the parent and the VIG practitioner experience and celebrate their strengths on video with an 'interested' other (Figure 10.3).

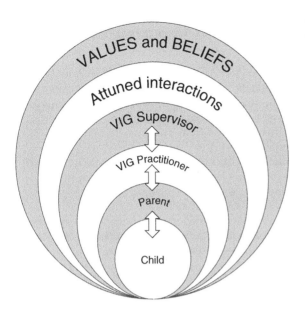

Figure 10.3 The embedded 'attunement' within the VIG process.

It is important that the arrows (interactions between people) go two ways and exemplify the core values and beliefs of VIG and FDAC. What happens is that VIG builds vital, energising relationships at all levels and this provides the energy and hope to sustain change. This will be brought to life when the VIG practitioner discusses her work in the next section.

Using VIG in FDAC

Where parents demonstrate sufficient change or promise with regard to their abstinence from drugs and/or alcohol, they will be offered VIG. At this stage parents receive one to two cycles (cycle = video of them with their child and a video of the shared review with the VIG practitioner) with the focus on being attentive and encourage their child/ren's initiatives. A further three to four cycles are offered where the FDAC team feel they can build on emergent reflective capacity to promote a specific aspect of parenting such as meal times, play or setting boundaries or to support a period of transition such as a child returning home to their parent.

The two case studies below are typical of FDAC work. They are 'blended' examples of what we commonly see, and are not individual or traceable families. The first case shows VIG being offered as part of a parenting assessment with two cycles being undertaken with each parent. The second case study demonstrates VIG as a longer intervention of four cycles.

Case Study A

The family consisted of mother, father and baby Clea (10 months). The case came into proceedings as a result of the parents' substance misuse, drug-related criminal lifestyles and domestic violence in the mother's previous relationships. The parents lived together, but Clea was removed and placed into foster care at birth. They were working towards Clea being returned to their full-time care.

The mother and father were both first-time parents who had experienced emotionally harmful and neglectful caregiving as children. The mother left home at a very young age and the father had spent time in care as a child. VIG was used to look at the quality of the parent–infant relationship for each parent.

VIG Work Undertaken

Although the mother reported that she found the initial filming session intrusive and threatening, she very much enjoyed watching her and Clea pass a favourite toy to one another in the first shared review. Once she had seen how she could respond to her child's interests, she said this motivated her to be more attentive and to try and replicate the same quality of interaction after filming and in the next session.

The father also said he was initially anxious about being videoed. However, in the first shared review he said he was filled with joy when he saw Clea turn, look at him and smile. He said it suddenly struck him that he was important to her, which he had doubted because he was only having a few hours of contact with her a week. The VIG practitioner and the father could share the experience of seeing him being attentive to his daughter, offering her space, mirroring her vocalisations, combined with his friendly posture and warm tone. He reported that seeing video clips of Clea responding to him really helped improve his confidence as a father.

The FDAC team observed a number of strengths in the parent–child relationship between each parent and Clea. This helped inform wider decisions around the parents resuming care of Clea.

Through providing supportive feedback, the parents were observed to be better able to attend to Clea's cues, which not only promoted more positive interactions, but also encouraged Clea's development. Enhanced communication was also seen between the parents along with increased self-awareness and mentalising capacities.

Case Study B

The family consisted of mother, father and two children, Ben (seven) and Amy (three). The case was in care proceedings because of the parents' long history of substance misuse and domestic violence. The parents were now separated. The FDAC team worked with both parents; however, the father engaged inconsistently and continued to use drugs. The mother was abstinent when FDAC began working with her and the children had recently returned home after living with their aunt while the mother undertook six months of residential treatment.

The mother was offered VIG to help her address a negative cycle of interaction with the older child Ben. The mother was depressed, lacking in self-esteem and at times seemed overwhelmed by the task of parenting. Ben had been more exposed than his younger sister to the parents' substance misuse and domestic violence. He struggled to regulate his emotions and would often lash out. He was self-critical and could be impatient and easily frustrated. Ben also looked like his father, and his mother reported that his aggression reminded her of the violence she had experienced with his father, evoking some of the negative feelings and responses she had towards his father.

VIG Work Undertaken

Because the mother had very low self-esteem she initially struggled to look at herself on film and was very self-critical. By focusing on video clips of happy moments where she and her children were observed laughing together, the mother was able to develop a more positive perception of her parenting and in particular her relationship with Ben.

When the clips were micro-analysed to identify what had resulted in the interaction going so well, the VIG practitioner saw that she was providing Ben with good eye-contact, space and time to explore and interact, while encouraging him and offering praise. The positive feedback the mother received from watching these clips inspired her to try and replicate these moments.

Significant positive changes in interaction were noted between the mother and Ben. An improvement in maternal sensitivity was observed and a change in the discordant pattern of communication that had developed over time. As the mother's attunement improved, so too did her self-efficacy as she was reminded through the video clips of the many good interactions she had with Ben and the positive role she played in that interaction.

The therapeutic relationship that developed between the mother and VIG practitioner was also important and contributed further to the mother's success. Through being actively involved in her own change and being able to recognise and name it during the shared reviews her confidence increased.

Parents usually expect to be criticised in the context of care proceedings, but by using VIG they can hope for a better future. By the end of the VIG work, the FDAC team regularly observed playful and fun interactions between the mother and Ben. There was a reduction in the mother's anxiety, she became more overtly affectionate towards Ben and in turn there was an improvement in Ben's behaviour.

Reflections on Why VIG Works Well in FDAC

Practitioners training in VIG can start implementing VIG with families under supervision straight after the initial two-day training course. This means that the knowledge and skills from the course are still fresh for the workers and they are well supported with regular VIG supervision. It also helps that VIG is very much a collaborative process where meaning is co-constructed with the parent, so the practitioner is not expected to be 'an expert'. This means that the parent naturally develops their own observations and reflections which are so important for maintenance of change.

The families say they enjoy receiving positive feedback about successful interactions with their children. This can be very affirming and empowering for parents who are lacking confidence and self-esteem. Also seeing themselves sharing moments of positive connection with their children provides parents with moments of joy, which is so important when their children are not living with them.

The use of VIG during the assessment process at FDAC gives the parent a chance to show their capacity for change in their attunement to their child, in the way they can talk to their child about what they are doing and might be thinking or feeling, in the way they can recover contact with their child when it is broken and in the way they can reflect on what they are doing and how they are changing. This can provide valuable evidence to the court of a parent's capacity to meet their child's emotional needs both now and in the longer term.

The relational approach of FDAC is very similar to VIG with trust between the practitioner and parent being central to the work. This is only possible if the assessment process is transparent, authentic and at the same time hopeful. Looking at video of shared reviews in VIG supervision helps practitioners achieve more attuned practitioner–parent interactions. These are skills which practitioners can use in a variety of other FDAC clinical and court settings.

The use of VIG in FDAC affords parents an opportunity to really focus on the needs of and relationship with their child. This complements the work they are doing in treatment, which is generally more focused on their own difficulties. The combination provides a holistic way to understand families and a realistic basis for planning for the future.

Does VIG Support Change?

The case studies above illustrate the changes that can be seen in the videos of parent–child interaction and the development of the reflective function of the parent as recorded during the shared review. This mirrors the findings of VIG practitioners in the UK over the last 20 years. Recently, the first 50 families where neglect had been identified received a short VIG intervention from NSPCC staff during their VIG training. The results were impressive with the families improving significantly in the quality of interaction, communication and limit setting (Kennedy et al., 2015). Another UK study concerned parents with infants under three months who were mandated by a court order to be in a residential treatment because of child protection concerns. Parent–child interactions were measured using the CARE-index for 15 parent–child dyads who received 'treatment as usual' and eight parent–child dyads who received VIG alongside treatment as usual. The study found a significant effect size (d=0.5). Before the intervention only 25 per cent of the VIG intervention group were scoring in the 'good enough' range whereas 87.5 per cent were considered 'good enough' and all the families who were 'of concern' had made at least two points improvement. These results are fully reported in 'Video Interaction Guidance as a method to promote secure attachment' (Kennedy et al., 2010).

Internationally, there is increasing evidence that sensitivity-focused video feedback methods are one of the few methods that are effective in improving parental sensitivity, children's behaviour and attachment patterns between parents and children (Bakermans-Kranenburg et al., 2003; Fukkink, 2008; Fukkink et al., 2011; Moss et al., 2011; Høivik et al., 2015). At the 2015 Society for Research in Child Development (SRCD) conference in Philadelphia, several presentations described new evidence of the effectiveness of video feedback interventions in the field of maltreatment and neglect. Marinus Van IJzendoorn shared the University of Leiden's new meta-analysis of what works in preventing or reducing maltreatment. This showed that few interventions work with the exception of methods using video feedback and focusing on sensitivity, which consistently showed a significant effect size.

As a result of this research, video feedback, including VIG, is now recommended as an evidence-based intervention in the National Institute for Health and Care Excellence (NICE) guidelines: 'Children's attachment: attachment in children and young people who are adopted from care, in care, or at high risk of going into care' (NICE, 2015), and 'Social and emotional wellbeing – early years' (NICE, 2012).

VIG trained parent–infant psychotherapists are impressed by the speed with which some parents with significant mental health problems can change their representations of themselves as parents and their perception of their child. They document VIG's power to enable parents to move from a negative representation of their relationship with their child to a more positive and hopeful narrative (Pardoe, 2016) while decreasing anxiety in the parents (Celebi, 2013).

How Does VIG Promote Change?

For an in-depth discussion of the reasons why VIG works, the reader is referred to the theory chapter in the VIG book (Cross and Kennedy, 2011). To summarise the arguments from that chapter, VIG is based on a cooperative intersubjective model where the interaction in the space between people is the main focus (Trevarthen and Aitken, 2001). The method recognises the bidirectional influence of the two partners in any interaction. The celebration of joyful, playful interaction with the attuned, appreciative VIG practitioner opens them both to be able to think together about the new meanings and narratives. The pattern for parental pain and trauma triggering violence or neglect of themselves and their children is a hard cycle to break. VIG has shown to be a powerful catalyst for change for the better (De Zulueta, 2015).

At the 2014 VIG International Conference, Jane Barlow, Professor of Public Health at the University of Warwick, put forward the following hypotheses. VIG develops sensitive responsiveness within a balanced mid-range model, reflective function/mentalisation and mind-mindedness in *both* the parent with their child and the VIG practitioner with the parent. In the next subsection, these terms are unpacked with reference to the parent–child interaction, however the reader is urged to reflect on the parallel process from the VIG practitioner with the parent (Kennedy et al., 2017).

Sensitive Responsiveness

The parent learns to see and understand their children's initiatives and how to respond in a way that connects with their child, who in turn feels loved and understood. There is strong evidence that interventions that promote sensitivity promote secure attachment and reduce behaviour problems (Bakermans-Kranenburg et al., 2003; Moss et al., 2011; Beebe and Steele, 2013).

Mid-range Contingency

Parents are supported to find a flexible balance between giving the child space to regulate themselves and to be in attuned interaction with them. They become experienced at 'repairing ruptures', which are crucial to optimal development. This is in contrast the poles of 'excessive' monitoring by the parent at the expense of allowing self-regulation (high contingency) or 'withdrawal' of the parent (low contingency). The mid-range model predicts secure attachment while both high and low contingency predict insecure attachment (Beebe and Lachmann, 2002).

Learning that their children thrive when they have the space to offer 'good enough' parenting (Bettleheim, 1987) is important, as so often the parents in FDAC set very high standards for themselves and can so easily give up at the first sign of failure. They must be encouraged to find a healthy balance in the way they respond to the initiatives (or demands) of their children.

Reflective Function/Mentalisation

The parent learns to reflect not only on their and their child's behaviour but also on their own and their child's mental states and intentions. In turn, the child who is understood will learn to understand others. Peter Fonagy and colleagues have produced evidence for an association between the quality of attachment relationship and reflective function in the parent and the child (Fonagy and Target, 1997; Fonagy et al., 2007).

Mind-mindedness

The parent is more able to tune in to their child's feelings and thoughts and engages in sensitive, appropriate talk about what their child may be feeling or thinking (Meins et al., 2013).

Good quality mind-minded talk has been shown to predict secure attachment, an increase in play abilities at two years and a decrease in behaviour problems in the pre-school years.

To VIG practitioners, Jane Barlow's proposal is congruent with their experience in practice. Through the VIG process, the parent can develop their abilities to respond in an attuned way to their child's initiatives, to be able to think about their child's actions and feelings and to be able to name to their children what they are doing, thinking or feeling. As a bonus, the parents develop the same skills in working with a trusted professional, developing their own narrative about themselves and their child within an attuned dialogue. In turn, they improve in their communication skills with other professionals (e.g. their social worker) and adults around them in their own lives. It helps them listen to others and use the support offered to change their previous risky and neglectful behaviour.

What Evidence is There that VIG Could Provide an Accurate Assessment within FDAC?

Chantal Cyr presented relevant recent research at the 2015 SRCD meeting in Philadelphia (Cyr, 2015), at 2016 World Association of Infant Mental Health (WAIMH) in Prague and at the AVIGuk 2017 International Conference in Glasgow. She works with a team at Montreal, Quebec where they have developed an attachment-based video feedback intervention (very similar to VIG) which has been used as an intervention with families in the child welfare system and also as an assessment of parenting capacity to care, to protect and to change. There were 60 high-risk families randomly allocated to either video feedback intervention or a psycho-educational intervention and 46 very similar high-risk families in a non-randomised control group who received care as usual. The research questions were around the impact of the interventions (i.e. does the parent become more sensitive, does the child's behaviour improve and does the attachment pattern change) and the accuracy of the professionals' prediction of the recurrence of maltreatment 12 months on. The intervention results showed a significant change in sensitivity/reciprocity in interaction and in externalising child behaviour problems for the video feedback as compared to the psycho-educational and the control. The assessment results show that only the video feedback practitioners were accurate in predicting the recurrence of maltreatment a year later. This is an important finding and one that supports the use of VIG as an assessment tool in FDAC and will be returned to in the final section.

VIG in Early FDAC

VIG is now an integral part of the FDAC process and we remain optimistic about the ongoing development of VIG in the FDAC model. The FDAC model is expanding and continues to develop and try new approaches. The FDAC National Unit is working with three local authorities on 'Early FDAC', working from booking in with pregnant mothers who have previously had a child removed through care proceedings. It is known that these women sometimes hold back from emotionally connecting with their unborn child because of the shame and grief associated with the removal of the previous child and fear the unborn child will also be removed. VIG has been successfully used in Early FDAC to help promote mother–child interaction during ultrasound scans and a detailed case study of Mia has been published (Kennedy and Underdown, 2017). Mia, who had been in care from the age of 15 years, experienced childhood trauma including sexual abuse. She had a history of homelessness, drug addiction and being in violent relationships. Mia had two previous babies removed because of neglect, despite being in rehabilitation and a mother–baby placement. After three antenatal VIG sessions, Underdown writes:

> The prenatal sessions validated Mia's perceptions about her baby and enabled her rich representations to be heard and affirmed. Watching the film in supervision, Fay identified how she attuned with Mia and scaffolded her growing sense of wonder about her developing baby. For Mia the VIG sessions offered opportunities to build new representations of herself as a mother alongside imagining what this baby might be like. (Kennedy and Underdown, 2017, p. 233)

VIG is offering a good start for trauma work without opening up the wounds too deeply during pregnancy, and to support the developing relationship in a compassionate and transparent way. There are promising possibilities in engaging fathers in this process, and especially in the effects of pre- and post-birth VIG with men who have a history of perpetrating domestic abuse.

So, What Next?

The next step is to embed VIG more consistently in the assessment process of wider FDACs and research the validity of assessments made by the FDAC team when using VIG. The research question could be 'does the VIG process improve the reliability of assessments of parenting capacity within the FDAC process?'

Chantal Cyr in Montreal found that it was only those professionals using an attachment-based video feedback intervention who were able to accurately predict the recurrence of maltreatment a year later. Will this be true in the FDAC process?

References

Bakermans-Kranenburg, M. J., Van IJzendoorn, M. H. and Juffer, F. (2003) Less is more: meta-analyses of sensitivity and attachment interventions in early childhood. *Psychological Bulletin*, 129(2), 195–215.

Beebe, B. and Lachmann, F. (2002) *Infant Research and Adult Treatment: Co-Constructing Interactions*. Hillsdale, NJ: Analytic Press.

Beebe, B. and Steele, M. (2013) How does microanalysis of mother–infant communication inform maternal sensitivity and infant attachment? *Attachment and Human Development*, 15, 583–602.

Bettleheim, B. (1987) *A Good Enough Parent: A Book on Child-Rearing*. New York: Knopf.

Celebi, M. (2013) Helping to reduce parental anxiety in the perinatal period. *Journal of Health Visiting*, 1(8), 438–42.

Cross, J. and Kennedy, H. (2011) Video Interaction Guidance: why does it work? In H. Kennedy, M. Landor and L. Todd (eds),

Video Interaction Guidance: A Relationship-based Intervention to Promote Attunement, Empathy and Well-being. London: Jessica Kingsley Publishers.

Cyr, C. (2015) An attachment-based intervention protocol for the assessment of parenting capacity in child welfare cases. SRCD 2015, Philadelphia, PA. Available at: https://vigknowledge.wikispaces.com/ file/detail/Chantal%2C+C.%28+2015%29 +Attachment+based+intervention+assessin g+parental+capacity+in+child+welfare+ca ses+.pdf (accessed 31 May 2017).

De Zulueta, F. (2015) From pain to violence and how to break the cycle. Available at: www .youtube.com/watch?v=8d2grzTn3M4 (16.23 min.–end).

Feuerstein, R., Feuerstein, S., Falik, L. and Rand, Y. (1979 [2002]) *Dynamic Assessments of Cognitive Modifiability*. Jerusalem, Israel: ICELP Press.

Fonagy, P. and Target, M. (1997) Attachment and reflective function: their role in self-organisation. *Development and Psychopathology*, 9, 679–700.

Fonagy, P., Gergely, G. and Target, M. (2007) The parent–infant dyad and the construction of the subjective self. *Journal of Child Psychology and Psychiatry*, 48(3/4), 288–328.

Fukkink, R. G. (2008) Video feedback in the widescreen: a meta-analysis of family programs. *Clinical Psychology Review*, 28, 904–16.

Fukkink, R., Kennedy, H. and Todd, L. (2011) Video Interaction Guidance: does it work? In H. Kennedy, M. Landor and L. Todd (eds), *Video Interaction Guidance: A Relationship-based Intervention to Promote Attunement, Empathy and Well-being*. London: Jessica Kingsley Publishers.

Høivik, M., Lydersen, S., Drugli, M., Onsøien, R., Hansen, M. and Berg-Neilson T. (2015) Video feedback compared to treatment as usual in families with parent–child interactions problems: a randomized controlled trial. *Child and Adolescent Psychiatry and Mental Health*, 9(3).

Kennedy, H. and Underdown, A. (2017) 'Video Interaction Guidance: promoting secure attachment and optimal development for children, parents and professionals. In P. Leach (ed.), *Innovative Research in Infant Wellbeing*. London: Routledge.

Kennedy, H., Ball, K. and Barlow, J. (2017) How does Video Interaction Guidance (VIG) contribute to infant and parental mental health and well-being? *Clinical Child Psychology and Psychiatry*, 22(3), 500–17.

Kennedy, H., Macdonald, M. and Whalley, P. (2015) Video Interaction Guidance: providing an effective response for neglected children. In R. Gardner (ed.), *Neglect*. London: Jessica Kingsley Publishers.

Kennedy, H., Landor, M. and Todd, L. (eds) (2011) *Video Interaction Guidance: A Relationship-based Intervention to Promote Attunement, Empathy and Wellbeing*. London: Jessica Kingsley Publishers.

Kennedy, H., Landor, M. and Todd, L. (2010) Video Interaction Guidance as a method to promote secure attachment. *Education and Child Psychology* 27(3), 59–72.

Meins, E., Muñoz-Centifanti, L. C., Fernyhough, C. and Fishburn, S. (2013) Maternal mind-mindedness and children's behavioral difficulties: mitigating the impact of low socioeconomic status. *Journal of Abnormal Child Psychology*, 41, 543–53.

Moss, E., Dubois-Comtois, K., Cyr, C., Tarabulsy, G. M., St-Laurent, D. and Bernier, A. (2011) Efficacy of a home-visiting intervention aimed at improving maternal sensitivity, child attachment, and behavioral outcomes for maltreated children: a randomized control trial. *Development and Psychopathology*, 23, 195–210.

NICE (2012) NICE Guidelines. Social and emotional wellbeing. Available at: www .nice.org.uk/guidance/PH40 (accessed 31 May 2017).

NICE (2015) NICE Guidelines. Children's attachment: attachment in children and young people who are adopted from care, in care or at high risk of going into care. Available at: www.nice.org.uk/guidance/ng26 (accessed 31 May 2017).

Pardoe, R. (2016) Integrating Video Interaction Guidance (VIG) and psychoanalytic psychotherapy in work with parents and infants. *Bulletin of the Association of Child Psychotherapists*, May.

Trevarthen, C. and Aitken, K. J. (2001) Infant intersubjectivity: research, theory, and clinical application. *Journal of Child Psychology and Psychiatry*, 42(1), 3–48.

Chapter

11

A Life Course Approach to Promoting Healthy Behaviour

Lorraine Khan

Severe and persistent behavioural difficulties are our most common, costly and overlooked childhood mental health problem. All children go through stages of challenging behaviour and for most it is merely a phase. However, some children get stuck in unhelpful and damaging cycles of poor behaviour. Such severe problems emerge from complex interactions over time between genetic and environmental risk. The more risks a child accumulates, the greater the likelihood that a child's mental health will be compromised and poor outcomes will persist into adult years. Severe and persistent behavioural difficulties not only affect children's outcomes, they can also impact on others around them, causing stress to families, prompting victimisation of peers, affecting community safety and storing up significant societal costs over time.

There is now good evidence on what can be done to reduce the chance of behavioural difficulties developing in the first place and on what interventions make the biggest difference to children's recovery and progress once behaviour escalates into unhealthy ranges on the behavioural spectrum. There is also growing evidence of the protective factors which help reverse accumulating risk over a child's life course. However, there is also evidence that we still wait far too long for problems to fester and multiply, leaving the youth justice system and courts to deal with resulting behavioural crises at much too late a stage.

This chapter will make the case for a systematic life course de-escalation and diversionary strategy for reducing costly, damaging, severe and persistent behavioural problems in children and young people. It will consider the evidence on what has the strongest chance of changing negative behavioural trajectories and poor mental health, right from the first spark of life up to young adult years, exploring commissioning implications, current opportunities and finally current barriers to doing things differently.

Cumulative Risk, Accessing Help and Early Intervention

Childhood mental illness is common and damaging. One in 10 children aged five to 16 will have a diagnosable mental illness. Severe and persistent behavioural problems (or conduct disorders) represent the most common childhood and youth mental illness, affecting 6 per cent of children and young people – mainly boys (Green et al., 2005). Risk factors for conduct problems include:

- Family structure
- Harsh parenting or poor parental sensitivity or supervision
- Exposure to trauma and maltreatment
- Exposure to maternal depression
- Low household education
- Smoking during pregnancy
- Location in societies with higher income inequalities

- Exposure to multiple stressors and risks over time (Gutman et al., 2018; Green et al., 2005; Finkelhor, 2008; Finkelhor et al., 2009; Yoshikawa et al., 2012; Lennox and Khan, 2013).

Evidence tells us that some children are at much higher risk of childhood mental illness than others. So:

- children in local authority care are at least four times as likely to experience diagnosable mental illnesses (mostly severe and persistent behavioural problems); those in residential settings are at least seven times more likely to present with diagnosable conduct problems (Ford et al., 2007);
- under-18 year-olds in the youth justice system (both in the community and in custody) are at least seven times as likely as other children to have diagnosable-level conduct problems (Fazel et al., 2008; Stallard et al., 2003);
- 90 per cent of 16–20-year-olds in custody have a mental illness; 80 per cent will have more than one diagnosable mental illness (Singleton et al., 1998);
- between half and three-quarters of homeless young people have diagnosable-level mental health conditions (Hodgson et al., 2013);
- nearly three-quarters of sexually exploited young women have diagnosable mental health conditions (Department of Health, 2013).

Most parents of a child with a diagnosable behavioural problem will seek advice; yet still only a quarter of children get help likely to be effective (Green et al., 2005). Furthermore, there have been recurrent concerns, during recent national child mental health reviews, about children's inability to get timely mental health support (HM Government, 2014; Frith, 2016). Such delays are of concern because there is strong evidence that the longer the duration of mental illness during teenage years and the more episodes reoccur, the more likely the young person will face prolonged impairment as an adult (Patton et al., 2014).

Delays in getting help occur despite the existence of a range of interventions across the life course with potential to intervene early and effect positive change.

In general, evidence suggests that earlier intervention to change the trajectory of risk in a child's life is better – however, there are still interventions that can make a real difference quite late during adolescent and young adult years. In this respect, it is never too late to link up young people with effective help (Washington State Institute of Public Policy, 2015).

Intervening early can mean:

- preventing problems emerging by intervening early in life to build strengths in a child, family or in his/her environment; and
- intervening early in the course of illness – when the very first signs emerge.

It is particularly important to restore good mental health quickly in childhood thereby preventing the accumulation of potentially damaging further risks (e.g. school underperformance, school exclusion, social exclusion).

Taking all of this evidence into account, the Centre for Mental Health advocates that local commissioners work together to develop an integrated preventative approach to promoting and maintaining healthy behaviour and outcomes right from the first spark of life.

From the First Spark of Life

There is now growing neuroscientific evidence that untreated maternal mental illnesses such as depression and anxiety can expose the foetal and infant brain to excessive amounts of cortisol (the fight or flight hormone) and overstimulate stress response systems – even in the womb. This overexposure can lead children to develop long-standing difficulties regulating emotion and behaviour later on (Zeanah, 2009), difficulties which lie at the heart of most common child and adolescent mental health problems including conduct problems. Furthermore, if maternal illness is not swiftly and effectively treated, it can also undermine maternal–infant sensitivity and the quality of parent–child attachment in the crucial months following birth – both of which are critical for jump-starting cognitive and emotional development and buffering a child against excessive environmental stresses (e.g. maltreatment, chronic deprivation, exposure to violence, etc.) (Zeanah, 2009).

At present, in the UK only half of new mothers with maternal mental illness get identified and hardly any get good quality treatment likely to assist their recovery (Bauer et al., 2014). Expertise in identifying such vulnerabilities and good quality services are inconsistent across England (Maternal Mental Health Alliance, 2014). Embarrassment and shame also stop mothers seeking help (Khan, 2015). A recent report noted that better identification and evidence-based treatment had the potential to save significant costs to society with most savings emerging from reductions in poor later child mental health – particularly diagnosable conduct problems (Bauer et al., 2014). Early identification and treatment of mothers during the perinatal period should be seen as an essential diversionary starting point to reduce the prevalence and associated costs of youth behavioural problems.

Early Starting Childhood Behavioural Problems

Early starting behavioural problems are our most common diagnosable mental health condition affecting around 5 per cent of children under secondary school age – mainly boys (Green et al., 2005). They result from a child's inability to self-calm, self-soothe or regulate emotions or behaviour – challenges which can be prompted by exposure to early environmental risks (Zeanah, 2009). Children communicate their distress, fear and developmental frustration through their behaviour. This important communication is frequently misinterpreted, ineffectively responded to and gets overlooked by many in contact with children, with three-quarters missing out on effective early help (Green et al., 2005). In a study completed by the Centre for Mental Health, parents often took many years to get heard after voicing initial concerns about their child's behaviour – even when these behaviours were exceptionally severe (Khan, 2014). Some specialist Child and Adolescent Mental Health Services also actively excluded children with behavioural problems from their services (Brown et al., 2012). This is of concern in that we know from many longitudinal studies tracking children from birth to young adult years that children with early severe and persistent behavioural difficulties under secondary school age have a greater chance of some of the very worst outcomes and life chances (see Figure 11.1) (Fergusson et al., 2005). Without early intervention, around 50 per cent of these early starters are likely to continue to experience multiple poor outcomes as adults (Parsonage et al., 2014).

Interventions for children with early behavioural problems are some of the best tested and most effective (National Institute for Health and Care Excellence, 2013). These positive parenting support programmes help parents pick up critical techniques to help settle their child's behaviour. Programmes are most effective for children with the most severe behavioural problems often helping them move back into healthy behavioural ranges (Brown et al., 2012). Such programmes (e.g. Triple P and Incredible Years) are also very good value (Parsonage et al., 2014). Economic analysis of their effectiveness shows that, if well implemented, they can result in savings of £3 for every £1 invested with the greatest benefits and savings emerging for the later justice system (Parsonage et al., 2014).

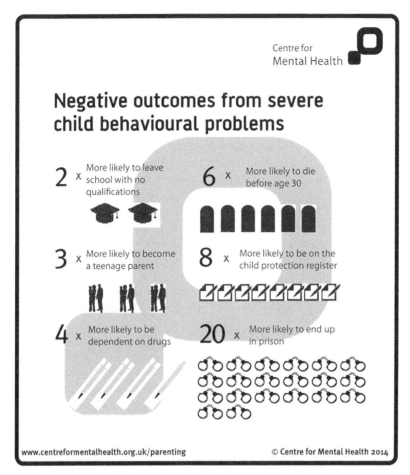

Figure 11.1 Long-term negative outcomes associated with early starting severe behavioural difficulties, taken from Parsonage et al. (2014).

At the present time, availability of such programmes in England rarely matches likely scale of need for this age group (Brown et al., 2012). In Scotland, there has been a concerted public health effort through the Psychology of Parenting Project (PoPP) to roll-out early years screening to track when children move outside healthy behavioural ranges, matched with making available engaging early support via positive parenting programmes from nursery school onwards.

Effective School-Based Programmes and Activity

There is good evidence that some whole-school universal mental health promoting approaches such as the Good Behaviour Game have the ability to significantly reduce later conduct problems through supporting children's ability to self-regulate emotions and behaviour. The Good Behaviour Game has produced consistent positive results in the United States and has also been piloted in the Republic of Ireland, replicating promising outcomes (Washington State Institute of Public Policy, 2015; Morgan and O'Donnell, 2015). Economic analysis of the programme's effectiveness indicates that for every pound invested in this programme in schools, savings of around £30 are produced for society. Again, most cost savings benefit the youth justice system.

There is also early evidence emerging from the US of the potential for greater earlier partnership between schools, behavioural experts and mental health practitioners to pre-empt and prevent behavioural crises and exclusions, breaking the school failure to youth justice 'pipeline' (Cocozza et al., 2016).

The Age of Criminal Responsibility Onwards

As children move into teenage years, prevalence of diagnosable conduct problems rises to 8 per cent (Green et al., 2005). By this time, those children who missed out on early effective intervention have often accumulated multiplying risks, becoming more entrenched in unhealthy behaviours. Others may join this higher risk group due to the combined effect of peer mimicry and increased tendencies for sensation-seeking/risk-taking and non-consequential thinking linked with dramatic neural pruning taking place between the ages of 13 and 25 years (Johnson et al., 2009). For those developing later starting behavioural problems, anti-social behaviour often stabilises as the brain matures by age 25 years and as young people settle into adult responsibilities and relationships (Centre for Mental Health, 2009). For those with earlier starting problems (for example, those in early contact with the police, those excluded from primary school, those running away from home, early substance users, those involved in severe early bullying, etc.), the prognosis is poorer. It is important, therefore, that those with early starting behavioural difficulties are prioritised for evidence-based help early on in their contact with the youth justice system. At this later adolescent stage, successful interventions tend to be more complex and intensive (although still largely cost-effective). Such interventions include:

- multi-systemic therapy: this approach takes a whole family and system-wide problem-solving approach to helping families move forward and has been shown to have good effectiveness, if implemented well, with a saving of around £3 for every pound invested (Khan et al., 2015);
- functional family therapy which also involves working with the family to support improved behaviour and reduced crime (Khan, et al., 2015);
- multidimensional foster treatment: for children who are unable to remain with their families. Highly trained and supported foster parents produce much better outcomes in terms of reducing offending compared with residential group homes or custodial and remand units which remain highly expensive and overall limited in effectiveness (with some regimes actually making things worse) (Washington State Institute of Public Policy, 2015);
- aggression replacement therapy: this is rarely available in the UK but has a proven record of reducing violence and offending behaviour in US trials. This should be a standard offer for children on the edges of the youth justice system (YJS) and for those on statutory youth offending team caseloads (Khan et al., 2015);
- family nurse partnerships: for young women in the YJS who are also teenage parents, this has shown particularly positive outcomes for mothers themselves and for their children's later criminal activity when outcomes were tracked over many decades. Criminal justice outcomes were particularly improved for female offspring (Eckenrode et al., 2010). In fact, improved intergenerational outcomes were apparent across many domains with particularly high reductions in maltreatment, with better rates of school

attainment, higher lifetime salaries, reduced substance abuse, etc. (Washington State Institute of Public Policy, 2015). The UK trial has so far produced less promising results than studies of implementation in the US (Robling et al., 2016). However, this should not yet be seen as a sign of failure in this country since many of the broader benefits of the intervention emerged over decades in US studies. Instead, follow-up research should continue tracking outcomes over time.

Childhood trauma, maltreatment and attachment difficulties can be major triggers for later severe behavioural problems, aggression and criminal behaviour (Zeanah, 2009). Stress response systems and behaviour which may once have been functional, helping children survive in highly unsafe and stressful family or community circumstances, can often lead children to respond inappropriately or explosively or to overreact, even when threat levels are much lower – sometimes with very damaging consequences for victims and communities. For this reason, there should be systematic and sensitive assessment of trauma and attachment difficulties in young people in contact with the youth justice system as well as good pathways to engaging trauma-based interventions (particularly for young women and Black, Asian and Minority Ethnic (BAME) young people, some of whom have higher rates of post-traumatic stress disorder symptoms; Chitsabesan et al., 2006). Available interventions should include eye movement desensitisation and reprocessing (EMDR) and trauma-based cognitive behaviour, both of which are gaining proof of efficacy for this age group (Washington State Institute of Public Policy, 2015).

Finally, highly engaging and well implemented mentoring is now gaining evidence of effectiveness in supporting better outcomes, behaviour and life chances for those most at risk (Washington State Institute of Public Policy, 2015). Such mentoring opportunities help foster more trusting, prosocial and healthy attachments, particularly for vulnerable young people, providing practical coaching with aspirations and life goals. These interventions, along with generally improved mental health support, should be available in schools and colleges that have important opportunities to identify early need and strengthen children and young people's mental health. In England, third sector organisations such as MAC-UK and Safer London have used these approaches with early promise for girls and young men in the justice system and at risk of gang involvement.

Point of Arrest: Identification and Diversion

For many years, there has been inadequate identification of health vulnerabilities as young people enter the youth justice system in England and Wales. As already outlined, point of arrest screening should not be the starting point of any strategy to improve outcomes and reduce community victimisation; rather, it should form part of a broader pathway seeking to promote healthier behaviour right from the start of life. Point of arrest screening and support is, however, a useful opportunity to create a safety net to catch those who have been missed as part of any early intervention strategy and, as importantly, those who start to develop symptoms of poor mental health for the first time during adolescence. This is important as, particularly with diagnosable mental health difficulties, adolescent and young adult years represent the peak time for the emergence of early adult mental illnesses with 50 per cent of lifetime mental illness starting by the age of 14 years (Kessler et al., 2005) and three-quarters showing first symptoms by the mid-twenties (Kessler et al., 2007). Yet it is the time when young people are most likely to experience significant gaps in mental health support as commissioning responsibility switches between meeting children's and adult's needs. This is frustrating, since there is good evidence that effective treatment can change the likely impairment and trajectory of these conditions during this crucial adolescent life stage (Knapp et al., 2011; Patel et al., 2007).

It is important to note that many young people in the justice system also face other multiple health and social challenges which often remain under the radar for many years. For example, six out of ten will have moderate to severe speech and language difficulties (Bryan et al., 2007). A further 60 per cent screened in custody also met criteria for acquired brain injury (impairment following a historic blow to the head and subsequent loss of consciousness). Acquired brain injury has been associated with higher levels of violence and higher risk of suicide in young people in custody and may be associated with historic child abuse, past car accidents and other violent victimisation (Williams, et al., 2010). Many children in the youth justice system will also have higher risk of suicide, attempted suicide and self-harm (Lennox and Khan, 2013; Youth Justice Board, 2012) driven by histories of abuse, victimisation and maltreatment (Khan et al., 2013).

Recent Health Developments Affecting Children and Young People in the Youth Justice System

The development and introduction of a detailed and robust health assessment tool (the Common Health Assessment Tool, or CHAT) by the Department of Health and NHS England in the youth custodial estate in England and Wales (and its more recent piloting in some community youth offending teams) potentially strengthens the focus on health issues which we know are over-represented among young people in the youth justice system.

Furthermore, point of arrest screening for health issues affecting both children and adults has now been rolled out across England by NHS England through the all-age 'liaison and diversion' programme (NHS England, 2015). This initiative aims to enhance integration between health and justice activity, improving early identification and support for mental health problems, learning disabilities and other vulnerabilities. Young people can be referred to liaison and diversion teams:

- from the point that a young person first has contact with the police through community resolutions (including street-level restorative justice) and other out-of-court disposals;
- through routine screening in police custody by liaison and diversion health workers;
- and as a result of referrals from court for those missed at earlier points.

Local liaison and diversion services can build up good knowledge of a range of children's services, youth services, parenting support, voluntary sector, health and mental health provision (addressing both routine and urgent needs), substance misuse and school support pathways (such as resources for special educational needs and school counselling resources). For those at an early stage of contact with the youth justice system, liaison and diversion workers help young people bridge to local community services. For those at a later stage in the youth justice pathway (in police custody, facing remand or entering court), practitioners can begin early work to inform police, the Crown Prosecution Service and youth offending team decisions ensuring health screening feeds into reports, informs intervention proposals and advises the court when 'reasonable adjustments' are required to facilitate improved participation in the justice process. For all young people in the youth justice system, the design of any service is critical as they need help and solutions which are co-produced, based on reliable and positive attachments and relationships, trauma-informed and which are outreaching (rather than clinic-based), placing a high priority on delivering effective help in a warm and engaging way.

The Crisis Concordat

Support for young people on the edges of or in the youth justice system has been boosted by a national drive for local areas to develop multisector Crisis Concordat Agreements to support children and adults in mental health crisis (Department of Health, 2014). The Concordat sets out how local agencies can work together to deliver high-quality responses when people with mental health problems need help. It expects that in every locality in England local partnerships of health, criminal justice and local authority agencies will agree and commit to local commitments and actions to deliver services that meet the principles of the national Concordat. The Concordat has been used to address historic concerns about holding young people inappropriately in police custody settings for lengthy periods as an attempt to keep them safe. Instead, activity has increased pressure to make available alternative and more appropriate places of safety for children. The Concordat has sometimes improved gateways for urgent mental health referrals and it has helped identify gaps in local mental health systems which compromise children's safety. In some areas, it has also led to the development of 'street triage' teams where mental health practitioners and police work in close partnership at street level to respond to those identified with vulnerabilities in the community.

The Child and Adolescent Mental Health Service (CAMHS) Taskforce

In 2014/15, as a result of growing concerns about the quality, accessibility and scale of funding for child and adolescent mental health services in England, a national review was mobilised to address challenges. Several reports including 'Future in Mind' and the Independent Mental Health Taskforce's Five Year View report to NHS England, provided broad-ranging recommendations designed to facilitate children and families getting 'the right help in the right place at the right time' (Department of Health, 2015; Independent Mental Health Taskforce, 2016). A total of £1.4 billion was made available for child mental health and local areas were required to produce plans to convert this national transformational ambition into practice. A key area of national priority has been better care to meet the needs of particularly vulnerable groups of children with higher risk of severe and persistent mental health difficulties, such as children in local authority care, those exposed to violence, those with early starting behavioural difficulties and children in the youth justice system. There was recognition that many of these children needed a different service design – more outreach work and less clinical-feeling forms of trauma-informed help. The success of this transformational ambition for children's mental health services, and particularly for vulnerable children, is still being monitored.

Ongoing Challenges and Priorities

Despite these positive developments, significant challenges remain on the horizon. At the moment, transformation plans vary considerably in terms of their quality and the priority placed in action plans on meeting the needs of vulnerable children and young people more effectively, particularly those in the youth justice system.

Most worryingly, over the last five years there have been persistent and incremental cuts affecting Children's Services, Youth Services, the voluntary sector and specialist CAMHS services in England and Wales. This in turn has led to a pattern of disinvestment in all but essential/crisis services with rising thresholds and waiting periods for accessing help. Although significant new money has followed Taskforce recommendations, it is as yet difficult to assess whether the scale of new money will compensate for these severe and continuing cuts to early intervention, school support and local children's service provision. Furthermore, government green paper proposals in 2017 on transforming children and young people's mental health seeking to strengthen mental health support in schools have also been criticised for their limited scale and ambition (Education and Health and Care Committee 2018). This may mean that what is given with one hand, may well be taken away with the other, leading to yet another failed attempt at CAMHS transformation. Such fiscal pressures result in critical breaks in the 'chain' of early intervention across the child developmental course. These breaks occur because historical funders of very early intervention (often health, children's services or schools) rarely feel they see sufficient short-term and concrete benefit from preventative activity (benefits which largely accrue later in life, get hidden across many budgets and mainly impact the field of criminal justice). At times of economic difficulty, it is therefore easier for early years' commissioners to consider such services 'a luxury' as they seek to prioritise management of ongoing crises and balance the books in a context primarily concerned with short-termism. Ironically, disinvestment in prevention and early intervention eventually stores up problems upstream, resulting in higher likelihood of young people ending up in costly crisis settings such as Accident and Emergency units, inpatient settings, children's homes or custody. Although Police Crime Commissioners in England and Wales might benefit most from early intervention, they would not routinely see early intervention services as a core part of commissioning responsibilities. Neither would they systematically partner with early years, local schools and colleges, public health or CAMHS providers to jointly commission such support.

National CAMHS transformation activity is attempting to improve the availability in local areas of evidence- and lived-experience-informed help for child and adolescent mental health. However, the same priority is not currently being placed on making proven interventions available for those on the edge of or in the youth justice system. So, most Children's Services and youth offending teams in the UK still do not have routine, reliable and timely access to the league table of interventions considered most effective in addressing crime and trauma and improving severe and persistent behavioural difficulties (e.g. see those explored above on pages 90, 92, 93 and 94; Washington State Institute of Public Policy, 2015). Indeed, some interventions encouraged at national level (e.g. Troubled Families) have lacked robust evaluation before investment, with concern often arising about reliability of claims of success and cost-effectiveness (Crossley, 2015). It is essential that there is a shift towards investing in more robustly proven, well implemented and trauma-informed programmes for these young people and their families. It is also critical that interventions are made available to children, young people and families in a way that maximises participation and engagement.

If new programmes are driven or embarked upon at national level, these must be accompanied by high-quality evaluation to ensure they reliably improve children's outcomes.

Conclusion

In summary, diversion of young people from the youth justice system must not begin at the point of arrest and in courts but must instead be founded on a firm 'chain' of joined-up family-based commissioning using proven interventions to build strong mental health and respond to first signs of deterioration right from the first spark of life. Research findings clearly highlight the folly, damage and expense associated with commissioning approaches that allow gaps to develop across this chain of interventions and which merely wait to respond to later behavioural crises. And yet too often deterioration in children's and families' mental health is overlooked with still only a quarter of children getting the help they need and many facing delays for first responses. Too often commissioning remains fragmented across the life course and across sectors with stakeholders focused on short-term book-balancing and sector 'survival' rather than longer-term community benefits and outcomes. When investing new money, commissioners should seek to minimise weak links in this 'chain' of evidence-based help in local areas for children and families' mental health from conception and across the child, adolescent and young adult life course. Second, at every link in this chain of early intervention, efforts should be made to reduce current treatment gaps, improving the proportion of children with diagnosable difficulties who actually get the timely help they need. Only then will we have a chance of minimising the drift of children into unnecessary and damaging crisis and will the youth justice system and courts act as an appropriate and very late safety net for young people missed at earlier stages in the system – rather than the starting point for any strategy of support and diversion.

References

Bauer, A., Parsonage, M., Knapp, M. I. V. et al. (2014) *The Costs of Perinatal Mental Health Problems*. London: PSSRU and Centre for Mental Health.

Bryan, K., Freer, J. and Furlong. C. (2007) Language and communication difficulties in juvenile offenders. *International Journal of Language and Communication Disorders*, 42(5), 505–20.

Brown, E. R., Khan, L. and Parsonage, M. (2012) *A Chance to Change*. London: Centre for Mental Health.

Centre for Mental Health (2009) *Childhood Mental Health and Life Chance in Post-War Britain: insights from Three National Cohort Studies. Executive Summary*. London: Centre for Mental Health.

Chitsabesan, P., Kroll, L., Bailey, S., Kenning, C., Sneider, S., MacDonald, W. and Theodosiou, L. (2006) Mental health needs of offenders in custody and in the community. *The British Journal of Psychiatry*, 188, 534–40.

Crossley, S. (2015) A kind of trouble: the recontextualisation and operationalisation of the Troubled Families Programme. No method in the Troubled Families Madness. Available at: https://akindoftrouble. wordpress.com/2015/03/11/no-method-in-the-troubled-families-madness/ (accessed January 2016).

Cocozza, J., Keator, K. J., Skowyra, K. R. and Greene, J. (2016) Breaking the school to prison pipeline: the school-based diversion initiative for youth with mental disorders. *International Association of Youth and Family Judges*, January, 21–22.

Department of Health (2013) *Health Working Group Report on Child Sexual Exploitation: An Independent Group Chaired by the Department of Health Focusing On: Improving the Outcomes for Children by Promoting Effective*

Engagement of Health Services and Staff. London: Department of Health.

Department of Health (2014) *Mental Health Crisis Care Concordat: Improving Outcomes for People Experiencing Mental Health Crisis.* London: Department of Health.

Department of Health (2015) *Future in Mind: Promoting, Protecting and Improving Children and Young People's Mental Health and Well Being.* London: Department of Health.

Eckenrode, J., Campa, M., Luckey, D. W., Henderson Jr, C. R., Cole, R., Kitzman, H., Anson, E., Sidora-Arcoleo, K., Powers, J. and Olds, D. (2010) Long-term effects of prenatal and infancy nurse home visitation on the life course of youths: 19-year follow-up of a randomized trial. *Archives of Pediatrics and Adolescent Medicine,* 164, 9–15.

Education and Health and Care Committee (2018) The government's green paper on mental health: failing a generation. Available at: https://publications. parliament.uk/pa/cm201719/cmselect/ cmhealth/642/64202.htm (accessed May 2018).

Fazel, S., Doll, H. and Långström, N. (2008) Mental disorders among adolescents in juvenile detention and correctional facilities: a systematic review and metaregression analysis of 25 surveys. *Journal of the American Academy of Child and Adolescent Psychiatry,* 47(9), 1010–19.

Fergusson, D., Horwood, J. and Ridder, E. (2005) Show me the child at seven: the consequences of conduct problems in childhood for psychosocial functioning in adulthood. *Journal of Child Psychology and Psychiatry,* 46(8), 837–49.

Finkelhor, D. (2008) *Childhood Victimization. Violence, Crime and Abuse in the Lives of Young People.* Oxford: Oxford University Press.

Finkelhor, D., Ormrod, R., Turner, H. and Holt, M. (2009) Pathways to poly-victimization. *Child Maltreatment,* 14, 316.

Ford, T., Vostanis, P., Meltzer, H. and Goodman, R. (2007) Psychiatric disorder among British children looked after by local authorities: comparison with children living in private households. *The British Journal of Psychiatry,* 190(4), 319–25.

Frith, E. (2016) *Centreforum Commission on Children and Young People's Mental Health: State of the Nation.* London: Centreforum.

Green, H., McGinnity, Á., Meltzer, H., Ford, T. and Goodman, R. (2005) *The Mental Health of Children and Young People in Great Britain 2004.* Basingstoke: Palgrave.

Gutman, L.M., Joshi, H., Parsonage, M. and Schoon, I. (2018) Gender-specific trajectories of conduct problems from ages 3 to 11. *Journal of Abnormal Child Psychology,* 1–14.

HM Government (2014) *Children and Adolescents' Mental Health and CAMHS. Third Report of Session 2014–15.* London: The Stationery Office.

Hodgson, K. J., Shelton, K. H., van den Bree, M. B. and Los, F. J. (2013) Psychopathology in young people experiencing homelessness: a systematic review. *American Journal of Public Health,* 103(6), 24–37.

Independent Mental Health Taskforce (2016) *Five Year Forward View for Mental Health.* London: NHS England.

Johnson, S., Blum, W. and Giedd, J. (2009) Adolescent maturity and the brain: the promise and pitfalls of neuroscience research in adolescent health policy. *Journal Adolescent Health,* 45(3), 216–21.

Kessler, R. C., Berglund, P., Demler, O., Jin, R., Merikangas, K. R. and Walters, E. E. (2005) Lifetime prevalence and age-of-onset distributions of DSM-IV disorders in the National Comorbidity Survey Replication. *Archives of General Psychiatry,* 62, 593–602.

Kessler, R. C., Angermeyer, M., Anthony, J. C. et al. (2007) Lifetime prevalence and age-of-onset distributions of mental disorders in the World Health Organization's World Mental Health Survey Initiative. *World Psychiatry,* 6(3), 168–76.

Khan, L. (2014) *Wanting the Best for My Children: Parents' Voices.* London: Centre for Mental Health.

Khan, L. (2015) *Falling Through the Gaps: Perinatal Mental Health and General Practice*. London: Centre for Mental Health.

Khan, L., Brice, H., Saunders, A. and Plumtree, A. (2013) *A Need to Belong: What Leads Girls to Join Gangs*. London: Centre for Mental Health.

Khan, L., Parsonage, M. and Stubbs, J. (2015) *Investing in Children: A Review of Evidence on the Costs and Benefits of Increased Service Provision*. London: Centre for Mental Health.

Knapp, M., McDaid, D. and Parsonage, M. (2011) Mental health promotion and prevention: the economic case. Available at: www.pssru.ac.uk/index.php (accessed 22 February 2011).

Lennox, C. and Khan, L. (2013) Youth justice. In *Annual Report of the Chief Medical Officer 2012: Our Children Deserve Better: Prevention Pays*. London: Chief Medical Officer, pp. 200–14.

Maternal Mental Health Alliance (2014) Everyone's business. Available at: www .everyonesbusiness.org.uk/wp-content/ uploads/2014/07/UK-Specialist-Community-Perinatal-Mental-Health-Teams-current provision (accessed 21 December 2013).

Morgan, M. and O'Donnell, M. (2015) *Evaluation of the PAX Good Behaviour Game Pilot Study in Ireland*. Dublin: Northside and Midlands Area Partnership.

National Institute for Health and Care Excellence (2013) *CG158 Antisocial Behaviour and Conduct Disorders in Children and Young People. Recognition, Intervention and Management. National Clinical Guideline Number 158*. London: NICE.

NHS England (2015) Liaison and diversion. Available at: www.england.nhs.uk/ tag/liaison-and-diversion/ (accessed 1 November 2015).

Parsonage, M., Khan, L. and Saunders, A. (2014) *Building a Better Future: The Lifetime Costs of Childhood Behavioural Problems and the Benefits of Early Intervention*. London: Centre for Mental Health.

Patel, V., Flisher, A., Hetrick, S. et al. (2007) Mental health of young people: a global public-health challenge. *The Lancet*, 369(9569), 1302–13.

Patton, G. C., Coffey, C., Romaniuk, H. et al. (2014) The prognosis of common mental disorders in adolescents: a 14-year prospective cohort study. *Lancet*, 383, 1404–11.

Robling, M., Bekkers, M. J., Bell, K. et al. (2016) Effectiveness of a nurse-led intensive home-visitation programme for first-time teenage mothers (Building Blocks): a pragmatic randomised controlled trial. *The Lancet*, 387(10014), 146–55.

Singleton, N., Meltzer, H. and Gatward, R. (1998) *Psychiatric Morbidity among Prisoners in England and Wales*. London: Department of Health.

Stallard, P., Thomason, J. and Churchyard, S. (2003) The mental health of young people attending a Youth Offending Team: a descriptive study. *Journal of Adolescence*, 26, 33–43.

Washington State Institute of Public Policy (2015) *Return on Investment: Evidence-Based Options to Improve Statewide Outcomes*. Olympia, WA: Washington State Institute of Public Policy.

Williams, W. H., Cordan, G., Mewse, A. J., Tonks, J. and Burgess, C. N. (2010) Self-reported traumatic brain injury in male young offenders: a risk factor for re-offending, poor mental health and violence? *Neuropsychological Rehabilitation*, 20(6), 801–12.

Yoshikawa, H., Aber, J. L. and Beardslee, W. R. (2012) The effects of poverty on the mental and emotional and behavioural health of children and young people: implications for prevention. *American Psychologist*, 67(4), 273–284.

Youth Justice Board (2012) *Youth Justice Statistics 2010/11 England and Wales Youth Justice Board / Ministry of Justice Statistics Bulletin*. London: Youth Justice Board.

Zeanah, C. H. (ed.) (2009) *Handbook of Infant Mental Health*. New York: Guilford Press.

Chapter

Female Genital Mutilation

Najette Ayadi O'Donnell and Deborah Hodes

Over 130 million girls and women worldwide have undergone FGM.

FGM is practised in more than 29 countries across Africa, parts of the Middle East, South East Asia and countries where migrants from FGM affected communities live.

(FORWARD UK, n.d.)

60,000 girls under 15 are at risk of FGM in the UK.

127,000 girls and women in the UK are living with the consequences of FGM.

(Macfarlane and Dorkenoo, 2015)

Medical campaigning against female genital mutilation (FGM) is not new: the Egyptian Society of Physicians condemned the practice in the 1920s (Berer, 2015). In the UK it is 30 years since Efua Dorkenoo founded FORWARD (Foundation for Women's Health Research and Development) to campaign for gender equality and safeguarding the rights of African girls and women, and 20 years since an article about the practice appeared in the *British Medical Journal* (Black and Debelle, 1995). Despite this, and anti-FGM legislation in 1985, 2003 and 2015, we continue to see and treat victims of FGM in the UK.

In this chapter we argue that the key to eradicating this tradition is a fundamental change of attitude within practising communities. FGM is rooted in cultural beliefs and practices in the countries and communities of origin of some immigrant communities. It may be based on the economic dependence of women and patriarchal values and includes many misconceptions, such as ideas of purity and sexuality. If FGM is considered a prerequisite for marriage, and marriage a necessity for economic security, families from these communities will be under pressure to continue the practice. A change in these cultural beliefs by both women and men should lead to a reduction in the practice.

Background

FGM is the ritual alteration of the genitalia of females for no medical reason (Creighton and Hodes, 2015). The World Health Organisation (WHO) classifies it into four types (WHO, 2008). Table 12.1 helps to identity the four types, and compares them to male circumcision and cosmetic alterations of genitalia. All FGM has immediate consequences and apart from Type 4 and Type 1a, the long-term medical and psychological consequences for women are frequent (Simpson et al., 2012; Johnsdotter and Essen, 2016).

Its practice has been documented globally, mostly in 29 sub-Saharan African countries, South East Asia and some Middle Eastern communities. It bears no correlation to religious practice, having been documented in communities which are practising Christians, Muslims and those without any religion at all (Vissandjée et al., 2014).

Table 12.1 Description of type of FGM in order of anatomical severity compared with male circumcision and cosmetic surgery (United Nations Children's Fund, 2013; WHO, 2014)

WHO Type (UNICEF)	Description female	Description male	Cosmetic genital surgery female	Main likely physical and psycho-social effects/harm
4 (nicked)	Cut, prick around clitoris Labial stretching Insertion of corrosives Cauterisation of vagina	Piercings	Piercings	Pain Infection Flashbacks
1a (flesh removed)	Removal prepuce (clitoral unhooding)	Male circumcision – removal of the prepuce. Modern form more extensive than originally	Removal of prepuce for aesthetic and sexual function reasons	Pain Haemorrhage Infection including blood-borne viruses (BBV) Keloid and cysts Flashbacks
1b (flesh removed)	Partial removal of the clitoris or total removal of the glans and most of the erectile tissue in the body envelope			Pain Haemorrhage Infection including BBV Keloid and cysts Flashbacks Loss of sexual function
2 (flesh removed and sealed)	Removal of the clitoris as 1a and also labia minora; with some stitching if bleeds		Labiaplasty – both or one labia minora	Pain Haemorrhage Infection including BBV Keloid and cysts Flashbacks Loss of sexual function Gynaecological and obstetric complications
3 (flesh removed and sealed closed)	Infibulation (sealing together the vulva), usually with but maybe without 1a, 1b and 2			Pain Haemorrhage Infection including BBV Keloid and cysts Flashbacks Loss of sexual function Serious obstetric complications for mother and baby

Migration to the UK from high prevalence countries has led to an estimated 127,000 women living with the consequences of FGM in the UK alone (Macfarlane and Dorkenoo, 2015). However, there have been few studies on attitudes towards and observance of the practice among the UK diaspora.

UK Law

Years of lobbying by the charity FORWARD led to the passing of the Prohibition of Female Circumcision Act 1985 which outlawed FGM in the UK. Further legislation followed in

2003, which made it illegal to take girls abroad to perform FGM. Furthermore, the Serious Crime Act of 2015 made any person who is responsible for the girl at the time the FGM occurred liable for the offence committed. It also introduced 'a mandatory reporting duty which requires regulated health and social care professionals and teachers in England and Wales to report "known" cases of FGM in under 18s which they identify in the course of their professional work to the police' (Home Office, 2015).

FGM made UK newspaper headlines over the summer of 2015. Baroness Jenny Tonge (former Liberal Democrat Member of Parliament) publicly reported her concerns to the police having witnessed young girls being taken from the UK to the Horn of Africa for their summer holidays (O'Neill, 2015). Headlines, quoting the Health and Social Care Information Centre (HSCIC), misled the public into believing that thousands of women were having FGM performed in the UK, despite HSCIC (2015) noting: 'Caution is advised in interpreting these findings because data completeness is often low and may vary by region and submitter.' Furthermore, Liberal Democrat MP and Crime Prevention Minister Lynne Featherstone publicly stated: 'If a boy came to a professional with half of his penis missing there would be no question about whether it should be reported' (Topping, 2014).

Prosecutions

At the time of writing, the Crown Prosecution Service (CPS) for England and Wales had only brought one case to court; this was in 2014 and resulted in acquittal. It concerned a woman in labour with her first baby who had had infibulation (sewing up of the vulva) as a child. After the baby was born, a trainee doctor was called to stop the bleeding, which he did with one surgical stitch. At issue was whether he had been guilty of restoring her infibulation (BBC News Online, 2015). Summing up, the judge said that the doctor had been 'let down by a number of systematic failures which were no fault of his own' (Laville, 2015). It took very little time for the jury to find him not guilty and the CPS was heavily criticised for bringing the charge in the first place. The case underlined the need for health professionals to be better trained and leaves a concern as to whether there will now be a reluctance to stitch a bleeding woman who has undergone FGM, with resulting health risks. Since 2014, two further cases have also resulted in acquittals.

In 1982 France became the first 'Western country' to have a conviction for FGM after a baby girl died following infibulation (Rowling, 2012). Since then, it is said that there have been more than 40 prosecutions in France, which is unusual among Western countries, most of which have had no or few convictions. One possible reason for this is that in France all children under six years are examined during routine child surveillance.

Reasons for the lack of prosecutions may include a failure of health, education and social care professionals to refer cases to the police where they suspect FGM to have taken place, although since the Serious Crime Act 2015 this is now mandatory. There may also be a misunderstanding of the genital anatomy and the type of procedure among some examining doctors. In Type 4 FGM, the examination may show no anatomical change such as a scar; in a recent study of the specialist children's FGM clinic (Hodes et al., 2015), 11 of 18 children under 18 years old had undergone Type 4, and so in many the diagnosis was made on the basis of medical history alone. Another factor may be difficulty in obtaining evidence because of the reluctance of victims and practising communities to come forward. If the procedure occurred outside the UK it can be difficult to obtain reliable and admissible evidence from the country in which it took place. The victim's evidence may not be forthcoming as often the child is too young to remember; or when older she may well not want to give evidence against her parents; or they may be unable to identify or remember the cutter because of the traumatic nature of the act. However, it may also be that the prevalence of new cases of FGM once families have moved to Western countries has been overestimated.

Without adequate professional understanding, a statutory approach risks alienating families and the overuse of the power of the state against families and particular cultural communities (see 'The South African family' case example later in this chapter). There is also a risk that girls and women who have had Type 4 FGM see themselves as damaged physically and sexually as a result of society's misunderstanding of the variation of types of FGM (see 'Am I normal?' case example later in this chapter).

Socio-cultural Tension

There is still a strongly held belief in some practising communities that men will refuse to marry an uncircumcised woman because they fear God's punishment (Rainbo, 2009). This puts pressure on mothers to ensure FGM is performed on their daughter to secure future marriage suitability. To not allow it could therefore compromise her future. We would argue that in order to really eradicate FGM, we have to enter into a debate about the role and economic status of women in practising communities.

We recognise at-risk factors for girls and these include: having a mother who has been cut, low parental education level, local practice and men's belief in FGM, early and forced child marriage, and acceptance of violence. Challenging the attitudes of men in practising communities is, therefore, paramount.

Attitudes: A Change from Within

The eradication of the cruel practice of foot-binding, which happened for centuries in China, occurred when men were actively encouraged to marry women who did not practise foot-binding. This was effective because the 'fear of not finding a spouse was the most important concern of those who considered rejecting footbinding' (Broadwin, 1997, p. 423). Could something similar to the anti-foot-binding narrative from the turn of the twentieth century be helping to change attitudes to FGM in the twenty-first century?

Anecdotal evidence suggests that among the UK-based diaspora from high-prevalence communities, mothers are not allowing their daughters to undergo FGM or only allowing Type 4 (ceremonial cut and no removal of genitalia). Furthermore, a Norwegian study found almost all Somali girls born in Norway were not circumcised (Gele et al., 2012). When Somali males living in Oslo were interviewed the majority were against FGM: they thought FGM was harmful to women and not a religious requirement (in contrast to male circumcision which they felt was a religious obligation). Some even felt it was prestigious for a woman not to be cut (Gele et al., 2015). Johnsdotter and Essen (2016) have written very eloquently on the cultural changes after migration, concluding that the future challenge lies in balancing prevention with the examination of suspicious cases of FGM.

Ethical Frameworks

There are many difficulties surrounding the ethical debate on FGM. Some have argued the need to respect the cultural element of this practice, grounded in the idea that all cultural beliefs are equal, with no one being better or worse than the other (Deller Ross, 2008). This approach, sometimes referred to as cultural relativism, identifies the tension between this 'traditional practice' versus the belief FGM is simply child abuse.

A great variety of reasons have been identified as to why certain cultures promote FGM. These include: social obligation, acceptance, rite of passage, reducing sexual desire, fear of the clitoris and sexuality, keeping virginity, a religious requirement, readiness for marriage and adulthood, to purify the body, aesthetics and to protect against material want (Vissandjée et al., 2014). The procedure is often performed by family members and there can be significant pressure from within communities for this practice to occur (International NGO Council on Violence against Children, 2014).

In direct opposition to the cultural relativism argument is a universal rights-based approach. This suggests human rights are objective rather than subjective and apply in all places and at all times. On this basis an ethical justification for FGM based on cultural understandings fails and the practice therefore represents child abuse (Reading et al., 2009). This approach is supported by the United Nations Convention on the Rights of the Child (UNCRC), with Article 19 stating:

> That Parties shall take all appropriate legislative, administrative, social and educational measures to protect the child from all forms of physical or mental violence, injury or abuse, neglect or negligent treatment, maltreatment.

Furthermore, Article 24 states:

> Parties shall take all effective and appropriate measures with a view to abolishing traditional practices prejudicial to the health of children.

However, in contrast with most forms of maltreatment, FGM is a single abusive event conducted with the misconception that it is in the best interests of the girl. Although it is child abuse, the context, risk factors and signs are very different from 'traditional abuse' factors.

Finally, it could be argued that the rights-based approach falls into difficulty when discussing male circumcision, which conversely does not generate the same degree of debate. For example, in the UK FGM is illegal but male circumcision is not. Do Articles 19 and 24 of the UNCRC not apply in this instance?

Male Circumcision

A chapter on FGM would not be complete without addressing male circumcision. The practice has been largely accepted as a culturally appropriate procedure and neglected from mainstream debates on harmful practices during childhood (International NGO Council on Violence against Children, 2014).

There is a strong association with religious practice (Judaism and Islam) alongside rituals for boys progressing into adulthood. In his autobiography *Long Walk to Freedom*, Nelson Mandela describes in detail (as is traditional in his Xhosa tribe) his removal from home as a teenager for this ritual and thus entry to manhood (Mandela, 1994). There has also been recent evidence that male circumcision decreases the transmission rates of acquiring HIV in males (International NGO Council on Violence against Children, 2014).

However, perhaps times are changing. There has been a move to categorise male circumcision in similar terms to FGM. In 2012, a German court established male circumcision to be a 'violation of physical integrity as a child is permanently and irreparably changed by the circumcision and that the practice is also in conflict with the child's right to religious freedom' (International NGO Council on Violence against Children, 2014). Furthermore, there have been movements among certain medical communities to make male circumcision illegal until the child becomes an adult and able to make the decision themselves (International NGO Council on Violence against Children, 2014).

Case Study 1: Distraught Parents

A 30-year-old Indonesian woman, a permanent resident in the UK and pregnant with her second child, attended an antenatal appointment with the midwife. When asked, the mother confirmed that both she and her daughter had both been subjected to circumcision. This prompted a referral to social care and investigation by the police.

Her five-year-old daughter was seen in the clinic and was found to be anatomically normal which confirmed Type 4 circumcision had been performed (Table 12.1). This constitutes a prick or small cut near the clitoris, which leaves no physical change or a small scar that can only be seen with light and magnification (using a colposcope).

Being law-abiding citizens, both parents were horrified to hear that they may have done something illegal to their five-year-old. In fact, the daughter had undergone the procedure before she became a British citizen, which meant there was no prosecution. This was seen as a loophole in the law that has since been closed with the 2015 Serious Crime Act.

Case Study 2: 'Am I Normal?'

A mother and her five daughters were referred to the clinic in order to confirm FGM in the oldest three girls who had recently come from Ethiopia to the UK. The visit was also to ensure the youngest children (aged four and seven) had not had FGM performed in the UK, where they were born and where the practice is illegal.

The 17-year-old daughter was subjected to FGM at the age of 10. She had Type 3 and symptoms of a slow urinary stream. When offered, she refused de-infibulation. Her view may have been that this would make her less marriageable as her future husband would not be able to see on their wedding night that she had undergone FGM. An appointment was offered for the woman to attend with her future husband in order to allay such concerns.

Of the 11-year-old twins, one had a small scar (Type 4) over the clitoral hood and no anatomical changes and the other had no scar but a history of having had the same procedure as her twin. We were able to reassure them that they were anatomically intact. This came as a great relief to them both. After explaining the findings to them, one poignantly asked: 'So I am normal?'

Reassuringly, the four- and seven-year-olds had not had an FGM procedure performed.

The family illustrates an interesting change of opinion, even across the birth interval between siblings. The strongly held belief by the 17-year-old to keep what she had was palpable, as was the relief of her younger sisters upon hearing they were anatomically normal.

Case Study 3: The South African Family

A South African Asian family were referred to a tertiary FGM clinic by social care. This followed concerns raised by an anonymous member of the public that their daughter had been subjected to FGM. The family underwent a lengthy investigation by social care and their child was examined. They came from a non-FGM practising community (Indian, Hindu community) and their child had no evidence of FGM on examination nor disclosed such during her consultation. The case was closed by social care with no evidence of either FGM or child safeguarding concerns.

Case Study 4: FGM Explained

A teenager, born in Sudan, learnt about FGM in school. The girl talked to her teacher and disclosed she had undergone FGM prior to coming to live in the UK. She requested an appointment at the specialist FGM clinic in order to find out what had happened to her. At the clinic, when she was examined she asked for a full explanation of her anatomy while she looked at the video recording (which was deleted) of her genitalia on a screen. She later brought her older sister (also born in Sudan), who was about to get married, to the clinic for the same explanation.

Experience in the multidisciplinary clinic has demonstrated the importance of the right of the child to know and understand what has happened to them (Hodes and Creighton, 2017). In the two cases above, neither needed any medical intervention and both would have no physical difficulties with sexual intercourse or childbirth. However, their FGM may result in a decrease in sexual pleasure due to the absent clitoris.

Conclusion

Anyone who has worked with women who have had FGM recognises the vital importance and benefit of working alongside leaders and spokeswomen from affected communities. At the end of FGM guidelines in the UK are references to the collaborative work of the authors alongside community leaders and advocacy groups. This collaboration is perfectly illustrated by the groundbreaking work of Naana Otoo-Oyortey MBE, Executive Director of FORWARD, who introduced the Health Education England e-learning training module on FGM.

The fear of prosecution is very real for the community and for the medical professions. However, we believe that the government should be as determined to implement a UK prevention strategy as to obtaining a successful prosecution. It was not until 2012 that MPs signed the Home Office 'health passport' which is a statement opposing FGM that can be given to all women from practising communities travelling abroad.

Just like foot-binding in China, a change in attitude can and should come from within communities. The fear of prosecution and victimisation of communities runs a real risk of driving the practice underground. However, communities also need it made clear that FGM is illegal and not tolerated. It is a fine balancing act. A change in attitude from mothers and fathers alike, and communities as a whole, has a greater chance of success in eradicating FGM than prosecution alone. To address FGM is to address societal imbalances and the status of women. Educating, empowering and changing the attitude of women and men so that marriage options will not be restricted by the absence of FGM is paramount in the current debate.

Acknowledgements

Thanks to John Cape and Andrew Child for helpful comments.

References

BBC News Online (2015) FGM trial: prosecutors defend decision to charge acquitted doctor. Available at: www.bbc.co.uk/news/uk-31143911 (accessed 8 March 2016).

Berer, M. (2015) The history and role of the criminal law in anti-FGM campaigns: is the criminal law what is needed, at least in countries like Great Britain? *Reproductive Health Matters*, 23, 145–57.

Black, J. A. and Debelle, G. D. (1995) Female genital mutilation in Britain. *British Medical Journal*, 310, 1590.

Broadwin, J. (1997) Walking contradictions: Chinese women unbound at the turn of the century. *Journal of Historical Sociology*, 10(4), 418–43.

Creighton, S. M. and Hodes, D. (2015) Female genital mutilation: what every paediatrician should know. *Archives of Disease in Childhood*, 101(3), 267–71.

Deller Ross, S. (2008) *Women's Human Rights: The International and Comparative Law Casebook*. Philadelphia, PA: University of Pennsylvania Press.

FORWARD UK (n.d.) Available at: www.forwarduk.org.uk/key-issues/fgm (accessed 28 February 2016).

Gele, A., Kumar, B., Hjelde, K. H. and Sundby, J. (2012) Attitudes towards female circumcision among Somali immigrants to Oslo: a qualitative study. *International Journal of Women's Health*, 4, 7–17.

Gele, A., Sagbakken, M. and Kumar, B. (2015) 'Is female circumcision evolving or dissolving in Norway? A qualitative study on attitudes toward the practice among young Somalis in the Oslo area. *International Journal of Women's Health*, 7, 933–43.

Laville, S. (2015) Doctor found not guilty of FMG in London hospital. *The Guardian*, 4 February. Available at: www.theguardian.com/society/2015/feb/04/doctor-not-guilty-fgm-dhanuson-dharmasena (accessed 23 April 2017)

Topping, A. (2014) FGM: UK plan to require professionals to report suspected cases. *The Guardian*, 5 December. Available at: www.theguardian.com/society/2014/dec/05/fgm-uk-professionals-report-suspected-cases (accessed 28 February 2016).

Health Education England (n.d.) E learning module to improve awareness and understanding of FGM. Available at: www.e-lfh.org.uk/programmes/female-genital-mutilation (accessed 8 March 2016).

Health and Social Care Information Centre (HSCIC) (2015) Female genital mutilation (FGM) – July 2015 to September 2015, experimental statistics, 2 December. Available at: http://content.digital.nhs.uk/catalogue/PUB18533/fgm-apr-2015-jun-2015-exp-rep.pdf (accessed 11 May 2016).

Hodes, D., Armitage, A., Robinson, K. and Creighton, S. M. (2015) Female genital mutilation in children presenting to a London safeguarding clinic: a case series. *Archives of Disease in Childhood*, published online first.

Hodes, D. and Creighton, S. M. (2017) Setting up a clinic to assess children and young people for female genital mutilation. *Archives of Diseases of Childhood (Education Practice Edition)*, 102(1), 14–18.

Home Office (2015) Mandatory reporting of female genital mutilation – procedural information. Available at: www.gov.uk/government/publications/mandatory-reporting-of-female-genital-mutilation-procedural-information

International NGO Council on Violence against Children (2014) Violating children's rights: harmful practices based on tradition, culture, religion or superstition: a report from the International NGO Council on Violence against Children. Available at: http://resourcecentre.savethechildren.se/library/violating-childrens-rights-harmful-practices-based-tradition-culture-religion-or (accessed 8 March 2016).

Johnsdotter, S. and Essen, B. (2016) Cultural change after migration: circumcision of girls in Western migrant communities. *Best Practice and Research Clinical Obstetrics and Gynaecology*, 32, 15–25.

Macfarlane, A. and Dorkenoo, E. (2015) Prevalence of female genital mutilation in England and Wales: national and local estimates. City University London and Equality Now.

Mandela, N. (1994) *Long Walk to Freedom*. Boston, MA: Little, Brown.

O'Neill, B. (2015) The crusade against FGM is out of control. *The Spectator*. Available at: https://blogs.spectator.co.uk/2015/07/the-crusade-against-fgm-is-out-of-control (accessed 28 February 2016).

Rainbo (2009) Available at: www.rainbo.org/ fgm–female-genital-mutilation (accessed 1 December 2015).

Reading, R., Bissel, S., Goldhagen, S. et al. (2009) Promotion of children's rights and prevention of child maltreatment. *The Lancet*, 373, 332–43.

Simpson, J., Hodes, D., Robinson, K. and Creighton, S. (2012) Female genital mutilation: the role of health professional, assessment and management. *British Medical Journal*, 344, e1361.

Rowling, M. (2012) France reduces genital cutting with prevention, prosecution lawyer. *Thomson Reuters Foundation News*, 27 September. Available at: http:// news.trust.org//item/?map=france- reduces-genital-cutting-with-prevention- prosecutions-lawyer/ (accessed 11 May 2016).

United Nations Convention on the Rights of the Child (UNCRC) (n.d.) Available at: www .unicef.org/crc/files/Rights_overview.pdf (accessed 28 February 2016).

United Nations Children's Fund (2013) Female genital mutilation/cutting: a statistical overview and exploration of the dynamics of change. UNICEF, New York, July. Available at: www.unicef.org/media/files/ UNICEF_FGM_report_July_2013_Hi_res .pdf (accessed 28 February 2016).

Vissandjée, B., Denetto, S., Migliardi, P. and Proctor, J. (2014) Female genital cutting (FGC) and the ethics of care: community engagement and cultural sensitivity at the interface of migration experiences. *BMC International Health and Human Rights*, 14(13).

World Health Organisation (WHO) (2008) Eliminating female genital mutilation: an interagency statement. Department of Reproductive Health and Research, WHO, Geneva. Available at: http://apps. who.int/iris/bitstream/10665/43839/1/ 9789241596442_eng.pdf (accessed 23 April 2017).

World Health Organisation (WHO) (2014) Female genital mutilation. Fact sheet no. 241, updated February. Available at: www.who.int/mediacentre/ factsheets/fs241/en/ (accessed 28 February 2016).

Litigation for Failure to Remove

Richard Scorer

13

'Failure to remove' litigation involves a child seeking monetary damages from a local authority social services department for failure to protect that child from abuse. The abuse in question will usually have occurred within the child's birth family but in some cases, for example those involving child sexual exploitation by organised gangs, it will have occurred in the wider community. Wherever the abuse has occurred, the basis of the claim will be that social workers negligently failed to protect the child from abuse which they knew or ought to have known was occurring. Such legal claims have become more common since 2005, following landmark appellate court decisions which finally removed the long-standing immunity from suit previously enjoyed by social workers.

In this chapter I will argue that failure to remove litigation supports the aims of family justice in two ways: first, by compensating children who have been failed by negligent decisions or inaction by social services; second, by helping to monitor and uphold the quality of service provided by social work professionals. Failure to remove litigation thereby helps to underpin society's commitment to the rights of some of the most vulnerable members of society, namely abused and neglected children. At the same time, I will argue that failure to remove litigation supports the aims of family justice in an imperfect way. This is because this type of litigation, as a species of tort law, suffers from some of the deleterious features of that branch of law, for example, an excessive attention to the technical calculation of compensation at the expense of justice and – because of the manner in which most cases are concluded – insufficient opportunity for society to learn from the failings and mistakes which these cases reveal.

Legal Basis of Failure to Remove Litigation

The starting point for failure to remove claims is provided by section 47 of the Children Act 1989. This requires a local authority, which has reasonable cause to suspect that a child in the area is suffering or likely to suffer significant harm, to make enquiries to enable it to decide whether it should take any action to safeguard or promote the child's welfare. If, as a result, the local authority (acting through its social workers) concludes that it should take action to safeguard or promote a child's welfare, it is required to take that action, insofar as it is within its power and reasonably practicable for it to do so. Among the steps the local authority can take to safeguard the child's welfare is to apply to the court for a care order under section 31. If a care order is made, the local authority is under a duty to receive the child into its care.

However, this section does not, in itself, create a civil cause of action – in other words a right to sue for damages – for a child who asserts that the duty has not been complied with. Such a civil cause of action has, nonetheless, been recognised by the courts since 2005. In a landmark judgment in that year, the Court of Appeal held that a common law duty of care is owed to a child in relation to the investigation of suspected child abuse and the initiation and pursuit of care proceedings, and that breach of that duty may result in social services being ordered to pay damages.

The duty on a social worker is a common law duty to take reasonable care to protect the child from foreseeable injury. As with other professionals, the standard of care is assessed by reference to the well-known test laid down in *Bolam* v. *Friern Barnet Hospital Committee* [1957], the 'Bolam test'. This holds that a social worker is not to be considered negligent if he or she acts in accordance with a practice accepted as proper by a responsible body of social work opinion at the relevant time, even though other social workers may take a different view. The Bolam test is now applied in failure to remove cases to the context in which the social worker was operating. Importantly, the Bolam test focuses on the standards of care applicable at the time the decisions were being made. Standards and practices in social work can and do change over time, as the 'pendulum' of social work practice has swung between 'family preservation' and 'child rescue'. The courts are astute to avoid hindsight and will consider the actions of social workers in the context existing at the time they were taken. If the actions of the social worker are deemed to have fallen below the requisite standard as judged by the Bolam test, and if, in consequence, the child suffered harm, then damages may be payable. It is important to note that the right to sue in negligence is the affected child's right. A parent aggrieved at a decision to remove his or her child into care has no such right of action, at least so far as the common law is concerned; however, it should be noted that a parent adversely affected by social work errors may be able to bring a claim against social services under the Human Rights Act 1998 (Scorer, 2017).

Social Worker Immunity: *X* v. *Bedfordshire County Council*

This civil cause of action was hard won over a decade of landmark decisions of the Court of Appeal and the House of Lords (i.e. the UK's senior appeals courts); before 2005, it did not exist. Although the criminal and family courts have been involved in the investigation of child abuse for many decades, it was only in the mid- to late 1990s that victims of child abuse started to look to the civil courts for compensation. Throughout the 1990s and 2000s the civil courts began to grapple with the legal issues arising from civil litigation (compensation claims) brought by victims of abuse against those who abused them or, much more frequently (since it is often only organisations that have the money to meet claims), against organisations charged with responsibility to care for and protect children. From the 1990s onwards, the civil courts had little difficulty in acknowledging that in principle organisations like schools and hospitals acting *in loco parentis* should be capable of being held legally liable where they had knowingly failed to protect a child from abuse perpetrated by one of their employees. But the courts had much more difficulty in accepting that social workers, who may know or suspect that a child in their community is being abused, should be capable of being held legally liable for a failure to act upon that knowledge, or, as is more often the case, for failing to act upon their knowledge quickly enough.

The courts' reluctance to impose liability in these circumstances arose from a belief that tort liability would have a detrimental impact on the work and judgement of professionals engaged in the investigation and remediation of social ills. This mentality had already led the House of Lords in a 1987 decision to create a blanket of immunity from tort litigation for police officers engaged in the investigation and suppression of crime. The imposition of liability on police officers, so their Lordships reasoned, could lead to police operations being carried out in a 'detrimentally defensive frame of mind'. In 1995 in *X (Minors)* v. *Bedfordshire County Council* the House of Lords extended that blanket of immunity to cover local authorities engaged in the performance of their s47 statutory duty to protect children.

In his lead judgment in *X* v. *Bedfordshire County Council*, Lord Browne-Wilkinson listed several policy reasons for this immunity. First was that:

> a common law duty of care would cut across the whole statutory system set up for the protection of children at risk… The system is inter-disciplinary, involving the participation of the police, educational bodies, doctors and others… To introduce into such a system a common law duty of care enforceable against only one of the participant bodies would be manifestly unfair.

Second was that the task of the local authority in dealing with children at risk is 'extraordinarily delicate'; quoting the 1987 Cleveland report, Lord Browne-Wilkinson noted that social services must tread 'a delicate and difficult line… between taking action too soon and not taking it soon enough'. Third was the risk of defensive practice:

> If the (local) authority is to be made liable in damages for a negligent decision to remove a child (such negligence lying in the failure properly first to investigate the allegations) there would be a substantial temptation to postpone making the decision until further inquiries have been made in the hope of getting more concrete facts. Not only would the child be prejudiced by delay: the increased workload inherent in making such investigations would reduce the time available to deal with other cases and other children.

Fourth was that as the relationship between a social worker and the child's parents is often one of conflict, there was a very high risk of vexatious and costly litigation diverting money and human resources from the statutory purpose. And fifth was that a child complaining about social work decisions could utilise statutory complaints procedures (albeit that these do not provide compensation).

Overturning *Bedfordshire*

Clearly, the *Bedfordshire* judgment was based on the belief that negligence liability had little to contribute to upholding standards of professional competence among social workers – and indeed would undermine them. But over the succeeding decade the immunity established in *Bedfordshire* was gradually whittled away, ultimately to be replaced by an explicit recognition that potential negligence liability can and will underpin and support high professional standards. The key factor in that sea change was the European Convention on Human Rights (ECHR), implemented into UK domestic law by the Human Rights Act 1998. In a succession of cases influenced by ECHR jurisprudence, UK appellate courts chipped away at the *Bedfordshire* immunity. In *Barrett* v. *London Borough of Enfield* [1999] the House of Lords held that, while a decision on whether or not to take a child into care was non-justiciable given *Bedfordshire*, once a care order has been granted to the local authority then subsequent negligent decisions or omissions, for example the failure to arrange an adoptive placement, might be actionable: by that stage the delicate decisions about whether to take the child into care had already been made so the *Bedfordshire* immunity was no longer justified. In *Barrett*, the House of Lords also started to retreat from their earlier concern about 'defensive practice', Lord Slynn stating that this 'should normally be a factor of little if any weight' and disputing the notion that the imposition of a duty of care does not contribute to high professional standards.

In 2001 in *S* v. *Gloucestershire County Council* the Court of Appeal departed more explicitly from *Bedfordshire* by holding that children in care who had been abused by their foster carers could sue the local authority for negligence in selecting those foster carers and supervising them. In this case, the Court of Appeal explicitly stated that social workers were now akin to other professionals in that they no longer enjoyed blanket immunity. Meanwhile, in *Z and others* v. *United Kingdom* [2001] the claims of the children in *X* v. *Bedfordshire* reached the European Court of Human Rights in Strasbourg. The European Court of Human Rights held that the *Bedfordshire* children had suffered breaches of Articles 3 and 13 ECHR (i.e. prohibition of inhuman and degrading treatment; right to an effective remedy).

The *X* v. *Bedfordshire* decision was finally consigned to its grave in 2005. In *JD* v. *East Berkshire Community NHS Trust* [2003] and two other conjoined cases concerning intervention by social workers in families where children were misdiagnosed as suffering abuse, the Court of Appeal concluded (in the words of Lord Phillips MR) that:

> In so far as the position of a child is concerned, we have reached the firm conclusion that the decision in *X* v. *Bedfordshire* cannot survive the Human Rights Act. Where child abuse is suspected the interests of the child are paramount; see s1 Children Act 1989. Given the obligation on a local authority to respect a child's convention rights, the recognition of a duty of care to the child on the part of those involved should not have a significantly adverse effect on the manner in which they perform their duties. In the context of suspected child abuse, breach of a duty of care in negligence will frequently amount to a violation of articles 3 or 8. The difference, of course, is that those asserting that wrongful acts or omissions occurred before October 2000 will have no claim under the 1998 Act. This cannot, however, constitute a valid reason of policy for preserving a limitation of the common law duty of care which is not otherwise justified. On the contrary, the absence of an alternative remedy for children who were victims of abuse before October 2000 militates in favour of the recognition of a common law duty of care once the public policy reasons against this have lost their force.
>
> It follows that it will no longer be legitimate to rule that, as a matter of law, no common law duty of care is owed to a child in relation to the investigation of suspected child abuse and the initiation and pursuit of care proceedings.

Although the abandonment of immunity in *Bedfordshire* was probably a necessary consequence of human rights jurisprudence, it was accompanied by a striking sea change in the thinking of courts about the professional and societal consequences of imposing potential tort liability on local authorities performing social work functions. As Lord Phillips stated in his 2005 judgement in *JD*, the public policy reasons for that immunity as enunciated in *Bedfordshire* 10 years earlier had now 'lost their force'. The *JD* decision recognised that, on the contrary, tort law has an important role to play in monitoring and upholding the standard of care exercised by public authorities towards some of the most vulnerable members of society. As Lord Bingham explained in *JD*:

> The second policy ground relied upon in [*X* v. *Bedfordshire*] was... that the task of a local authority and its servants in dealing with children at risk is extraordinarily delicate. There is a difficult line to tread between taking action soon and not taking it soon enough. The truth of this may be readily accepted. It is however a standard function for any professional to assess what may be a fraught and difficult situation. That is not generally treated as a reason for not requiring the exercise of reasonable skill and care in the task. The professional is not required to be right, but only to be reasonably skilful and careful.

As regards the 'defensive practice' objection (the third policy reason listed by Lord Browne-Wilkinson in *X* v. *Bedfordshire*), Lord Bingham observed that: 'to describe awareness of a legal duty as having an "insidious effect" on the mind of a potential defendant is to undermine the foundation of the law of professional negligence'. Rather, awareness of a legal duty should be a 'badge of professional status'.

Failure to Remove Litigation Now

We are now 13 years on from *JD*, and in that period several hundred claims for failure to remove have been brought against local authorities up and down the country. It is clear from the experience of the past decade that the public policy immunity enunciated in *Bedfordshire* was never justified in the first place: it was based on untested and unproven assumptions about the deleterious consequences of tort liability. The several hundred failure to remove claims which have been litigated in the past 10 years represent a minute fraction of the total number of child abuse cases dealt with by local authorities in that period, and there is no evidence that failure to remove litigation has imperilled or undermined day-to-day social work practice in the manner originally feared. On the contrary, in private discussions I have had with local authorities and their insurers, the opposite impression emerges: at least some local authorities acknowledge that failure to remove litigation has highlighted some flaws in social work practice both individual and systemic, and thereby has promoted better practice and higher standards. In this way, failure to remove litigation supports and underpins family justice. That said, it should be acknowledged that this view is not universally shared among local authorities and their insurers, and at the time of writing there are some attempts underway to persuade the courts that liability of social services for professional negligence is wrong in principle and out of line with the case law relating to the negligence of other public bodies (*CN* v. *Poole* [2016]). It remains to be seen whether these attempts will make any headway. However, it is noteworthy and perhaps unsurprising that questions of principle regarding the availability of a legal remedy to children failed by social services – questions which appeared to have been resolved with finality by the courts – are being revived against the backdrop of austerity and the difficulties faced by local authorities in discharging their social work duties in the context of greatly reduced budgets.

For now, however, failure to remove litigation remains an important mechanism for promoting individual justice for child victims and wider learning of lessons for social services departments and society as a whole. However, in both respects, it is an imperfect tool, for two main reasons.

The first is because English tort law is based on compensatory principles – restoring the injured claimant, in so far as money can, to the position they would have been in but for the breach of duty. Litigation can seem to be fixated on arcane and technical disputes about causation and damage, thus for claimants detracting from a broader sense of justice being done. In failure to remove claims, the court will look at causation and extent of damage in fine detail. Sometimes it can be shown that a social worker has failed to act on knowledge of abuse but for other reasons this failure was not causative of the harm suffered by the child. Frequently the evidence will show that a social worker's failure only tipped over into negligence as defined by the Bolam test at a certain point in the timeline of abuse – thus some abuse will be actionable but other abuse not. This is an inevitable feature of the analysis required by tort law but is difficult and frustrating for claimants to understand and often seems to detract from the justice of the situation. This 'sliding scale' of liability is particularly invidious where sibling groups are involved. Typically, experts instructed in these cases will identify a 'date of removal' – a point in time at which it can be said that the social worker was negligent in failing to act on the accumulated evidence of abuse. At that point in time the older members of the sibling group may have already suffered years of abuse, so their 'damage' may be less actionable than that suffered by younger siblings, leading to a perception of different and unfair treatment.

Second, the very nature of failure to remove litigation as a private law remedy militates against its broader societal effectiveness: much of what we could learn from these cases is lost to the wider social work profession because most cases are settled out of court. Of the hundreds of cases which have been litigated since 2005, only seven or eight have ever been litigated to trial and resulted in a published judgment from which lessons might be learned. And there are many such lessons. Within the cases that I and other lawyers have litigated in this period, a number of themes have emerged time and again, for example, lack of timely decision-making and newly qualified social workers being expected to handle complex cases. Perhaps the two most common types of failure identified are a failure to consider past history in assessments – i.e. incidents are examined in isolation rather than as part of a pattern of abuse or neglect. This failure often stems from staff churn leading to frequent changes in case handling and a loss of past experience of the family. The other repeated and glaring issue is the failure to see children or seek their views. These are important issues of public interest yet, because as they are being litigated in private law tort proceedings, unless the claim goes to trial they rarely see the light of day.

Of course, for litigants themselves, it is far better that cases are resolved 'out of court' and that the expense and distress of a trial is avoided. However, it also means that the evidence that lawyers and experts instructed in these cases have painstakingly collated is never shared with the wider social work community and thus cannot be used to promote better practice to the extent that we would wish. With colleagues in the Association of Child Abuse Lawyers (ACAL, www.childabuselawyers.com), I have considered whether there might be ways to collate the evidence and lessons of failure to remove cases to facilitate wider learnings but we always come up against the same practical obstacles around confidentiality and data protection which we are rightly bound to observe.

Is there any workable solution to this? The government abuse inquiry under Professor Alexis Jay will be looking at the effectiveness of civil redress. Consideration should be given to how the evidence from civil claims can be utilised by society as a whole in tackling child abuse more effectively. We are increasingly moving towards specialist courts for abuse and sex crimes in the criminal law arena and I believe that a similar system of specialist courts should be adopted for civil claims arising from allegations of child abuse. The consolidation of these cases in one venue would better enable the legal system to draw and share lessons from these cases without prejudicing the confidentiality which is a necessary part of the court process.

Addendum, March 2018

The above chapter was written in mid-2017. As noted, at the time of writing there were 'some attempts underway to persuade the courts that liability of social services for professional negligence is wrong in principle and out of line with the case law relating to the liabilities of other public bodies'. Since this chapter was written, the case cited in this respect (*CN v. Poole Borough Council*) has been considered by the Court of Appeal, which handed down its judgment in late December 2017. The unsuccessful claimant in *CN v. Poole* is seeking leave to appeal to the Supreme Court, but if it stands the Court of Appeal judgment is likely to have a significant impact on failure to remove claims, potentially making many (but not necessarily all) of those claims impossible to pursue, at least at common law.

The facts of *CN* v. *Poole Borough Council* were atypical in that the case involved a claim that the defendant local authority was in breach of its common law duty of care in failing to remove children from a family where the mother was unable to protect the children from the anti-social behaviour of neighbours, rather than an allegation of failure to protect from abuse perpetrated by a family member. Nonetheless, in giving the lead judgement Lord Justice Irwin held that the 2005 decision of the Court of Appeal in *JD* v. *East Berkshire Community NHS Trust* was incompatible with two subsequent decisions of the Supreme Court concerning the liability of state agencies for the wrongful acts of third parties and as such, could no longer be considered good law. In citing the general principle that a defendant is not liable for the wrongdoing of a third party, Lord Justice Irwin also acknowledged that an exception to this general principle might arise where a defendant had 'assumed responsibility', but held that this exception was not applicable on the particular facts of *Poole*.

The implications of *Poole* are still being digested, but the decision is certainly being interpreted by local authorities as meaning that no duty of care in negligence can be owed by a local authority in the exercise of its child protection functions to investigate and take action to prevent significant harm to children, whatever its source. If correct, this would have the effect of returning the law to its pre-*JD* state and rendering impossible many claims for failure to remove. However, a number of caveats should be noted. First, the judgment in *Poole* may be appealed to the Supreme Court. Second, even if *Poole* is not considered by the Supreme Court, given the importance of the issues arising it is likely that another case, perhaps with more standard failure to remove facts, will come before the Supreme Court sooner rather than later. Third, cases are very fact-specific and other cases may further elaborate on the analysis of liability in failure to remove situations, particularly so far as the question of 'assumption of responsibility' is concerned: when might a local authority be said to have assumed responsibility such that it would still be liable in negligence for failure to prevent foreseeable abuse to a child? So, the Court of Appeal decision in *Poole* is unlikely to be the last word on these matters. Finally, the pre-*JD* decisions which followed *X* v. *Bedfordshire*, and which whittled down its impact, still stand: *Barrett* v. *Enfield*, which provides that where a care order has been granted to a local authority, it may be liable for subsequent negligent acts and omissions, remains good law. Moreover, the judgement in *Poole* does not prevent abused children from seeking a remedy against the local authority under the Human Rights Act 1998: this cause of action potentially remains available where the breaches of duty occurred after the HRA came into force in October 2000. The practical difficulty with pursuing claims under the HRA is the much shorter one-year limitation period applicable to such claims, but where the negligence route is closed off by *Poole*, children who have been abused in circumstances involving failures by local authorities are likely to seek redress via the HRA route. For all these reasons, it is likely that failure to remove litigation will, in some form, remain a feature of our legal landscape, and the important issues it raises about society's wider responsibility to protect children will not go away.

References

Barrett v. *London Borough of Enfield* [1999] 3 WLR 79.

Bolam v. *Friern Barnet Hospital Committee* [1957] 1 WLR 582.

CN v. *Poole* [2016] EWHC 569 (QB).

JD v. *East Berkshire Community NHS Trust* [2003] EWCA Civ 1151.

S v. *Gloucestershire County Council* [2001] 2 WLR 909.

Scorer, R. (2017) Claims against social work and medical professionals for wrongful allegations of abuse. *Journal of Personal Injury Law*, 2.

X (Minors) v. *Bedfordshire County Council* [1995] 2 AC 633.

Z and others v. *United Kingdom* [2001] 2 FLR 612, ECHR.

Chapter

14

Towards a Theory for the Development of Autonomy

Mike Shaw

I realise that this chapter has been forming in my mind for a long time. Early on in my child psychiatry career, when I was running a tertiary referral service for pre-adolescent children with complex psychiatric disorders, I was keen to promote children's autonomy and participation in treatment decision-making, even when children lacked 'competence' or when it was necessary to overrule a child's objections in the interest of their welfare (Shaw, 2001). For instance, how should we manage a girl with anorexia nervosa, who presents on the verge of metabolic collapse and has a history of being raped? We will have to use a nasogastric tube and it is likely that she will experience this as another rape. Is there anything we can do to make this less traumatising? Furthermore, presuming that we can nurse her back to a safer metabolic balance, how do we encourage her to take back responsibility for making sure she is adequately fed?

In the later part of my career I have worked as an expert witness in the family court where I see parents who love their children but are unable to keep them safe. Most of these parents have had horribly traumatic childhoods. They are left with terrible feelings of pain and emptiness, which they alleviate with alcohol, drugs, sex and violence. So, how do we protect these children without exacerbating their parents' sense of powerlessness? How do we get the parents to take responsibility and create order in their own and their children's lives? Finally, where children are already traumatised, how do we stop them from following their parents down the same path?

What follows is a theory for the development of autonomy, which I hope can help us answer some of these questions.

Outline

I will define autonomy as *having the capacity, for the most part, to be in charge of meeting one's own needs*. I say 'for the most part' because, as I will demonstrate, autonomy is relative rather than absolute, and 'in charge' because the heart of autonomy is decision-making rather than doing. For instance, I might have a problem with mobility, for which I require help, but I can still be in charge of where I am going.

Over the rest of the chapter:

1. I will set out what I mean by 'needs'.
2. I will suggest that children have a natural urge for autonomy.
3. I will argue that healthy autonomy requires four benign developmental influences.
4. I will use this framework to consider the development of autonomy for bodily needs, emotional needs and making decisions.

5. I will consider situations where the development of autonomy doesn't go so easily or so well.
6. I will finish with some implications for research, practice and policymaking.

Children's Needs

No inventory of children's needs could ever be definitive. This list is one that has built up over my clinical practice. For the purposes of this chapter, I have divided children's needs into three subcategories.

Bodily Needs

- To be kept safe and feeling safe.
- To be adequately fed, washed and clothed and to have somewhere comfortable to sleep.
- To have developmentally appropriate routines for eating, hygiene, sleeping, play and education.

Emotional Needs

- To give and receive love.
- To receive affection and comfort from a trustworthy adult.
- To feel understood, lovable and that the world is a reasonably good place.
- To be able to communicate painful feelings, thoughts and memories in a safe way and to feel listened to by a respected and trustworthy adult.
- To be able to rework and give meaning to previously overwhelming experiences.

Complex Needs Involving Decision-Making

- To have clear expectations about socially appropriate behaviour, and a calm but firm and consistent approach to discipline.
- To have developmentally appropriate levels of adult supervision.
- To have developmentally appropriate levels of control over one's own body, actions and conscience.
- To be encouraged to observe, learn and solve problems.
- To be encouraged to pursue interests and talents through play, education and other cultural and leisure activities.
- To be encouraged to make developmentally appropriate choices about identity, health and education and have access to adequate opportunities and services.

Where children have developmental or health problems, their needs are generally greater and more complex. For example, children who have been exposed to violence will have a greater than usual need to be safe and feel safe, to express painful thoughts, feelings and memories with a trustworthy adult and to be able to rework and give meaning to previously overwhelming experiences.

A Natural Urge for Autonomy

While autonomy is made possible by physical and mental maturation, it is likely that children also have a natural urge for autonomy. Helplessness and dependence are intrinsically perilous states, which are often experienced as deeply unpleasant. If adults and older children find them problematic why wouldn't something similar be true for babies and younger children?

At the same time autonomy can seem very attractive. We are all familiar with children who would rather struggle with a difficult problem than accept help. Similarly, I remember the enormous feelings of freedom and adventure when I was first able to ride my bicycle in the street. Autonomy is a popular theme in children's literature and film, and part of the allure of orphan characters that are 'free to run wild and live large and daring lives' (Rundell, 2014). Finally, it is likely that the urge for autonomy is part of a wider group of development-driving motivations that include Rousseau's (1993) ideas about children's curiosity and Bion's (1984a) ideas about a desire to discover the truth.

If children find autonomy attractive, parents see things rather differently. They have to hold the tension between protection and autonomy, keeping children comfortable and safe on the one hand, while encouraging perseverance and problem-solving on the other. What the children can do unaided is constantly being tested, fought over and renegotiated with their parents.

Benign Developmental Influences

I believe that healthy autonomy requires four benign developmental influences:

1. That parents and others provide for the needs that children cannot provide for themselves.
2. That parents and others promote the development of capacities that will allow children to be in charge of providing for their own needs.
3. That parents and others permit, help or cajole children to take charge of meeting their own needs at a point where they are ready to do so.
4. That parents and communities tolerate a level of individual autonomy that doesn't interfere with the autonomy of others.

I will now use this theoretic framework of children's needs, their desire for autonomy and the benign developmental influences to consider the development of autonomy for bodily needs, emotional needs and decision-making. In each case I will draw examples from the need to be adequately fed.

Handling Bodily Needs

The newborn baby's capacity to feed herself is limited to a few reflexes. If you touch her cheek she turns her head in the direction of the touch and opens her mouth. Touch the roof of her mouth and she begins to suck and swallow. New feeding capacities will emerge as her nervous and skeletal systems grow and become more sophisticated. At the same time, she will learn from the way her parents feed her and the extent to which they support and stimulate her innate capacities.

The emergence of new physical capacities triggers kaleidoscope-like shifts in her needs. One day she is happy being spoon-fed, the next she insists on holding a spoon. Being an effective parent requires flexibility. Rather than fighting over who holds the spoon, the creative parent provides two spoons, one for the baby to practise feeding herself and another for the parent to ensure that the meal doesn't take all day. However, at some point the parent steps back because the child is able to spoon food into her own mouth and prefers to do so.

Unless the child becomes sick, exhausted or asks for help, the parent won't spoon-feed the child again and to do so would feel, to the parent and the child, like an intrusion, or in the extreme case of a child who was refusing to eat, an assault.

With spoon-feeding, there is a more or less complete transfer of responsibilities from the parent to the child. Starting with one spoon controlled by the parent, moving through a phase of two spoons until there is just one spoon again, but this time controlled by the child. The *one-spoon, two-spoons, one-spoon pattern* applies to the development of autonomy for most bodily needs including learning to dress, wash and use the toilet. It is also the prototype for millions of other daily skills such as riding a bicycle, handling money and writing a message.

Managing Emotional Needs

The need to be adequately fed also has a powerful emotional dimension. As with bodily needs, the baby starts out helpless and dependent, and the mother has a lot of work to do:

1. Observing her baby's distress, for example, noticing a thin high-pitched quality to the baby's cry and that her back is slightly arched.
2. Forming hypotheses about her baby's possible unmet needs, for instance, 'that is probably wind, but she is also nearly ready for a nap'.
3. Using her tone of voice and touch to let her baby know that she understands how frightened and frustrated the baby feels, but that from her adult perspective things aren't so bad and that help is on its way.
4. Working with the baby to solve the problem by trying a different position, patting the baby's back, rubbing her tummy or offering the breast until a solution emerges.

As our baby matures, new capacities to manage emotional needs will emerge. She starts to understand a few words, not just about the outside world such as 'carrot', 'spoon' and 'mouth', but also about what is going on inside her body and mind, like 'thirsty', 'yucky' and 'enough'. Words are a way for our baby to communicate her needs and to give them meaning. Other helpful new capacities include starting to enjoy games and responding to humour so that being fed is easier and more fun when her mother pretends the spoon is an aeroplane.

Once our baby is a little older she is able to tolerate a greater degree of discomfort and frustration. Her mother can promote this capacity to 'sit with' uncomfortable feelings:

1. By creating predictable routines around her baby's needs.
2. By helping to maintain strong lines of communication.
3. By not being in a rush.
4. By tolerating failure and mess.
5. By giving little hints and encouragement, without taking over when there is a chance the baby will get there by herself.
6. By stepping in and helping when the baby's distress is reaching the point where she can no longer cope on her own.

This highly supported 'safe space' allows painful experiences to be processed and become an opportunity for emotional growth. It also leaves our baby free to experiment. She learns not only how to manipulate the spoon but also that persistence pays. With practice her capacity to 'sit with' difficult feelings grows, as does her capacity to represent feelings symbolically in words, play and humour. This allows her to push on from simply working in tandem with her mother and to take the first steps towards being able to think about and manage her feelings unaided.

The importance of the mother–child relationship in meeting the baby's emotional needs and laying the foundations of autonomy is central to a lot of psychoanalytic thinking. An example is Bion's (1984a, 1984b) and Wadell's (2002) idea that the baby uses her mother's mind to 'contain' and digest experiences that she is unable to tolerate on her own, and that repeated cycles of containment by the mother allow the baby to develop her own capacity to contain and regulate her feelings.

Where things go well, our baby gradually feels 'at home' in her body and mind. In time, she will be sitting with and processing countless sensations, thoughts and feelings on her own. However, there will still be some feelings and thoughts she needs help with. So, the *one-spoon, two-spoons, one-spoon pattern* only goes so far in describing the development of autonomy with managing emotional needs.

Decision-Making

Decision-making is the area of complex feelings and thought where the *one-spoon, two-spoons, one-spoon pattern* tends to prevail. In the beginning, parents make decisions for children; later, parents share decision-making with children, but at some point, children make decisions for themselves.

Decision-making starts early; even young babies prefer certain foods, toys and activities, while older children make complex and potentially highly significant decisions about food, hairstyles, fashion, school attendance and effort, sexual preference, sexual activity, tobacco, alcohol, drugs, social media, pornography, bullying, racism, antisocial behaviour and criminal activity.

Where things go well, parents help children to recognise situations where decision-making is needed. Where parents impose decisions on children it helps if parents are respectful and explain the decision-making process. It also helps if parents share some decision-making with their children and create a 'safe space' in which children are free to make their own decisions between more than one satisfactory option. Finally, all this needs to be geared to match and slightly stretch children's developmental capacities.

Returning to the need to be adequately fed, at first the mother will make most of the decisions, but increasingly the child becomes her mother's collaborator. The mother will 'offer' the breast and wait for her baby to respond. In time the baby will be given more decisions to make, such as 'shall we eat peas first or potatoes'. Whether it is peas or potatoes first is not really important, but the mother's question gives our baby a 'safe space' in which to practise decision-making. What's more, being given this measure of control makes our baby more inclined to take responsibility for making sure she is adequately fed. The older child has much more control over what, when and where she eats, and peers, role models and the wider zeitgeist will increasingly affect her decision-making. The older adolescent makes complex decisions such as choosing certain foodstuffs as a statement of social affiliation or taking an ethical position, for example, on not eating meat. She also has to learn about tolerating other people who make different choices.

Decisions about education and health have long-lasting effects on children's life chances so it is common for parents and children to share these types of decisions over a longer period. For example, Alderson (1993) interviewed 120 children aged eight–15 years undergoing repeated elective surgery for relief of chronic musculoskeletal conditions; on average these children had already had five operations. She asked the children: 'How old do you think you were or will be when you're old enough to decide (about surgery)?' At the same time she asked their parents: 'At what age do you think your child can make a wise choice?' Parents and children gave a very similar answer, but girls and their parents thought they would be ready to decide two years earlier than boys and their parents (13.1 years for girls and 12.8 years for girls' parents compared to 15 years for boys and 14.9 years for boys' parents). Only a few children wanted to be the 'main decider' (17.5 per cent), and when asked what they might do if they disagreed with their parents, relatively few children said they would try to get their own way (22 per cent of boys, 11 per cent of girls).

The law uses the concept of 'capacity' to identify children who are 'ready' to make decisions independently. In theory, the term 'capacity' could be applied to any age group; however, in English law the term 'competence' is preferred when describing 'capacity' in children under 16 years old, and the test is the common law decision in *Gillick* v. *West Norfolk and Wisbech Area Health Authority* [1986], whereas the test for capacity in 16- and 17-year-old is the Mental Capacity Act (see Parker, Chapter 16 in this volume). However, the requirements for competence and capacity are very similar, which are that the individual:

- understands the information relevant to the decision;
- retains that information;
- uses or weighs that information as part of the decision-making process; and
- communicates their decision (whether by talking, sign language or any other means).

Judgements about capacity are made on a case-by-case basis, taking account of the individual, type of decision and particular circumstances. However, there is presumption of capacity in 16- and 17-year-olds (as with adults) whereas a judgement needs to be made whether under-16-year-olds are competent.

Capacity is very important because it allows children to 'consent', which is a particular type of decision-making involving:

> Agreeing to allow someone else to do something to, or, for you. Particularly consent to treatment. Valid consent requires that the person has the capacity to make the decision (or the competence to consent, if a child), and they are given the information they need to make the decision, and that they are not under any duress or inappropriate pressure. (*The Mental Health Act Code of Practice*, 2015)

It follows that treatment or other acts such as sexual activity without consent or under pressure is assault.

While these legal definitions provide a helpful conceptual framework, real life is a lot messier. Although 'consent' requires a capacity for rational thinking, the process of making decisions is rarely rational or straightforward. For example, tobacco smokers continue to smoke despite being able to 'understand' and 'weigh' the evidence about the dangers of smoking. Similarly, complex unconscious processes exert a powerful influence over all our choices. Furthermore, outside a few tightly controlled arenas, such as health care, children make lots of decisions without the capacity to do so.

Nevertheless, where things go well, children are given developmentally appropriate options and learn to take decisions. Children mess things up and make mistakes, but overall make the best of their interests and talents and maintain or optimise their health and life chances. In time, parents recognise that their children have the capacity to take particular decisions for themselves and will respect those decisions, even if they have some concerns or disagree. This experience of having their decisions respected not only gives children confidence but also teaches them about the importance of tolerating the autonomy of others. It is the final stage of the *one-spoon, two-spoons, one-spoon pattern*. In the end autonomy provides both the freedom to take risks, make mistakes and learn, and the obligation to take responsibility for the decisions made.

Billions of Tiny Steps

To recap, by learning to use a spoon, 'sit with' uncomfortable feelings and deciding whether to eat peas or potatoes first, our baby takes her first tiny steps on the road to meeting her own need to be adequately fed, and she will take further tiny steps as new physical emotional and decision-making capacities emerge. By taking billions of these tiny steps over a couple of decades, she will be capable, for the most part, to be in charge of meeting her need to be adequately fed.

Where Things are More Difficult or Don't Go So Well

So far, we have talked about normal development. But what happens when children have complex needs, or families are neglectful and abusive, or communities are blighted by prejudice, poverty and war?

I have argued that achieving autonomy requires parents and others to permit, help or cajole children to take charge of meeting their own needs at a point where they are ready to do so, and that children are encouraged to learn by taking risks and making mistakes. However, nudging children into the world is more problematic when they have complex needs, for instance, sensory impairments such as deafness, developmental problems such as autism spectrum disorder or life-threatening physical and mental disorders such as diabetes mellitus or anorexia nervosa. Having complex needs doesn't necessarily diminish children's desire for autonomy or the contribution it can make to their quality of life. However, there is more to learn. For instance, children with diabetes mellitus need to know more about healthy diet and lifestyle and understand their insulin therapy; what is more, they also have bigger risks to face. While most parents hold their nerve, and judge it well, some will hand over responsibility too early or too late, while some overstretched health services tackle the risk but lose sight of the need to promote autonomy.

Neglected and abused children face an even greater challenge. How can they learn to look after themselves when their parents fail to show them how? For instance, I see severely neglected and abused infants of three or four years who can't stop eating. They are overly preoccupied by food, eat huge quantities without feeling full and vomit up the excess, but carry on eating, even when they are being adequately fed in foster care. I would suggest these children have failed to develop a capacity to 'sit with', 'process' and 'regulate' their anxieties around eating. Instead, they experience a blind panic, which Bion (1984b) called 'a nameless dread'.

Something similar can be seen in the adverse childhood experiences (ACE) study (Felitti and Anda, 2010), which shows a dose-dependent relationship between: first, exposure to one or more 'adverse childhood experiences' (10 common forms of abuse, neglect and or household dysfunction); second, making damaging decisions about eating, tobacco, alcohol, education, sexual activity, drugs, violence and criminal activity in adolescence and early adulthood; and third, diminished life chances, poor health and reduced life expectancy.

A theory for the development of autonomy would suggest that high ACE score individuals are relying on food, tobacco, alcohol, drugs, sex and violence to meet their emotional needs, because of a failure to develop healthy autonomy. Presumably the damage was done, not only by exposure to ACEs, which stirred up helplessness, terror and rage, but also by the absence of a 'safe space' where these toxic feelings could be 'contained', given meaning and become an opportunity for emotional growth.

But a second possible explanation for this pattern is that children pick up on their parents' sense of helplessness and unwillingness to take responsibility for their actions. Parents whose own development of autonomy is incomplete are unlikely to show their children that life is full of choices, or explain how they are making decisions or involve children in decision-making. They are more likely to give children decisions to make before they are ready to make them, or fail to respect their children's autonomy or fail to teach them to respect the autonomy of others. Instead, they introduce their children to a brutal world of self-interest, where individuals or groups exploit their superior physical, intellectual, social or economic power to get their emotional, sexual, social or economic needs met, at the expense of others.

Finally, many children never get an opportunity to pursue their interests and talents or think for themselves, because they grow up in communities weighed down by poverty, poor health care, lack of education, rigid social codes, discrimination, corruption, gangs, sectarianism, brutal governments or war.

Adults who lack *the capacity, for the most part, to be in charge of meeting their own needs* feel helpless and hopeless and have less to offer to their children and their communities. Families and communities dominated by such adults are at a catastrophic disadvantage, because feelings of helplessness and hopelessness are passed on, as part of a culture of despair.

Implications of a Theory for the Development of Autonomy

If we accept that there is a normal course for the development of autonomy, but that for some children the course is less straightforward and seriously disturbed for others, then perhaps there is a role for supplementary or remedial assistance.

It could be that individuals with non-typical development or serious illnesses can achieve better outcomes if more effort was directed at promoting autonomy (see both Parker, Chapter 16 and De Ceglie, Chapter 17 in this volume).

Similarly, where children have been abused, remediation and reinforcement of the four benign developmental influences (see this chapter, section Benign Developmental Influences above) might help establish healthy autonomy. Interventions such as mindfulness or mentalisation help children tolerate difficult feelings and give them meaning. Abused children might also need additional help with learning how to make decisions especially around health and education, or respecting the decisions of others, particularly sexual activity (see Pearce and Coy, Chapter 15 in this volume).

An obvious target population would be children who have been subject to child protection concerns or care proceedings. We know that the current care system leaves children poorly equipped for adult life (National Audit Office, 2015).

Where parents are struggling to meet their children's needs, a theory of autonomy would suggest that parents need to get better at managing their own needs before they help their children. For example, the Family Drug and Alcohol Court (see Harwin et al., Chapter 9 in this volume) encourages parents to regulate their own difficult feelings without recourse to drugs and alcohol, as an important step on the way to helping them regulate their children's feelings with techniques such as Video Interaction Guidance (see Kennedy et al., Chapter 10 in this volume).

Similarly, helping communities break out of a pattern of poverty, prejudice and poor educational and health outcomes involves building a sense that there are real decisions to make, involving communities in those decisions and making them feel responsible.

These solutions could have been arrived at from different starting points. However, I would argue that a theory for the development of autonomy provides a new frame, which allows us to see familiar problems in a fresh and more coherent way.

References

Alderson, P. (1993) *Children's Consent to Surgery*. Buckingham: Open University Press.

Bion, W. R. (1984a) *Learning from Experience*. London: Karnac (original published 1962).

Bion, W. R. (1984b) *Second Thoughts*. London: Karnac (original published 1967).

Felitti, V. J. and Anda, R. F. (2010) The relationship of adverse childhood experiences to adult health, well-being, social function, and healthcare. In R. Lanius, E. Vermetten and C. Pain (eds), *The Impact of Early Life Trauma on Health and Disease: The Hidden Epidemic*. Cambridge: Cambridge University Press (www.theannainstitute.org/Lanius.pdf).

Gillick v. West Norfolk and Wisbech Area Health Authority [1986] AC 112.

National Audit Office (2015) Care leaver's transition to adulthood. HC 269 Session 2015–16, 17 July. Available at: www.nao .org.uk/wp-content/uploads/2015/07/ Care-leavers-transition-to-adulthood-summary.pdf

Rousseau, J.-J. (1993) *Émile*. London: Everyman.

Rundell, K. (2014) Katherine Rundell's top 10 orphans. *The Guardian*, 6 March. Available at: www.theguardian.com/ childrens-books-site/2014/mar/06/ top-10-orphans-katherine-rundell

Shaw, M. (2001) Competence and consent to treatment in children and adolescents. *Advances in Psychiatric Treatment*, 7, 150–9.

The Mental Health Act Code of Practice (2015) London: The Stationery Office.

Wadell, M. (2002) *Inside Lives: Psychoanalysis and the Growth of the Personality*. London: Karnac.

15

Child Sexual Exploitation and Consent to Sexual Activity

A Developmental and Context-Driven Approach

Jenny Pearce and Maddy Coy

In this chapter we explore some of the complex debates about if, when and why a child or young person who is being sexually abused and exploited online and/or offline may be seen to hold responsibility for consenting to sexual activity. We use the terms 'sexual abuse' and 'sexual exploitation' following established definitions that recognise sexual abuse as unwanted sex (HM Government, 2015) and sexual exploitation as abuse involving some form of exchange in return for sex (Department for Children, Schools and Families, 2009; Department for Education, 2017; Beckett et al., 2017). 'Fraser guidelines' are available to advise health professionals on when and why to give contraceptive advice to children under the legal age of consent to sexual activity. There is less advice about child-centred therapeutically informed responses to help professionals recognise and respond to a young person under the age of 18 experiencing exploitative, abusive sex. Activists advocating for more sophisticated child protection assert that no child can consent to, or be held responsible for, their own abuse. Sadly though, recent research and reviews of interventions note failures to protect children and recognise confusion about how to prevent blame being paced on the child (Ofsted, 2014). We argue that these failures are often based on a poor understanding of the psychosocial pressures facing children who are being exploited and manipulated into appearing to consent to their own exploitation. For too long children under the age of 18, particularly those in later adolescence, have been deemed to be responsible for their own abuse and sexual exploitation, attention being placed on their 'delinquent' behaviour, their dress and demeanour or their apparent maturity for their age. While many children can, and do, take informed decisions about when and why they engage in sexual activity, we will argue that abusive and exploitative sexual activity, either perpetrated by adults or by children themselves, is overlooked because 'consent' to sexual activity has historically been based on three flawed assumptions: first that the child's capacity to consent can be determined solely by their age; second that the child's capacity to consent is independent of the social context within which that child is functioning; and finally, that the onus is on giving, rather than getting consent. We argue that while dynamics of abuse online and offline have some differences (as explored in Beckett et al., 2017 and Palmer, 2015), the essential power differential surrounding questions of consent are similar. We want to look further into the dynamics occurring in the process of giving and getting consent.

Defining Childhood

Throughout this chapter we refer to children as anyone under the age of 18 according to the United Nations Convention on the Rights of the Child (UNCRC) 1987. While we appreciate the vast number of changes taking place throughout a child's adolescence as they approach adulthood, with recent research on the brain telling us even more about the significant changes happening through puberty (Coleman, 2011), we uphold the UNCRC focus on protecting all children up to 18, irrespective of their chronological age. We also appreciate that 'childhood' itself is a contested, socially constructed concept (Jenks, 2005), and that the changing capacity of different children throughout childhood is influenced by familial, social and environmental factors (Kroger, 2004). Despite these variations, we hold onto and promote Article 19 of the UNCRC, which stipulates that all children, including those approaching adulthood, have the right to be protected from harm.

However, children themselves recognise that this right is easily undermined, both by adults who may sexually abuse them within the family or other environments and by peers in contexts where masculinity is associated with (hetero) sexual success. As noted by one young person in a research project exploring the meaning of consent among children:

> I think it's a given now that you are expected if you ever go out with a guy or whatever, it's expected that you are supposed to be having sex with him. Even when you are little. (Young woman, Year 11, in Coy et al., 2013, p. 63)

This young woman is saying that 'even when you are little' you are still expected to have sex if you are going out ('or whatever') with a young man. For us, this quote identifies two distinct losses for this young woman: the loss of being able to have non-sexual friendships with young men and the loss of the capacity to choose whether or not to be sexually active, even when 'little'. These are both big losses to bear, particularly as the commencement of sexual activity is often deemed as a rite of passage to adulthood, meaning that once sexually active, aspects of childhood have to be left behind. She is also learning about how sexual expectations are shaped by gender. The fact that the childhood of young women and young men in these situations is being radically interrupted is rarely discussed. Work undertaken by Barter et al. (2009) and currently documented under a European project titled 'stiritup' (http://Stiritup.eu) is engaging with this process, but all too often discussion with children and adolescents about negotiating sex is avoided (including the resulting distress from unwanted and/or forced progression into sexual activity). If it is addressed in schools at all, it is as an 'add on' to standard personal social and health education and sex and relationship classes. There are some examples of good practice in schools (e.g. 'Healthy Minds Curriculum Journey') and some women's organisations use their expertise on sexual violence and exploitation to deliver prevention work in schools. Despite this, much more is needed to demystify abuse and exploitation, be it peer on peer or adult to child sexual abuse and exploitation. This demystification process needs to shift the focus from 'othering' abuse, to help all children identify and manage the fear of harm and of exploitation. It also needs to support practitioners, parents, carers and communities to engage meaningfully with those who are affected. This takes more than a one day-, one week- or even term-long course. It means owning the fact that sexual abuse and exploitation happen, that everyone has a responsibility to identify it when it does happen, and a responsibility to help to manage the consequences. How this is managed has a knock-on impact on children and young people who are trying to negotiate their transition into living free from abuse as adults.

Rite of Passage and Gender Inequality

The obvious corollary of preventing sexual violence is for sex to be mutually consensual; for how we choose to offer the boundaries of our bodies to others to be respected; and for the social pressures impacting on decisions about when and why and how sexual intimacy is negotiated to be understood and addressed. We recognise here that the dominant heterosexual norms permeate these discussions and that both similarities and differences in negotiating consent between gay and lesbian young people may occur. The research material drawn upon here is addressing the gender-based power dynamics expected within heterosexual activities between young men and young women. As noted by young people themselves, entry into sexual activity marks a recognised transition into pending adulthood. Gender inequalities mean that this transition has to be carefully negotiated, for heterosexual young men as a means of gaining credibility among peers (often noted through award of 'man' or 'lad' points) and for heterosexual girls as a means of avoiding labels such as 'sket' (slut), or 'ho' (whore). Research is increasingly linking sexual scripts and coercion to young people's exposure to online pornography, with consistent gendered dimensions: boys are more likely to seek pornography and show correlations between its use and influences on sexual behaviours (e.g. Horvath et al., 2013; Stanley et al., 2016).

Coy and colleagues (2013) argue that it is impossible to talk about consent without also exploring its gendered dimensions. At the most basic level this is important because research shows the majority of victim-survivors of sexual violence are women and girls, and perpetrators disproportionately men and boys (Radford et al., 2011). It is also vital, however, to understand the social meanings associated with gendered practices. In their study with almost 600 young people about their understandings of sexual consent, Coy et al. (2013) noted the double bind for young women who both were expected to be sexually active but whose sexual activity then runs the risk of then being labelled and disrespected. The opposite remains true for young men; heterosexual prowess is associated with accumulation of 'man (or 'lad') points', which afford young men ratings with their friends for 'scoring' with young women.

The following quotes illustrate this:

> If you'd done something with a girl a boy would just be like 'ah you get lad points for that…'
>
> If you respected the girl's decision and just said yeah, I'm not going to do anything, then… they would probably just give up and not give you lad points. (Two different young men, aged 14, in Coy et al., 2013, pp. 53 and 54)
>
> Boys get rated and girls get slated. So basically, could be the same age, girls and boys have sex, if anyone finds out, the boys will get, 'oooh, good boy, good boy' but the girl will be like 'oi, you're a sket, you're this, you're that'. (Participant S, 14-year-old young woman, in Beckett et al., 2013, p. 21)
>
> It depends what the girl is. If she's a slag, she ain't equal. Boys treat her like shit and that's the only thing. Don't get your name around if you're not ready to get violated. (Participant F2, 15-year-old young man, in Beckett et al., 2013, p. 21)

The above explains some young people's fears and hopes about entry into heterosexual activity. What is clear is that 'giving and getting consent' is not a one-to-one independent activity. Giving or getting consent within these examples is influenced by conscious or unconscious awareness of the need to negotiate gendered and heterosexual power dynamics. This 'consent' to sexual activity, which itself carries a rite to passage towards adulthood, can establish dynamics that then continue to label young people and impact on future sexual activity. Fraser guidelines that help practitioners to address whether a child is capable of taking responsibility for their sexual activity do not fully embrace these social pressures. The implications of failing to manage this transition can be severe, particularly when research shows that many young people do not understand the meaning of rape (lack of consent, rather than force) as evidenced through work by Barter and Berridge (2011) and by these quotes:

> I don't really use the term rape. Yeah, it's not talked about as rape, they just say, 'this is what happened, we took her to the house and told her to do this and she did it'. They don't say, 'we forced her'. Most of the time they don't even force them, as I said, once they've implanted that fear into them it's easy to get what you want. (Participant S2, 18-year-old young man, in Beckett et al., 2013, p. 31)
>
> This girl came to school upset really. She had sex with every boy in a gang just to be part of their gang, and it was really terrible when I heard about this… I think it probably was under pressure, because she wanted to be a part of them and they gave her an option. (Participant W3, 16-year-old young woman, in Beckett et al., 2013, p. 28)

What this means for understandings of sexual consent is that young women's actions are constantly under scrutiny for signs that they had invited sex; choosing to wear flattering clothes, being attracted to someone or initiating sexual intimacy, flirting and accepting a drink are all taken as signs that young women actively wanted sex. Any coercion or pressure by young men following this was excused by many of the young people surveyed by Coy et al. (2013).

The parallels here with rape myths that condone sexually abusive behaviours – and feed into miscommunication theory – are clear. Miscommunication theory is the notion that perpetrators of sexual violence misread behaviours and actions as signalling willingness to have sex, and cannot therefore be fully responsible, as there must have been ambiguity in the first place. This is what underpins questions of 'what did you do to make him think you wanted to have sex?' all too often asked of victim-survivors. The empirical evidence base for this theory has been critiqued; yet young women report a normative standard for them to show how they explicitly verbalised sexual refusal (Burkett and Hamilton, 2012). 'Being worn down' is often understood as still constituting consent. This is at odds with the formulation of consent in the Sexual Offences Act 2003, which requires 'freedom' to consent to be present. With other unwelcome or uncomfortable requests, we rarely say an outright 'no' immediately, but find ways to make excuses, offer alternatives and accommodate the feelings of others (Kitzinger and Frith, 1999). When it comes to sexual advances, different standards are applied. One study with young men found they were acutely aware of verbal and non-verbal sexual refusals, but drew on miscommunication theory to justify using pressure and grinding reluctant young women down. The researchers suggested that sexual miscommunication needs to be understood as a new rape myth, and that discussion with young people about how and when communication is clear would be one step towards better prevention of unwanted sexual activity and sexual violence (O'Byrne et al., 2006).

The Assumption that Capacity to Consent Can Be Determined by Age

Moving forward to embrace the concerns related to the above means addressing the question of when and why children might be deemed capable of making decisions about consenting to sexual activity, and when and why they are capable of taking responsibility

Table 15.1 Age of consent to sexual activity and age of criminal responsibility (taken from Pearce, 2017)

Country	Age for consent to sexual activity	Age of criminal responsibility
Turkey	18	12
Ireland	17	12
Belgium	16	18
UK	16	10 (except Scotland, where it is 12)
Czech Republic, Denmark, France, Greece	15	15
Estonia, Italy, Germany, Hungary	14	14
Angola	12	16
Tunisia	20	13
Bahrain	21	15
Bangladesh	14	9

for the consequences of this decision. Governments across the world respond to a number of moral, religious, economic and social pressures to determine the age of responsibility for both sexual and criminal activity. As can be seen in Table 15.1, despite the UNCRC ascribing specific rights to all children up to the age of 18, there are significant discrepancies between nations about when a child can or cannot take responsibility for their actions.

The ironic result of such discrepancies is that in many countries, including the UK, a child can be responsible for a criminal sexual offence that they are not deemed old enough to have capacity to consent to! While it is helpful to have an agreed age by which children are legally entitled to consent to sexual activity, it would be interesting to further compare this with other legislation determining capacity, such as criminal responsibility or age for which children can be responsible for driving vehicles on the roads, vote and or buy and consume potentially dangerous substances such as alcohol and nicotine. While there are these confused and confusing variations in the perceived age for taking responsibility, it is hardly surprising that children themselves become confused by the mixed messages adults give about children's capacity to make decisions for themselves.

The Social Context within which Consent is Sought or Given: Contextualised Consent and Contextualised Safeguarding

As noted above, a young person's capacity to consent to sexual activity can be influenced by external factors. While it may be easier for practitioners and other adults to ascribe responsibility to the child for their actions, it is essential that a full assessment of these external pressures is taken into consideration when assessing if a child has been abused or exploited, and therefore if action is needed to override the wish of the child and take protective action. Firmin (2013) calls this 'contextualised safeguarding', arguing that alongside assessment of a vulnerable young person and their family, an assessment of the young person's peer group, local community and environment needs to take place. Interventions to protect the

UNDERSTANDING CONSENT: A SOCIAL MODEL (Pearce 2013)

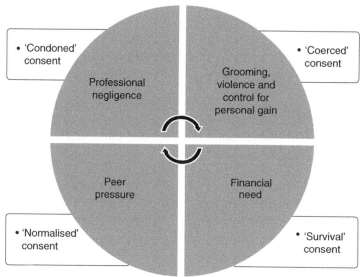

Figure 15.1 The social model of understanding consent.

child must, she argues, include interventions with the peer group, the local community and immediate environment surrounding the child and their family. Local authority strategies to manage anti-social behaviour, children who go missing, gun and knife crime and gang affiliation need to be joined up rather than siloed, so that interventions in the community, with peer groups and with children and families themselves, are coordinated. In a similar vein, Pearce (2013) argues that the child's capacity to consent must not rely only on an assessment of the individual, but on the pressures surrounding them. The dominance of a 'medical model' for understanding consent, such as that proposed by Gillick and Fraser guidelines for assessing whether or not to prescribe contraceptives tends to focus on the individual child's capacity to understand. Pearce argues that as well as this focus on the child, an assessment must accommodate awareness of the pressures surrounding the child. For example, were they, or are they, groomed and coerced into believing they are loved by their abuser? Are they struggling in poverty and deprivation, leading them to a believe that selling or swapping sex is the only way to gain access to resources enjoyed by peers, such as new clothes, jewellery or a bed for the night? Is sexual violence normalised within their immediate network to the point that rape is not named and coercion or abuse deemed the norm? Finally, and most worryingly, do professionals turn away from recognising the abuse experienced by those children, particularly adolescents they deem to be difficult and whose behaviour they feel unable to engage with? This latter concern, noted here as professional negligence, must not be the reason for blaming practitioners under a 'heads must roll' attack; instead it needs to be recognised as a reason for enhanced training about vulnerable adolescence, about the meaning and context for sexual exploitation and abuse and for improved support and supervision of staff dealing with these complex cases. Figure 15.1 identifies how these four areas of influence, located within a 'social model for understanding consent', can be interwoven and self-perpetuating.

Moving Forward and Addressing Myths

While the recent introduction of statutory sex and relationships education (SRE), is to be welcomed, school-based sessions are all too often limited to biological 'plumbing and prevention' aspects of sex, and studies consistently document children and young people's disappointment with the lack of content on emotions and relationships (Berelowitz et al., 2013; Coy et al., 2013). Indeed, evidence shows that while it can be helpful to have specific classes focused on sex and relationships, these classes need to be regular, consistent and taught by trained and experienced practitioners who understand the nature of abuse, violence and discrimination within many children's relationships. Evidence also shows that actually to change behaviours, these classes need to be embedded in a 'whole school' approach that accommodates a focus on behaviour management, safe environments and supported staff (Mahony and Shaughnessy, 2007; Coy et al., 2011; Bovarnick and Scott, 2016).

Without the whole school approach, safe and supported time to explore these complex issues is rarely fully integrated into statutory 'task-based' interventions with children. Schools are increasingly encouraged to focus on academic performance while health services respond to presenting physical, as opposed to mental health, problems (Hagell, 2012). Child and adolescent mental health services (CAMHS) have repeatedly been seen lacking in capacity to support vulnerable adolescents because of high thresholds for intervention and diminishing resources to provide child-centred, diversionary therapeutic support to vulnerable children (Hagell, 2012). It is recognised that SRE has a long way to go before issues of consent and the developmental and social context within which it occurs are fully integrated into educational programmes for children. Similarly, it is now recognised that the child protection process and procedures have not embraced the needs of the adolescent age group (Jay, 2014). It is absolutely the right time to challenge the traditional approach to child protection which focuses on the need to protect babies and toddlers within the home rather than older adolescents abused within their peer group and in relationships outside the home (Firmin, 2013).

Children and young people themselves argue that child protection systems and processes fail to fully address their understandings of abuse or exploitation, and that children's views are rarely considered or heard within discussions on how, why, if or when consent was given (Warrington, 2013; Beckett and Warrington, 2015). Yet sexual consent is precisely an issue of how 'one to one' and 'peer group' emotional and relational connections, and gendered practices, are negotiated. Not only do the voices of children and young people tell us how much they need open, honest conversations about the messiness of sexual intimacy, and the messy social context within which this messiness fits, but there is also now a policy imperative to build these child-centred discussions into national strategies on violence against women and girls and child protection (HM Government, 2015). Looking at legislation and policy and procedures, it is evident that despite good guidance, practice continues to fail to listen to or protect many children, including older adolescents, from exploitation and abuse (Melrose and Pearce, 2013). As argued by Munro (2011), and explored further by chapters within Blyth (2014), this failure can be accounted for by lack of resources, lack of training or awareness. It can also be a systemic failure of agencies to supervise and support their staff to be able to engage with the pain that is associated with managing cases of abuse and exploitation. Difficulties and barriers to listening to this pain can be further compounded if the young person is antagonistic, angry and rejecting of support (Pearce, 2009). Adolescence itself is a poorly understood concept (Coleman, 2011), and when the tensions associated with this developmental stage are compounded by vulnerabilities associated with disadvantage, discrimination, manipulation and abuse, it can be easier to resort to denial of the pain presented by the young person concerned, excusing this denial with statements about lifestyle choice (Beckett and Warrington, 2015). As many of the social and economic contexts inhabited by many vulnerable adolescents appear also to present insurmountable problems, they are rarely incorporated into assessments of the child's abusive or abused behaviours (Pitts, 2008; Firmin, 2013).

More work is needed to better improve therapeutic responses, ones that engage with children at all levels before they reach the 'high risk' threshold of demonstrable mental health problems as needed prior to a referral to receive CAMHS support. Essentially this means integrating awareness of the nature of sexualised abuse into discussions about unwanted sexual activity, where 'consent' has been undermined. We need to be able to offer time where children can consider the impact of sexualised trauma on their feelings of self-worth, linking it to feelings about betrayal as explored by Finkelhor and Browne (1985). More work is needed to explore the possibilities that children then, in trauma, continue to be vulnerable to traumatic sexualised attachments that themselves continue to undermine acknowledgement of abuse or recovery from it.

How Do We Translate This into Conversations with Young People?

Moira Carmody's (2008) innovative prevention work offers a range of ways, including role plays based on refusing tickets to see a favourite band play, where friends use flattery and cajolement to encourage acquiescence. One person in the group is required to continue rejecting the offer. When we talk with young people about sex, we should be asking about the ways in which they feel equipped not just to say no, but how and why they expect others to indicate willingness or refusal.

This means being prepared to ask young people questions which require all of us to reflect on long-held and often deeply internalised social constructions. Examples might include the following:

- How do young men make sense of what being a 'man' means?
- What expectations do they have of young women?
- What ideas about young women's sexual behaviour have both young men and young women heard? What about for young men?
- How far do they agree with these ideas?
- How have they seen any of this play out in their peer groups?

Specifically for young men, it is vital to explore how ideas about what it means to be a man influence their perceptions about when and how to ask for consent to sexual activity. If 'man points' and ratings as a successful boy/man rely on initiating sex and accumulating evidence of sexual conquest, how does this contribute to excusing the exertion of pressure, however subtle? When constructions of masculinity are so closely aligned with strength, not vulnerability, with being in charge, not subject to pressure and coercion, how can we create spaces for young men who have been victimised to speak out? How do young men resist these models of what it means to be man, and what can we learn from how they show intimacy, respect and emotional connections in the face of stereotypes that mock these as desirable attributes for men and boys?

The core conclusion of this chapter is twofold: first, that the discourse on consent needs to be changed, from a focus on *giving* – what actions young people take to show agreement or acquiescence – to *getting*. This would bring how we talk about consent in line with the Sexual Offences Act 2003, which requires that those prosecuted for crimes of sexual violence show the steps they took to ensure 'reasonable belief' that complainants were consenting. Second, the difficulties and pressures facing adolescents as they progress towards adulthood need better understanding, as do the implications for practitioners working with these complexities. It is not until we fully address the context within consent to sexual activity that is sought or given, will we better support children affected by abuse and exploitation. The child protection strategy of the future must embrace contextualised safeguarding and must understand the social as well as the individual pressures on children to engage in sexual activities.

References

Barter, C. and Berridge, D. (2011) *Children Behaving Badly: Peer Violence Between Children and Young People.* Chichester: Wiley-Blackwell.

Barter, C., McCarry, M., Berridge, D., and Evans, K. (2009) *Partner Exploitation and Violence in Teenage Intimate Relationships.* London: NSPCC Inform.

Beckett, H., with Brodie, I., Factor, F., Melrose, M., Pearce, J., Pitts, J., Shuker, L. and Warrington, C. (2013) *'It's wrong… but you get used to it.' A qualitative study of gang-associated sexual violence and exploitation.* University of Bedfordshire.

Beckett, H. and Warrington, C. (2015) *Making justice work. Experiences of criminal justice for children and young people affected by sexual exploitation as victims and witnesses.* University of Bedfordshire.

Beckett, H., Holmes, D. and Walker, J. (2017) *Child sexual exploitation: definition and guide for professionals – extended text.* International Centre Researching Child Sexual Exploitation, Violence and Trafficking, University of Bedfordshire.

Berelowitz, S., Clifton, J., Firmin, C., Gulyurtlu, S. and Edwards, G. (2013) *'If only someone had listened': Office of the Children's Commissioner's Inquiry into Child Sexual Exploitation in Gangs and Groups.* Final Report, London: Office of the Children's Commissioner.

Blyth, M. (ed.) (2014) *Moving on from Munro: Improving Children's Services.* Bristol: Policy Press.

Bovarnick, S. and Scott, S. (2016) *Child sexual exploitation: preventative education. A rapid evidence assessment.* University of Bedfordshire. Available at: www.beds.ac.uk/ic

Burkett, M. and Hamilton, K. (2012) Postfeminist sexual agency: young women's negotiations of consent. *Sexualities*, 15, 815–33.

Carmody, M. (2008) *Sex and Ethics: Young People and Ethical Sex.* Basingstoke: Palgrave Macmillan.

Coleman, J. (2011) *The Nature of Adolescence*, 4th edn. Hove: Routledge.

Coy, M., Thiara, R. and Kelly, L. (2011) *Boys think girls are toys? An evaluation of the NIA project sexual exploitation prevention programme.* CWASU, London.

Coy, M., Kelly, L., Elvines, F., Garner, M. and Kanyeredzi, A. (2013) *Sex without consent, I suppose that is rape: how young people in England understand sexual consent.* London: Office of the Children's Commissioner.

Department for Education (2017) *Child Sexual Exploitation: Definition and a Guide for Practitioners, Local Leaders and Decision Makers Working to Protect Children from Child Sexual Exploitation.* London: DfE and HMSO.

Department for Children, Schools and Families (2009) *Safeguarding Children and Young People from Sexual Exploitation: Supplementary Guidance to Working Together to Safeguard Children.* London: DCSF.

Finkelhor, D. and Browne, A. (1985) The traumatic impact of child sexual abuse: A conceptualization. *American Journal of Orthopsychiatry*, 55(4), 530–41.

Firmin, C. (2013) Something old or something new: do pre-existing conceptualisations of abuse enable a sufficient response to abuse in young people's relationships and peer groups? In M. Melrose and J. Pearce (eds), *Critical Perspectives on Child Sexual Exploitation and Related Trafficking*. Basingstoke: Palgrave Macmillan, pp. 38–52.

Hagell, A. (ed.) (2012) *Changing Adolescence: Social Trends and Mental Health*. Bristol: Policy Press.

HM Government (2015) *Tackling Child Sexual Exploitation*. London: Cabinet Office.

Horvath, M. A. H., Alys, K., Massey, K., Pina, A., Scally, M. and Adler, J. R. (2013) *'Basically, porn is everywhere…' A rapid evidence assessment on the effects that access and exposure to pornography has on children and young people*. London: Office for the Children's Commissioner.

Jay, A. (2014) *Independent inquiry into child sexual exploitation in Rotherham 1997–2013*. Rotherham Metropolitan Borough Council.

Jenks, C. (2005) *Childhood*, 2nd edn. London: Routledge.

Kitzinger, C. and Frith, H. (1999) Just say no? The use of conversation analysis in developing a feminist perspective on sexual refusal. *Discourse and Society*, 10, 291–2.

Kroger, J. (2004) *Identity in Adolescence: The Balance Between Self and Other*, 3rd edition. London: Routledge.

Mahony, P. and Shaughnessy, J. (2007) *'The Impact of Challenging Violence: Changing Lives*. London: Womankind Worldwide.

Melrose, M. and Pearce, J. (eds) (2013) *Critical Perspectives on Child Sexual Exploitation and Related Trafficking*. Basingstoke: Palgrave Macmillan.

Munro, E. (2011) *The Munro Review of Child Protection. Final Report: A Child-centred System*. London: The Stationery Office.

O'Byrne, R., Rapley, M. and Hansen, S. (2006) 'You couldn't say "no", could you?': young men's understandings of sexual refusal. *Feminism and Psychology*, 16(2), 133–54.

Ofsted (2014) *Sexual Exploitation of Children: Ofsted Thematic Report*. London: Ofsted.

Palmer, T. (2015) *Digital Dangers: The Impact of Technology on Sexual Abuse and Exploitation of Children and Young People*. Barkingside: Barnardo's.

Pearce, J. (2009) *Young People and Sexual Exploitation: It Isn't Hidden, You Just Aren't Looking*. London: Routledge Falmer.

Pearce, J. (2013) A social model of 'abused consent'. In M. Melrose and J. Pearce (eds), *Critical Perspectives on Child Sexual Exploitation and Related Trafficking*. Basingstoke: Palgrave Macmillan.

Pearce, J. (2017) Consent to sexual activity, child sexual exploitation and abuse: are international guidelines protecting children? In P. Dolan and N. Frost (eds), *The Handbook of Global Child Welfare*. London: Routledge, 153–165.

Pitts, J. (2008) *Reluctant Gangsters: The Changing Face of Youth Crime*. London: Routledge.

Radford, L., Corral, S., Bradley, C., Fisher, H., Bassett, C., Howat, N. and Collishaw, S. (2011) *Child Abuse and Neglect in the UK Today*. London: NSPCC.

Stanley, N., Barter, C., Wood, M., Aghtaie, N., Larkins, C., Lanau, A. and Överlien, C. (2016) Pornography, sexual coercion and abuse and sexting in young people's intimate relationships: a European study. *Journal of Interpersonal Violence* (online first).

Warrington, C. (2013) Partners in care? Sexually exploited young people's inclusion and exclusion from decision making about safeguarding. In M. Melrose and J. Pearce (eds), *Critical Perspectives on Child Sexual Exploitation and Related Trafficking*: Basingstoke: Palgrave Macmillan, pp. 110–25.

Chapter

Treatment without Consent

Camilla Parker

Consent to treatment, particularly in relation to mental health care, is an area of law in which the dynamics between the role of the state, the rights of the child and the rights and responsibilities of parents is both complex and uncertain.

The complexity of the law is illustrated by the array of legislation, which is listed in the Mental Health Act 1983: Code of Practice 2015 (the MHA Code) as being relevant to the legal framework for the admission to hospital and treatment of under-18s (Department of Health, 2015, para. 19.4). It recommends that practitioners working with this age group should be familiar with the Children Acts of 1989 and 2004, the Mental Capacity Act 2005 (the MCA 2005) and the Human Rights Act 1998 (the HRA 1998), as well as the Mental Health Act 1983 (the MHA 1983) and relevant case-law.

A major area of uncertainty is the extent of parents' powers to consent to medical interventions on behalf of under-18s who lack the capacity or competence to make the relevant decision for themselves. Although the European Court of Human Rights (ECtHR) in *Nielsen* v. *Denmark* (1988) and the national courts (*Hewer* v. *Bryant* 1970; *Gillick* 1986) have acknowledged that there are limits to parents' decision-making powers – hence the MHA Code refers to the 'scope of parental responsibility' (Department of Health, 2015, paras 19.38–19.42) – the parameters of such powers are ill-defined.

Thus, as noted by the Law Commission (2017, para 7.22), a 'complicating factor' is that in its decision in *Nielsen* v. *Denmark* (1988) the ECtHR 'has recognised the right of parents – in certain cases – to consent to restrictions placed on their child which would otherwise amount to a deprivation of liberty'. The circumstances in which restrictions placed on under-18s give rise to a deprivation of liberty and the relevance of parental consent in making such a determination is a developing area of law (see for example, the decisions of the Court of Appeal in *Re D (A Child)* (2017) and Sir James Munby, President of the Family Division in *Re A-F Children* (2018)).

Another area of concern, which is the focus of this chapter, is the situation of a child or young person who has the competence (in the case of a child aged 16 or less) or capacity (in the case of a young person aged 16 or 17) to make such decisions and is refusing medical treatment. This merits examination because it highlights a significant difference between the law's approach to adults and those aged under 18, as well as providing an example of the tension between 'autonomy' (enabling children and young people to exercise their rights) and 'protection' (ensuring that the welfare of children and young people is protected).

In considering these issues, reference is made to the United Nations Convention on the Rights of the Child (UNCRC) as well as the European Convention on Human Rights (ECHR). The ECHR has been incorporated into national law by virtue of the HRA 1998. Although the UNCRC is not part of English law, its principles 'guide domestic law and practice, and are often referred to by the courts when interpreting obligations imposed by human rights and other legislation' (Human Rights Joint Committee, 2015, p. 7). Thus, it is apposite to consider the UNCRC's approach in seeking a balance between autonomy and protection.

Children's Rights: Autonomy versus Protection

Two core principles of the UNCRC are that the best interests of the child (which refers to those aged under 18) shall be 'a primary consideration' in all actions concerning children (Article 3(1)) and that the views of the child are 'given due weight in accordance with the age and maturity of the child' (Article 12). In addition, the UNCRC places great emphasis on the 'evolving capacities' of the child. Article 5 UNCRC recognises the role of parents in giving guidance and direction to their children but provides that this should be 'in a manner consistent with the evolving capacities of the child'. Thus, the responsibilities of parents to make decisions on behalf of their child, and in their child's best interests, is balanced against the need to ensure that their child is able to exercise his or her rights, in accordance with their child's age and maturity.

Although the best interests of the child is not referred to specifically in the ECHR, the UNCRC's concept of best interests is recognised by the ECtHR as an important principle when taking action in relation to children and young people. The ECtHR considers there to be 'a broad consensus – including in international law – in support of the idea that in all decisions concerning children, their best interests must be paramount' (*Neulinger and Shuruk* v. *Switzerland* 2010, para. 135). Similarly, the UK Supreme Court has held that 'it is clear from the recent jurisprudence that the Strasbourg Court will expect national authorities to apply Article 3(1) of UNCRC and treat the best interests of the child as "a primary consideration"' (*ZH (Tanzania)* 2011, para. 25).

Although at first glance the rights under ECHR appear to apply to children and young people in the same way as to adults, closer inspection reveals a more nuanced situation in which the protection of under-18s plays a significant role, in particular through the concept of best interests. Nonetheless, the body responsible for overseeing states' compliance with the UNCRC, the Committee on the UNCRC (the CRC Committee), considers that the evolving capacities of the child, together with the requirement to respect the views of the child under Article 12 UNCRC, are two significant factors to be taken into account when determining the child's best interests. Thus, rather than pitting the views of the child against the child's best interests, the CRC Committee emphasises that the child's views form an essential element of assessing his or her best interests (CRC Committee, 2013, paras 53–4).

Self-determination: Only for Adults?

In the area of mental health care, the state can intervene where individuals of any age are considered to require assessment of, and/or treatment for, their mental disorder. Like adults, a child or young person who is competent or has capacity to make decisions about their admission to hospital and/or treatment for mental disorder and is refusing to give consent to such proposed interventions, can be detained in hospital under the MHA 1983 if the criteria are met, and treated without their consent in accordance with the procedures set out in Part 4 of the MHA 1983. A range of safeguards is available for those who are subject to these compulsory powers, such as the right to assistance from an Independent Mental Health Advocate (IMHA) and the right to apply (together with the right to free advice and legal representation) to an independent Tribunal to be discharged from detention under the MHA 1983.

For adults, detention under the MHA 1983 is the only time in which their capacitous refusal of medical treatment can be overridden. In other circumstances, provided that she or he has the capacity to make such a decision, the adult has 'an absolute right' to choose whether or not to receive medical treatment and 'these are not limited to decisions which others might regard as sensible' (*Re T* 1992, pp. 652–3). However, this fundamental legal principle for respect for an individual's personal autonomy (or 'right of self-determination') remains the prerogative of adults. Although the law recognises that young people (Family Law Reform Act 1969, section 8) and children (*Gillick* 1986) can consent to their own treatment if they have the capacity or competence to do so, the courts have held that the refusal of treatment by such 'mature minors' may be overridden (*Re R (A Minor) (Wardship: Consent to Treatment)* (1992) and *Re W (A Minor) (Medical Treatment: Court's Jurisdiction)* (1993)). As noted by David Feldman (2002, p. 293): 'It seems that the refusal of a competent teenager is relevant, but the courts regard the preservation of a minor's life as being more important than respecting her autonomy, even if she is competent.' The extent to which consideration of a minor's ECHR rights has influenced the approach taken by the courts in such treatment refusal cases is considered below.

In relation to policy, the HRA 1998 has engendered an important change. Having noted that in the past the courts have 'found that parents can consent to their competent child being treated even where the child/young person is refusing treatment', Department of Health guidance (2009, p. 34) states:

> there is no post-Human Rights Act 1998 authority for this proposition, and it would there-fore be prudent to obtain a court declaration or decision if faced with a competent child or young person who is refusing to consent to treatment, to determine whether it is lawful to treat the child.

A similar view is expressed in the MHA Code, which states that it would be inadvisable to rely on parental consent in such circumstances, and recommends seeking authorisation from the court in cases where the criteria for admission under the MHA 1983 are not met (Department of Health, 2015, paras 19.39, 19.59 and 19.65–19.66). The exception to this is where the failure to treat a child or young person 'would be likely to lead to their death or to severe permanent injury'. In such cases, medical treatment can be given if 'there is no time to seek authorisation from the court or (where applicable) to detain and treat under the [MHA] Act'. However, this would only authorise the treatment necessary to deal with the emergency situation and 'legal authority for on-going treatment must be established', such as a court order or, if the under 18-year-old is detained under the MHA 1983, Part 4 of that Act (Department of Health, 2015, paras 19.71–19.72).

The MHA Code explains that since the introduction of the HRA 1998 'court decisions concerning children and young people have given greater weight to their views' (Department of Health, 2015, para. 19.39). Another argument against relying on parental consent in such cases is that to do so would violate the child or young person's right to respect for private life under Article 8 ECHR. The ECtHR has emphasised the need for judicial scrutiny of decisions to treat individuals without their consent, so that the person concerned could 'require a court to rule on the lawfulness, including proportionality, of the forced admin-istration of medication and to have it discontinued' (*X* v. *Finland* 2012, para. 220). It is also supported by the UNCRC's 'evolving capacities' of the child (discussed above), which recognises that as children develop in their knowledge, experience and understanding the more the parent has 'to transform direction and guidance into reminders and advice and later to an exchange on an equal footing' (CRC Committee, 2009, para. 84). Moreover, children and young people's right to liberty under Article 5 ECHR must also be respected. Although, as noted in the introduction to this chapter, the extent of parental powers to consent to restrictions placed on their child that would otherwise give rise to a deprivation of liberty (thereby engaging Article 5) are not clear, they are limited to where under 18s are not able to make such decisions for themselves (Re D (A Child) (2017)).

Competence and Capacity to Decide

The right to respect the child's view under Article 12 UNCRC requires that children and young people are involved in decisions about their health care if they are capable of forming their own views (CRC Committee, 2009, paras 84, 98–103). However, children and young people will only be in a position to consent or refuse the proposed intervention if assessed as having the requisite competence or capacity.

The legal tests for assessing the ability to decide about matters such as treatment and care depends on the person's age. For children, the question is whether they have the 'competence' to make the decision (*Gillick* 1986), whereas for individuals aged 16 and over capacity is assessed in accordance with the MCA 2005 and the detailed guidance set out in the MCA 2005's Code of Practice (Department of Constitutional Affairs, 2007). A person is considered to lack capacity under the MCA 2005 if s/he is unable to make a particular decision for him/herself at the relevant time and that inability to decide is 'because of an impairment of, or disturbance in the functioning of, the mind or brain' (MCA 2005, sections 2 and 3).

Whereas young people and adults are presumed to have the capacity to make the relevant decision unless established otherwise (MCA 2005, section 1(1)), the law's starting point for children is that they lack the competence to decide (*Gillick* 1986). However, the House of Lords decision in *Gillick* (1986) established that children under 16 can consent to their medical treatment when they have 'sufficient understanding and intelligence to enable him or her to understand fully what is proposed'.

Despite its importance, and in stark contrast to the MCA 2005's clear legal framework for assessing the capacity of individuals aged 16 and over to make decisions for themselves, there is a paucity of guidance on how to assess a child's competence. However, the MHA Code (Department of Health, 2015, para. 19.36) suggests that practitioners consider four questions, which are adapted from section 3 of the MCA 2005 ('Inability to make decisions'):

- Does the child understand the information that is relevant to the decision that needs to be made?
- Can the child hold the information in their mind long enough so that they can use it to make the decision?
- Is the child able to weigh up that information and use it to arrive at a decision?
- Is the child able to communicate their decision (by talking, using sign language or any other means)?

In contrast to the capacity test under the MCA 2005 which requires that the inability to decide must be due to 'an impairment of, or disturbance in the functioning of, the mind or brain', a child might lack competence to make the relevant decision for reasons unrelated to a mental disorder. For example, this might be because 'they have not as yet developed the necessary intelligence and understanding to make that particular decision' (Department of Health, 2015, para. 19.37). A similar approach to the assessment of *Gillick* competence has since been taken by the court when determining whether a young mother, aged under 16 years, was able to consent to the adoption of her child (*Re S (Child as parent)* (2017)).

Refusal of Treatment: Decisions by the Courts

Although the question whether, and if so in what circumstances, a child's competent or young person's capacitous refusal of medical treatment can be overridden continues to provoke debate within the academic sphere (Fovargue and Ost, 2013; Fortin, 2014), this has not yet been explored fully by the courts in the post-HRA 1998 era. Of the two reported cases considered since the HRA 1998 came into force, the first did not mention the HRA at all (*Re P* 2003). Although the second case, *An NHS Foundation Trust Hospital* v. *P* (2014) referred to relevant ECHR rights, the court provided little analysis of these rights when holding that the 17½-year-old's refusal of life-saving treatment following her overdose should be overridden. On the basis of the available information the judge was 'not satisfied that [P] lacks capacity to make decisions concerning her medical treatment' (section 1 of the MCA 2005 states that a person 'must be assumed to have capacity unless it is established that she lacks capacity'). Nonetheless, the court considered that while P's wishes should be taken into account as part of her Article 8 rights (the right to respect for private and family life), 'those rights are not absolute' and 'are outweighed by her rights under Article 2' (the right to life).

This case provides a graphic illustration of the dilemma faced by those wishing to promote greater respect for children and young people's rights but also protect them from making decisions that will endanger their lives. The judge was at pains to stress that he had taken account of P's wishes and feelings but considered that the court was 'under a heavy duty' to take what steps it could to protect her life (*An NHS Foundation Trust Hospital* v. *P* 2014, paras 15–16).

The court's concern to preserve the life of a young person is one that many would share and support. Furthermore, the 'extreme urgency' of the case 'did not afford time for lengthy submissions or analysis' (*An NHS Foundation Trust Hospital* v. *P* 2014, para. 2). Nonetheless, 'forced administration of medication represents a serious interference with a person's physical integrity', thereby engaging Article 8 and requiring justification under Article 8(2) (*X* v. *Finland* 2012, para. 220). The interference must not only be lawful and pursue a 'legitimate aim', such as 'the protection of health', it must also be 'necessary in a democratic society', which in essence requires that the action is a proportionate response to the concern in question (in this case that the young woman will die if the treatment is not given). These points were neither acknowledged nor addressed by the court.

Whereas Article 2 was assumed to automatically trump the young woman's Article 8 rights, it is suggested that in cases where a child or young person is refusing life-saving treatment both ECHR rights would need to be considered so as to strike a balance between the child or young person's Article 8 right not to be subject to treatment without his or her consent and the positive duty on the state to protect the young person's life under Article 2 (*Rabone* v. *Pennine Care NHS Trust* 2012, para. 107). Article 2 would be one of a range of factors (albeit a major factor) to be considered when assessing whether the interference is justified under Article 8(2), in particular, whether the interference is a proportionate response to the legitimate aim of seeking to protect the child or young person's health, more specifically to prevent death. Relevant factors are likely to include taking into account matters such as the urgency of the situation and the likely consequence of not providing the treatment (*M. A. K. and R. K.* v. *United Kingdom* 2010, para. 79) and whether other less intrusive measures had been considered and ruled out (*Nada* v. *Switzerland* 2012, para. 183). Where the treatment is likely to require restraint, this may also engage Article 5 ECHR (the right to liberty), which requires consideration as to whether the deprivation of liberty can be justified on the basis of the child or young person's mental disorder (Fortin, 2009, p. 160).

Furthermore, it is suggested that when determining what is in the best interests of the child or young person, the court will need to balance the concern to prevent the child or young person's death against his or her wish not to receive the treatment. The CRC Committee considers that 'as the child matures, his or her views shall have increasing weight in the assessment of his or her best interests' (CRC Committee, 2013, para. 44).

Conclusion

The discussions in this chapter show that in the area of consent to treatment, the HRA 1998 does not remove the tension between autonomy and protection. In cases in which a child or young person is refusing life-saving treatment, the courts will be required to consider the best interests of that child or young person alongside their 'heavy duty' to take reasonable action to prevent the child or young person's death. Thus, in many cases, the outcome is likely to be the same as the pre-HRA 1998 treatment refusal cases, in that the child or young person's refusal is overridden. However, it is suggested that not only should the views of the child or young person be central to the judicial deliberations, but that the court should also provide a clear justification for overriding the child or young person's wishes in circumstances in which it would not be possible to do so for an adult.

References

Committee on the Rights of the Child (CRC Committee) (2009) General Comment No. 12: The right of the child to be heard, CRC/C/GC/12.

Committee on the Rights of the Child (CRC Committee) (2013) General Comment No. 14: On the right of the child to have his or her best interests taken as a primary consideration, CRC/C/GC/14.

Department of Constitutional Affairs (2007) *Mental Capacity Act 2005 Code of Practice.* London: The Stationery Office.

Department of Health (2009) *Reference Guide to Consent for Examination of Treatment,* 2nd edn. London: The Stationery Office.

Department of Health (2015) *Mental Health Act 1983: Code of Practice.* London: The Stationery Office.

Feldman, D. (2002) *Civil Liberties and Human Rights in England and Wales,* 2nd edn. Oxford: Oxford University Press.

Fovargue, S. and Ost, S. (2013), Does the theoretical framework change the legal end result for mature minors refusing medical treatment or creating self-generated pornography? *Medical Law International,* 13(1), 6.

Fortin, J. (2009) *Children's Rights and the Developing Law,* 3rd edn. Cambridge: Cambridge University Press.

Fortin, J. (2014) Children's rights: flattering to deceive? *Child and Family Quarterly,* 26(1), 51.

Human Rights Joint Committee (2015) Eight Report: The UK's compliance with the UN Convention on the Rights of the Child, HL Paper 144, HC 1016.

Law Commission (2017) *Mental Capacity and Deprivation of Liberty,* Law Com No. 372. London: The Stationery Office.

Cases

An NHS Foundation Trust Hospital v. P [2014] EWHC 1650 (Fam).

Gillick v. West Norfolk and Wisbech Area Health Authority [1986] AC 112.

Hewer v. Bryant [1970] 1 QB 357.

Nada v. Switzerland (2012) Application no. 10593/08, 12 September.

Neulinger and Shuruk v. Switzerland (2010) Application no. 41615/07, 6 July.

Nielsen v. Denmark (1988) Application no. 10929/84 28, 28 November.

M. A. K. and R. K. v. United Kingdom (2010) Application nos. 45901/05 and 40146/06, 23 March.

Rabone v. Pennine Care NHS Trust [2012] UKSC 2.

Re A-F (Children) [2018] EWHC 138 (Fam).

Re D (A Child) [2017] EWCA Civ 1695.

Re P (Medical Treatment: Best Interests) [2003] EWHC 2327 (Fam), [20014] 2 FLR 1117.

Re R (A Minor) (Wardship: Consent to Treatment) [1992] Fam 11.

Re S (Child as parent) [2017] EWHC 2729 (Fam).

Re T (Adult: Refusal of Medical Treatment) [1992] 4 All ER 649.

Re W (A minor) (Medical Treatment: Court's Jurisdiction [1993] Fam 64.

X v. Finland (2012) Application no. 34806/04, 3 July 2012.

ZH (Tanzania) v. Secretary of State for the Home Department [2011] UKSC 4, [2011] 2 AC 166.

Chapter

17 Autonomy and Decision-Making in Children and Adolescents with Gender Dysphoria

Domenico Di Ceglie

Personal autonomy has been an important issue for centuries in the psychosocial field and in medicine where it has been considered an essential ethical principle. Autonomy derives from a Greek word which is a combination of the words 'self' and 'law'. It means giving a law or regulation to oneself. Autonomy is the basis for decision-making and this area has become even more important in recent years with the development of new technologies, which can make considerable changes to the body and its functions, but also in other areas of human endeavours.

In philosophy, Kant regarded autonomy and rationality as the two characteristics that distinguished humans from the world of plants and animals. In his view, autonomy is what makes us responsible for our actions in contrast with plants and animals that are not autonomous beings. In medicine, autonomy is the basis for decision-making and necessary to be able to give informed consent to any form of treatment and participation in research projects.

In this chapter I will focus on the exercise of autonomy and decision-making in two areas of the management of gender dysphoria in young people: first, decision-making regarding the use of hypothalamic blockers, which suppress some aspects of pubertal development; and second, the gender role expression of perceived identity during childhood.

The capacity for autonomy is not an all-or-nothing phenomenon, as there are different degrees of autonomy and this capacity can be influenced by a number of factors. I briefly describe some of them.

Autonomy and Attachment Patterns

Attachment theory, based on 'the strange situation' research, has described four types of attachment: secure, insecure-avoidant, insecure-ambivalent, insecure-disorganised. The adult attachment interview (Main, 1990) has identified states of mind in adults that relate to the attachment patterns described by Ainsworth in children and these are: autonomous-secure, dismissing-detached, preoccupied-entangled and unresolved-disorganised.

Secure attachment seems to correlate well with autonomous thinking and behaviour while the other patterns seem to affect this capacity negatively. Furthermore, Holmes (2014, p. 99) suggests: 'Fonagy and colleagues noted that adults who were secure in relation to attachment seemed more able to appreciate and reason about mental states relating to their early childhood experiences and relationships.' These functions relate to the process of mentalising. A good capacity for mentalising also correlates well with an equivalent level of autonomy. Inversely, difficulties in mentalising may have a negative impact on the development of autonomy. Autonomy should not be confused with self-reliance or self-sufficiency, as autonomy includes the capacity to accept dependency when necessary, for example, when somebody requires assistance for more information by a more knowledgeable person or emotional support in a crisis.

Autonomy and Some Aspects of Psychoanalytic Thinking

Psychoanalysis has focused on the power of unconscious processes in influencing our thinking, emotions and behaviour. It has also drawn attention to how early infantile relationships affect current relationships. Klein and post-Kleinian analysts such as Bion, Britton and others have described in great detail the mechanism of projective identification as an early form of communication between the infant and the mother or caregiver. With development the intensity of communicating through this mechanism reduces, although it re-emerges in particular circumstances such as personal crisis, loss, etc. However, a child or adolescent who is on the receiving end of powerful projection by a parent may become entangled by this projection and his/her capacity for autonomous thinking affected in an unconscious way. On the other hand, a resilient child or teenager can disentangle him/herself from these projections and recognise them as not belonging to themselves. The following clinical vignette illustrates this point.

Case Vignette: Mary

A girl whom I shall call Mary was referred to the gender identity development service at the age of nine years after teachers had noticed uncertainty about her gender identity. During the interviews it emerged that at birth her mother was convinced that she was a boy but had been transformed into a girl through a black magic spell by her mother-in-law. The mother went on to treat Mary as a boy and gave her a name that in her culture could be given to both genders. When Mary was asked if she was a boy or a girl she said she did not know, possibly not to contradict her mother. The mother brought the girl to our service in the hope that we would transform her into the boy she believed she was. Apart from this particularly intense belief, the mother was warm and affectionate towards her child and other people. Mary's father totally colluded with his wife's beliefs and never seemed to challenge her. We offered Mary individual therapy in order to explore her gender identity and clarify who she believed she was. It became clear that Mary saw herself as an ordinary girl and eventually said that in her opinion her mother thought that she should be a boy because in her culture males had an advantage. In fact, from our interviews with the mother it was evident that her mother's beliefs were much more deep-rooted and not linked to the social advantages of being male. She believed that Mary had male organs inside her, which she hoped one day would emerge. The onset of her menstruation was a confirmation for Mary that she was a girl and dispelled any doubts about her gender. This case shows that in spite of her mother's beliefs and powerful projections, Mary had developed an autonomous self. In a less resilient child, however, one can hypothesise that the child's sense of autonomy could be affected to some extent. For a more detailed description of this case, see *A Stranger in My Own Body* (Di Ceglie, with Freedman, 1998).

The case has been anonymised and name and places changed for confidentiality.

Autonomy and Social Processes

Social processes have an impact on individual autonomy. For example, Milgram's experiment in the 1960s showed that people tend to obey orders coming from authority figures. These orders were in contrast to what their conscience would have suggested. One could say that social pressures had a negative impact on their exercise of autonomy (Milgram, 1974).

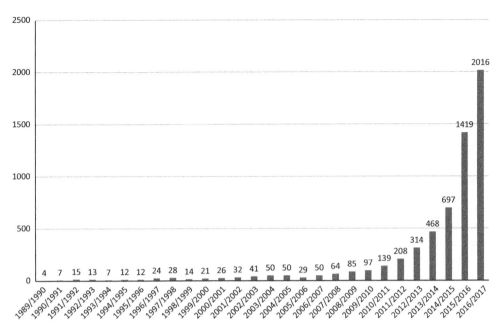

Figure 17.1 GIDS increase in referral rates; data provided by GIDS.

It is beyond the scope of this chapter to discuss this aspect in detail. However, I would like to mention as an example a scene from the film *Monty Python's Life of Brian* (1979) in which Brian (Graham Chapman) is mistakenly seen as a messiah. Brian talks from a window to a crowd gathered outside which has great expectation of his messianic speech. He says:

'Look, you've got it all wrong! You don't NEED to follow ME, You don't NEED to follow ANYBODY! You've got to think for yourselves! You're ALL individuals!' The crowd replies, 'Yes! We're all individuals!' Then Brian affirms, 'You're all different!' to which the crowd responds forcefully, 'Yes, we ARE all different!' A man in the crowd is heard saying: 'I'm not...'

Paradoxically, in the face of a crowd influenced by the power attributed to Brian in order to express his individuality and autonomy, the man in the crowd had to deny the crowd's collective belief that they were all individuals and diverse, a sign of obedience to the views of a charismatic figure. In society, cultural factors may facilitate or impede the expression of a diverse gender identity. A possible confirmation of this statement is the increase in referral rates of children and adolescents with gender dysphoria to gender identity services, as a consequence of cultural changes and attitudes to gender identity issues in Western societies which are now seen in a more positive light. See figures for the national Gender Identity Development Service in the UK (Figure 17.1).

Gender Dysphoria in Young People and Its Management

Gender dysphoria in young people is a complex condition where there is incongruence between the young person's perceived gender identity and their natal gender. The diagnostic criteria for gender dysphoria in adolescents and adults are defined in DSM-5. This includes the expression of an experienced gender that is in contrast to the gender assigned at birth, the conviction that one has the typical feelings and reactions of the other gender, a strong desire to get rid of one's primary and secondary sex characteristics and acquire those of the other gender, as well as a strong desire to be of the other gender and to be treated as the other gender or some alternative gender different from the gender assigned at birth. There are also separate criteria for gender dysphoria in childhood (American Psychiatric Association, 2013).

Over the last two decades the condition has tended to be regarded by professionals and members of society as a new identity development and the term 'gender identity disorder' has been removed from the classification, and the term of gender dysphoria introduced, which highlights the distress associated with this presentation. The diagnostic category has been maintained mainly to facilitate the development of services to help young people and their families.

Adolescents who have a persistent experience of incongruity between mind and body find puberty painful and unbearable. They are often at high risk of suicide attempts. A staged approach to management has been devised and this provides a containing framework for these unbearable states of mind. This approach involves four stages.

Stage 1 involves assessment of the gender identity and a therapeutic exploration. **Stage 2** is considered, following careful assessment, for adolescents whose gender dysphoria persists and becomes more distressing during adolescent development. This involves the use of hypothalamic blockers, which suppress the production of oestrogen or testosterone and produce a state of biological neutrality. This intervention is considered reversible. There has been controversy about timing this intervention during Tanner stage 2 of pubertal development. **Stage 3** includes partially reversible interventions such as hormonal treatment, which masculinises or feminises the body. Current guidelines allow this intervention usually after the age of 16. Finally, in adulthood after the age of 18, **stage 4** could be considered. This includes irreversible interventions, such as surgical procedures.

The staged approach model gives the young person and the family a sense of orientation and provides a space for reflection about the next intervention and the decision to be made.

Early Hormonal Intervention in Gender Dysphoria and Informed Consent

The exercise of autonomy in decision-making in this area is based on the recognition of children's rights and informed consent involving the child and the family. The World Congress on Family Law and Children's Rights 2009 in Halifax supported Resolution 19, which states:

a) children and adolescents with gender identity development dysphoria having a right to be protected from unnecessary suffering, stigma and bullying.

b) children and their families being able to participate fully in decision-making processes about treatment options; and

c) children and their families should have the right to have access to services that would assist their gender identity development.

Treatment with the hypothalamic blocker in the early stages of pubertal development (Tanner stage 2) was initially offered at the Gender Identity Development Service at the Tavistock Centre under an ethically approved research project to a selected group of adolescents who met the following criteria described in the protocol:

- You have a strong feeling that you are in the wrong body or that your gender and body do not match. Doctors call this a 'gender dysphoria' and they have agreed on a list of feelings and behaviours which young people with this condition show.
- Your body is starting to change – this is called early puberty. To check that your body is at this stage, you will need to have some medical tests and be physically examined by a doctor who specialises on the effect of hormones in young people.
- Being in puberty has made you more distressed and you want treatment to stop your body changing further.
- Your parents/carers are supportive of your wish to have hormone blockers in early puberty.
- The person/s you see at the Tavistock Centre have completed their assessment together with you and believe that you are suitable and ready to take part in the study.

During a long enough period of time the therapist and the paediatric endocrinologist discuss all the elements involved in the participation in the research project and in particular what are the possible benefits and disadvantages involved. These are described as follows in the information sheet given to the young person and the family. The wording of the information sheet was agreed with a number of families with whom the draft had been discussed.

What are the Possible Benefits of Taking Part?

We have looked at other countries that have given this treatment and the results suggest that:

1. Hormone blockers, which block the body's natural sex hormones, may improve the development of your body in your desired gender. They may also improve the way you feel about yourself.
2. If you decide to stop the hormone blockers early your physical development will return as usual in your biological gender. The hormone blockers will not harm your physical or psychological development.
3. Hormone blockers will make you feel less worried about growing up in the wrong body and will give you more time and space to think about your gender identity.
4. Hormone blockers may reduce the amount of operations that you may need as an adult (after the age of 18) should you wish to have operations to change your body.

What are the Possible Disadvantages and Risks of Taking Part?

1. We do not know how hormone blockers will affect bone strength, the development of your sexual organs, body shape or your final adult height. There could be other long-term effects of hormone blockers in early puberty that we don't yet know about.
2. Hormone blockers could affect your memory, concentration and the way you feel. They can also affect how you feel about your gender and how likely you are to change your mind about your gender identity.
3. Hormone blockers could affect your ability to have a baby. It could take 6 to 12 months or longer after stopping the hormone blocker before boys start making sperm or girls start maturing eggs in their ovaries.

The exercise of autonomy and decision-making requires that the adolescent and the family understand these issues and the potential consequences. A therapeutic exploration with the adolescent and the family, which take into account the potential influences on autonomy, as described above is aimed to increase the capacity of giving informed consent.

Gender Variant Role Expression in Childhood

This section deals with the question: should pre-pubertal children be allowed to live in their perceived gender? I will start with a quote from the memoir *Why Be Happy When You Could Be Normal?* (Winterson, 2011, p. 113).

Jeanette had been talking with her adoptive mother about her relationship with another girl. Then her mother asks:

'Jeanette, will you tell me why?'

'What why?'

'You know what why…'

But I don't know why… what I am… why I don't please her. What she wants. Why I am not what she wants. What I want or why. But there is something I know: '*When I am with her I am happy. Just happy.*'

She nodded. She seemed to understand and I thought, really, for that second, that she would be on the same side of the glass wall. I waited. She said: 'Why be happy when you could be normal?'

This quote shows a parental attitude influenced by perceived social norms and perhaps religious beliefs in contrast with a wish for self-expression and emotional well-being. In our society repressing one's own feelings and emotions is no longer seen as valuable but is considered as contributing to psychological difficulties and negatively affecting upon mental well-being. The mother's strong system of beliefs seemed to impede her capacity to accept her daughter's autonomy.

With regard to children with gender dysphoria who identify with the other sex, the expression of these perceptions in the social context has raised a number of controversies and caught the attention of the media in the UK and abroad.

Case Vignette: Martin

Martin was referred in the early 1990s to the Gender Identity Development Service at the age of eight when he was attending a primary school. The educational psychologist reported that his mother said that he had told her when he was seven that he wanted to be a woman when he grew up. He enjoyed dressing in women's clothing and ever since he could walk he liked to wear high heels and use tea towels to mimic long hair. He was very fond of Barbie dolls and his mannerisms and style of walking were feminine. At school he played only with girls. He lacked confidence and was teased by other children, who called him 'poof' and 'queer'. He suffered from symptoms of anxiety including stomach upsets, dizziness and headaches. His mother did not encourage his feminine behaviour but was supportive.

During his assessment at the GIDS we confirmed that Martin presented the features of a well-established gender identity disorder (now gender dysphoria in DSM-5). His anxiety about attending school resulted in poor attendance, and he also experienced teasing on the estate where he lived. He also had difficulties separating from his mother. At our service, we started working closely with the family, which consisted of Martin, his mother and his stepfather and had meetings with the school staff to facilitate his attendance at school.

Two years later Martin moved with his family to another town in England. Here, his wish to live in a female role became very intense and the parents agreed to let him live as a girl, by dressing in female clothes and changing his name to Martina.

In her new town Martina became involved in individual therapeutic work with a community nurse in the local child and adolescent mental health service (CAMHS). A colleague and I continued to see the parents every two months to help them to reflect on the gender identity and other developmental issues involved and to be able to make more informed decisions with their child (parental counselling). The parents attended a group for parents of GD children for six months. We continued to hold regular professional network meetings, including the school staff, two or three times a year. Martina attended a small special educational unit in a female role following careful preparation and discussions of the issues involved between the professional network (including us) and the family.

When Martina was 13 the social services department called a child protection conference as the school had become concerned that parental attitudes could have contributed to the development of Martina's gender dysphoria. After an investigation and a child protection conference, no child protection issues were found. As a result of this conference, the mother was offered further supportive individual counselling by local services.

When Martina was 14, while waiting to be seen by our paediatric endocrinologist, as she was entering puberty, she unexpectedly announced to her mother that she no longer wished to be a girl, and she now felt happier about being a boy. From now on, Martina reverted to living as Martin. The next time I saw him he had physically developed a lot and had the clear appearance of a boy. At the last professional/family network meeting I asked Martin if he thought that his parents had made a wrong decision in allowing him to attend school in a female role and he replied without hesitation that it had been right because that was how he had felt at the time.

The case has been anonymised and name and places changed for confidentiality.

From this case, which I saw in the 1990s, I drew the following conclusion:

1. Pubertal development can sometimes, even in well-established cases of gender dysphoria, change the course of gender identity development.
2. A parental response, which goes along with the intense wishes of the child to live in the perceived gender identity and role, does not necessarily influence the course of gender identity development. However, maintaining an open mind facilitates the process of change if this occurs.
3. My professional role was to maintain a reflective approach in working with the family and the professional network, evaluating pros and cons, and to facilitate decision-making within the family regarding what was in the best interests of the child in that particular social context.

There is very limited research evidence to suggest which approach to children living in their preferred gender role (social transition) during childhood is best. Long-term follow-up studies have shown that only in a small proportion (up to 30 per cent) of pre-pubertal children presenting with the features of a gender dysphoria did the gender dysphoria persist through adolescence and adulthood with or without any therapeutic intervention (Green, 1987; Zucker and Bradley, 1995; Cohen-Kettenis, 2001; Drummond et al., 2008; Wallien and Cohen-Kettenis, 2008). Steensma et al. (2011, p. 1) suggest that young people who changed:

considered the period between 10 and 13 years of age to be crucial… Both persisters and desisters stated that the changes in their social environment, the anticipated and actual feminization or masculinization of their bodies, and their first experiences of falling in love and sexual attraction had influenced their gender related interest and behaviour, feelings of gender discomfort and gender identification.

Regarding social transition in childhood the World Professional Association for Transgender Health (2011) makes the following statements and recommendations:

- Families vary in the extent to which they allow their young children to make a social transition to another gender role. Social transitions in early childhood do occur within some families with early success. This is a controversial issue, and divergent views are held by health professionals.
- Mental health professionals can help families to make decisions regarding the timing and process of any gender role changes for their young children.
- A change back to the original gender role can be highly distressing and even result in postponement of this second social transition on the child's part (Steensma and Cohen-Kettenis, 2011).
- Mental health professionals can assist parents in identifying potential in-between solutions or compromises (e.g. only when on vacation). It is also important that parents explicitly let the child know that there is a way back.
- Regardless of a family's decisions regarding transition (timing, extent), professionals should counsel and support them as they work through the options and implications.

My initial thinking about the management of gender role and social transition in childhood were based on a long-term observation of the case described from the 1990s. Since then I have seen a number of pre-pubertal children and have found that the exercise of autonomy in decision-making on the part of the parents and the child has been a helpful policy. The provision of a therapeutic exploration jointly with the family and a neutral professional is helpful. The exploration would aim at enhancing the capacity for autonomy in the family by reducing in some cases the potential effects of the factors described in the earlier section, and in this way leading to better informed consent to what is in the best interests in the development of the child and in particular of their gender identity. The value of therapeutic explorations and counselling with young people and their families can now be seen from a new vertex: 'their role in the service of the ethical principle of autonomy and better-informed decision-making'. Long-term follow-ups and further research in this area can contribute to the continuous development of appropriate guidelines.

References

American Psychiatric Association (2013) *Diagnostic and Statistical Manual of Mental Disorder*, 5th edn (DSM-V). Washington, DC: American Psychiatric Publishing.

Cohen-Kettenis, P. T. (2001) Gender identity disorder in DSM? *Journal of the American Academy of Child and Adolescent Psychiatry*, 40(4), 391.

Di Ceglie, D., with Freedman, D. (1998) *A Stranger in My Own Body: Atypical Gender Identity Development and Mental Health*. London: Karnac Books.

Drummond, K. D., Bradley, S. J., Peterson-Badali, M. and Zucker, K. J. (2008) A follow up study of girls with gender identity disorder. *Developmental Psychology*, 44, 34–45.

Green, R., Roberts, C. W., Williams, K. et al. (1987) Specific cross-gender behaviour in boyhood and later homosexual orientation. *British Journal of Psychiatry*, 151, 84–88.

Holmes, J. (2014) *John Bowlby and Attachment Theory*. London: Routledge.

Main, M. (1990) *A Typology of Human Attachment Organisation Assessed with Discourse, Drawings and Interviews*. New York: Cambridge University Press.

Milgram, S. (1974) *Obedience to Authority: An Experimental View*. London: Tavistock Publications.

Steensma, T. D., Biemond, R., de Boer, F. and Cohen-Kettenis, P. T. (2011) Desisting and persisting gender dysphoria after childhood: a qualitative follow-up study. *Journal of Clinical Child Psychology and Psychiatry*, 16(4), 499–516. doi: 10.1177/1359104510378303.

Steensma, T. D. and Cohen-Kettenis, P. T. (2011) Gender transitioning before puberty. *Archives of Sexual Behavior*, 40, 649–50.

Wallien, M. S. C. and Cohen-Kettenis, P. T. (2008) Psychosexual outcome of gender dysphoric children. *Journal of the American Academy of Child and Adolescent Psychiatry*, 47, 1413–23.

Winterson, J. (2011) *Why Be Happy When You Could Be Normal?* London: Vintage.

World Professional Association for Transgender Health (2011) Standards of Care for the Health of Transsexual, Transgender, and Gender Nonconforming People.

Zucker, K. J. and Bradley, S. J. (1995) *Gender Identity Disorder and Psychosexual Problems in Children and Adolescents*. New York: Plenum Press.

Criminal Responsibility

Enys Delmage and Hannele Variend

The development of rights and responsibilities in children encompasses two divergent aims – in one direction there is a duty to protect and on the other a duty to allow for autonomy and empowerment. This tension is reflected in UK civil law related to young people, which is relatively commensurate with the scientific understanding of the developing brain and is based on competency rather than chronological age. UK criminal law, however, takes a different position, with an age of criminal responsibility starting at 10. This is incompatible with the neuroscientific understanding of the neurological developmental process in young people, is very low in comparison to most other jurisdictions and has been the subject of criticism by the United Nations Committee (UN Committee General Comment, 2007). It is important to explore the challenges endemic in the criminal justice system as it relates to young people, and to consider potential solutions in respect of criminal responsibility.

Civil Law

Civil legislation manages emerging competencies through adolescence, which can have a high degree of individual variation often not in tune with chronological age, by defining a spectrum of development. This is ably reflected in the thinking behind the *Gillick* 1986 case: *Gillick* competency has no lower age limit, but instead reflects that some young people may have aptitudes which allow them autonomy, while some may not, irrespective of age. This position is similarly encapsulated in the Mental Capacity Act 2005 which, for 16- and 17-year-olds, describes a position in which the young person may be 'overwhelmed by the implications of the decision' (Mental Health Act Code of Practice, 2015). The implication of this is that a young person may lack capacity for reasons distinct from what is defined in Section 2 of the Mental Capacity Act (namely 'an impairment of or a disturbance in the functioning of the mind or brain') and must be managed via common law best interest principles. This symbolises the fact that even 16- and 17-year-olds may be developmentally immature and thus incapable of making certain types of civil decision. Criminal law has different aims than civil law (punishment versus legal redress or compensation), but, in relation to children, must still have at its heart the notion of the welfare of the child.

Criminal Law

Criminal responsibility can broadly be defined as the accountability an individual holds for the nature of his or her acts in breach of the law which would ordinarily result in punishment. An individual must be accountable for his or her acts to allow for prosecution – if they lack this capacity (so-called *mens rea* or the ability to form a guilty mind) then they are not culpable. Various states can impair this responsibility, including certain states of mental disorder or physical conditions. While either of these states may be present in children and could serve as a valid defence in a criminal court, a defence of developmental immaturity (namely a child's inability to understand the full implications of his or her actions due to his or her developmental stage) is not available in England, Wales and Northern Ireland for those aged 10 or over. This age has remained unchanged since the 1963 Children Act. Children under the age of 10 are subject to the defence of infancy, meaning that they cannot be culpable in relation to a criminal offence, since they are viewed as lacking the capacities to form criminal intent.

In the Republic of Ireland the minimum age of criminal responsibility is 10 for serious offences (murder, manslaughter, arson and sexual offences) but 12 for less serious offences. In Scotland the minimum age of criminal responsibility is eight, but children between the ages of eight and 12 that commit offences are dealt with in Children's Hearings rather than criminal courts. The average minimum age of criminal responsibility across the rest of Europe is 14, with some countries setting the age at 18.

While in the UK a protection for children aged 10 to 14 facing criminal sanction used to exist in the form of *doli incapax*, the notion that a child cannot have formed a guilty mind if they were not aware that what they did was seriously wrong, this was removed as a legal defence by the Crime and Disorder Act 1998, which reflected the social and political zeitgeist. The removal of *doli incapax* for 10- to 14-year-olds put the UK in a relatively small group of countries (including Namibia, Kenya, South Africa, Singapore, Indonesia and Papua New Guinea) that maintain such a young age of criminal responsibility.

Neurodevelopment

The minimum age of criminal responsibility in the UK has not changed since 1963 (Children and Young Persons Act 1963), despite the emergence of a higher degree of understanding of the brain's developmental capabilities and limitations through the course of adolescence. Given that mental disorders can act as valid defences, it is noteworthy that some of the cognitive deficits that would act as a defence in some states of mental illness or learning disability are also present in states of developmental immaturity.

Is it appropriate to have a chronological cut-off for criminal responsibility given that our current understanding of development demonstrates that it is a heterogeneous process which can vary widely on an individual basis? In order to properly understand the brain's emerging aptitudes in relation to autonomy and responsibility, we must look at patterns of development in the general population. In terms of the adolescent brain, neuroimaging studies are helping us to understand the areas involved in mental constructs such as empathy, working memory, consequential thinking, reasoning and judgement, planning, and inhibition of behaviour, all of which may impact on the ability to form a 'guilty mind' (i.e. be criminally responsible).

Physical brain development continues before and after puberty, into the early twenties (Blakemore and Choudhury, 2006; Sowell et al., 2001). The frontal lobes of the brain play a key part in various elements of cognition including judgement, consequential thinking, inhibition of impulses, empathy and coherent planning. This frontal lobe executive functioning increases over the course of adolescence (Anderson et al., 2001) – this has been linked with development of the brain's prefrontal cortex (Blakemore and Choudhury, 2006), in tandem with an emerging ability to engage in consequential thinking (Steinberg, 2009).

As commented on by the Royal Society (2011a), the frontal lobes of the brain are the slowest areas to develop (Gogtay et al., 2004), in contrast with the amygdala (the part of the brain responsible for reward and emotion-processing). The imbalance of the stage of development of the frontal lobes and the amygdala is thought to account for increased arousal and risk-taking behaviour in adolescence (Royal Society, 2011b). Adolescence represents a phase of increased impulsivity and sensation-seeking behaviour (van Leijenhorst et al., 2010; Baird et al., 2005; Steinberg, 2007), in tandem with a developing ability to empathise (Strayer, 1993) and a heightened vulnerability to peer influence (Steinberg and Monahan, 2007), all of which have an impact on decision-making.

The true picture is likely to be much more nuanced. As an example to highlight the complexity of brain function, it may not be too challenging for scientists to isolate the part of the brain that likes or does not like apples. The question 'do you like apples?' is a relatively straightforward one to ask the brain and probably does not require a large amount of processing power, or connections between different brain regions. However, the question 'would you feel empathy, guilt and remorse for stealing an apple from a friendly shop assistant in a large and affluent supermarket chain?' is a more challenging one which will probably involve multiple areas of the brain, and may in fact involve different areas depending on the individual's life experience thus far.

The experience of empathy is highly complex and almost certainly does involve multiple brain regions, all of which may be at different stages of development in the adolescent brain. Skills in 'mentalising' (perceiving and interpreting human behaviour, both of the subject and others, in terms of conscious and intentional mental states, namely desires, feelings, goals and reasons) are usually the task of adolescent rather than early childhood development, and researchers and clinicians are beginning to understand the pathways that help to facilitate this process. Networks for the social aspects of brain function have been identified that are crucial for mentalising and perspective-taking as part of decision-making, and there is growing evidence in relation to the structural and functional changes that these regions are progressing through.

The relationship between the frontal lobes and the amygdala is a complex one and the previously established model of frontal lobe immaturity in contrast with other brain areas as an explanation for emotional lability and problematic antisocial behaviour misses the impact of changes in social and emotional processing in teenage years in the context of influences on the brain from the environment. During the course of brain development, it has been demonstrated that certain areas (for instance, the medial pre-frontal cortex, an area at the back of the frontal lobes) may show higher activation than in adults, as the adolescent brain is potentially acquiring skills in social reasoning and self-knowledge. However, other regions (for instance, the temporoparietal junction, an area towards the back of the brain) may show lower activation than in adults. As this activation shifts and the temporoparietal junction becomes more active, adolescents show increasing responsiveness to the perspectives of others.

The aforementioned scientific position in terms of neurotypical brain development raises serious questions as to how we regard *mens rea* in children aged 10 and above. It is also worth delineating that many young offenders may be further disadvantaged as they may have a different brain structure compared to young non-offenders. Studies relating to conduct disorder (the most common mental disorder in childhood, affecting over a million children in the UK), which is a form of mental disorder strongly associated with offending behaviour (rates of conduct disorder can be as high as 80–90 per cent in young offenders' institutions) demonstrate differences in grey matter volumes in the brains of children with the disorder versus those without (Fairchild et al., 2011), making them potentially more developmentally immature and vulnerable in terms of their capacities.

Another impact factor comes in the form of negative developmental experiences – mistreatment in childhood, common in offending groups, is associated with changes in the hypothalamic-pituitary-adrenal axis (which can be over- or under-responsive as a result); overactivity can result in an increase in impulsive aggression while underactivity can result in a lack of empathy, non-responsiveness to punishment and increased instrumental aggression (Kiehl et al., 2001), and it is noteworthy that young people exposed to abusive experiences in childhood are 11 times more likely to be arrested for a violent crime than those not abused (English et al., 2002), an example of victim and perpetrator in the same vessel.

While it is important to consider culpability for offences, it is also worth examining the element of effective participation in legal processes, namely the ability of the child to be actively involved in the trial and be able to follow and understand the roles, the means of testing evidence and the basic principles and duties of the court, as well as the potential outcomes and their deciding factors. It is noteworthy that the European Court examination of the Thompson and Venables case (*T and V* v. *UK* 1999) – in which both boys were aged 10 at the time of the offence and were aged 11 at the time of trial – took the view that neither young person was able to effectively participate in their trial and a violation of Article 6 (the right to a fair trial) of the European Convention on Human Rights (1950) was found. The factors already highlighted as potentially impairing the capacity to form criminal intent are also likely to impair the ability to effectively participate in the trial process.

The MacArthur Adjudicative Competence Study (MacArthur Foundation Research Network) examined 927 youths and 446 adults in four locations across the US, and found that trial competence-related abilities improve with age – 11- to 13-year-olds show less understanding, less reasoning and less recognition than 14- and 15-year-olds, who in turn performed significantly more poorly than 16- and 17-year-olds (who functioned as well as adults). Low IQ scores were particularly associated with deficits. Young people were more likely to waive their rights than adults, more likely to accept plea agreements (even 16- and 17-year-olds) and were more likely to make choices in compliance with authority figures. Risk perception and future orientation deficits were found, and young people often did not understand the right to remain silent, and would see rights as conditional. Research has also demonstrated that young people are more likely to make false confessions than adults (Redlich and Goodman, 2003). It is also important to recognise that those identified as young offenders frequently meet the criteria for being classed as 'children in need' from a local authority perspective, but there exists no easy means to transfer cases from youth court (criminal) to family court (civil) which would allow the young person's overarching needs to be considered.

Potential Solutions

One proposed measure came via the Law Commission, which consulted widely and produced a robust discussion paper in 2013 which discussed a possible defence of 'not guilty by reason of developmental immaturity' which could be available to children up to the age of 18. This is a more scientifically sound position than the defence of *doli incapax* and would place the burden of assessment with psychiatrists and psychologists. While this burden would in all probability be small (*doli incapax* was rarely used as a defence) it is crucial that mental health professionals meet the responsibility to defend such children faced with criminal charges. It remains a matter of utmost importance to consider an increase in the minimum age of criminal responsibility to bring us in line with the United Nations Convention on the Rights of the Child, as well as the average international position.

Conclusion

What could account for the maintenance of the low age of criminal responsibility in the UK? It is possible that a small number of high-profile cases, inflamed by gratuitous media coverage, have paralysed politicians and law-makers in terms of increasing this age, for fear of upsetting the voting public.

While it is true that the options for disposal from court are different for children compared to adults (and may include secure social services accommodation or placement in a secure training centre or young offenders' institution, which differ from adult prisons and are tailored for children, with an aim in mind of having a benefit to the child), it is noteworthy that even low-scale contact with the criminal justice system can increase recidivism in this vulnerable group (McAra and McVie, 2007). This makes some sense if one considers one of the tasks of adolescence to be identity acquisition – in the absence of positive feedback in school, social care or the home setting, young people, excluded from prosocial groups, may seek meaning in antisocial peers and may begin to influence the young person's notion of who they are.

Dealing with these already vulnerable children without consideration of their developmental level, subjecting them to court without any mitigation and the possibility of criminal justice sanctions seems to many to be counterintuitive, especially in light of the reflections from scientific research over the past century, and the addition of neuroimaging work over the past 20–30 years. Our current legal position is certainly not commensurate with the scientific understanding of the child's developing brain.

Given the evident disparity between the civil law position and that of the criminal law, it is time that we as a society evolve our legal processes and take heed of children's developmental abilities and limitations in order to ensure that principles of justice and the right to a fair trial are upheld. There are resource implications to raising the minimum age of criminal responsibility, with a potential increased duty to provide local authority care, but this is a system adequately operated in other European member states and one must also factor in the reduced financial burden on the criminal justice system.

The defence of infancy should be available to more children (with some arguing for an increase of this conclusive presumption to the ages of either 14 or 16) and a defence of developmental immaturity must be made available. Without the developmental immaturity defence and an increase in the age of criminal responsibility, an already disenfranchised group is left with minimal protection in the criminal justice setting, and we as a society will be accountable for how we have treated these vulnerable young people in years to come.

References

Anderson, V., Anderson, P., Northam, E. et al. (2001) Development of executive functions through late childhood and adolescence in an Australian sample. *Developmental Neuropsychology*, 20(1), 385–406.

Baird, A., Fugelsang, J. and Bennett, C. (2005) What were you thinking? An fMRI study of adolescent decision making. Poster presented at the annual meeting of the Cognitive Neuroscience Society, New York.

Blakemore, S.-.J and Choudhury, S. (2006) Development of the adolescent brain: implications for executive function and social cognition. *Journal of Child Psychology and Psychiatry*, 47:3, 296–312.

English, D., Spatz-Widom, C. and Brandford, C. (2002) Childhood victimization and delinquency, adult criminality, and violent criminal behaviour: a replication and extension. National Institute of Justice, US Department of Justice Publications.

Fairchild, G., Passamonti, L., Hurford, G. et al (2011) Brain structure abnormalities in early-onset and adolescent-onset conduct disorder. *American Journal of Psychiatry*, 168(6), 624–33. doi: 10.1176/appi.ajp.2010.10081184.

Gillick v. *West Norfolk and Wisbech Area Health Authority* [1986] 1 AC 112.

Gogtay, N. et al. (2004) Dynamic mapping of human cortical development during childhood through early adulthood. *Proceedings of the National Academy of Sciences*, 101, 8174–9.

Kiehl, K., Smith, A., Hare, R. et al. (2001) Limbic abnormalities in affective processing by criminal psychopaths as revealed by functional magnetic resonance imaging. *Biological Psychiatry*, 50, 677–84.

Law Commission (2013) Criminal liability: insanity and automatism: a discussion paper. Law Commission Publications.

McAra, L. and McVie, S. (2007) Youth justice? The impact of system contact on patterns of desistance from offending. *European Journal of Criminology*, 4(3), 315–45.

Mental Health Act Code of Practice (2015) Paragraph 36.23.

Redlich, A. and Goodman, G. (2003) Taking responsibility for an act not committed: the influence of age and suggestibility. *Law and Human Behavior*, 27, 141–56.

Sowell, E., Thompson, P., Tessner, K. et al. (2001) Mapping continued brain growth and gray matter density reduction in dorsal frontal cortex: inverse relationships during postadolescent brain maturation. *Journal of Neuroscience*, 21, 8819–29.

Steinberg, L. (2007) Risk taking in adolescence: new perspectives from brain and behavioral science. *Current Directions in Psychological Science*, 16(2), 55–9.

Steinberg, L. (2009) Adolescent development and juvenile justice. *Annual Review of Clinical Psychology*, 5, 459–85.

Steinberg, L. and Monahan, K. (2007) Age differences in resistance to peer influence. *Developmental Psychology*, 43(6), 1531–43.

Strayer, J. (1993) Children's concordant emotions and cognitions in response to observed emotions. *Child Development*, 64(1), 188–201.

T and V v. *The United Kingdom (Application number 24888/94)*, European Court of Human Rights judgment, Strasbourg, 16 December 1999.

The Royal Society (2011a) *Brain Waves Module 2: Neuroscience: Implications for Education and Lifelong Learning*. Excellence in Science publications. London: The Royal Society.

The Royal Society (2011b) *Brain Waves Module 4: Neuroscience and the Law*. Excellence in Science Publications. London: The Royal Society.

United Nations Committee General Comment (2007) Number 10: Children's rights in juvenile justice CRC/C/GC/10 (para 30–35).

van Leijenhorst, L., Moor, B., Op de Macks, Z. et al. (2010) Adolescent risky decision-making: neurocognitive development of reward and control regions. *Neuroimage*, 51(1), 345–55.

19

How Reading This Book Can Contribute to Public Health Strategies for Children and Families

Sarah Jonas

I would like to offer some thoughts and responses to reading this book. I am a child psychiatrist with an interest in public mental health and policymaking, who has worked in a number of different policy settings and as an expert witness in the family courts.

By the end of preclinical medical training, I was very discouraged by the dry and scientific nature of the training and explicitly gave myself a term at clinical school to work out if I liked it. It was 1997, a time of great political optimism: my friends at the time were all going to be advisors to new MPs and I felt impotent.

I went to clinical school and was drawn in by the human scale and the interesting ethical dilemmas. In my first term I was lucky enough to have the course with Professor Len Doyal on medical law and ethics, and reading the chapters of this book brought my mind right back to those seminars and to those links between the micro of the doctor–patient consultation and the macro of society and the policy world.

The editors present a fascinating book exploring the ideas, values and structures promoting justice for children and families, which contains much that would be useful to those developing policy for children and families. In thinking about health and justice I am drawn to the ideas of Amartya Sen who helpfully draws the distinction in policy terms between 'good health policy' and 'good policy for health' (Sen, 2010). I will argue that the broad context of justice for children and families presented by the editors in this book fits with these ideas, giving a foundation for 'good policy for health' across a breadth of policymaking.

There has been a growing movement towards evidence-based policymaking, or evidence informed (initially in the UK promoted by the Blair government) (Banks, 2009). In terms of marrying how justice might be best served by policy, Amartya Sen in *The Idea of Justice* (2009) is again very helpful in his development of the concept of consequential justice and the capability approach, particularly his use of social consequences theory to develop a practical approach to achieving justice. These ideas are helpfully examined in Chapter 5 in this volume on 'Child Poverty, Well-Being and Social Justice'. Sen argues that rather than trying and failing to obtain perfect justice, a more just society can be obtained by making comparative choices for the best outcome whenever there are choices to be made, and assessing what the possible capabilities are that a person has access to.

In terms of policymaking, a pragmatic, evidence-informed approach where there is a consideration of what might practically work best and be most implementable is key to the final impact. I believe the ideas in this book can inform this kind of policymaking and thinking.

Interestingly, one of my more surprising responses when reading this book was noting initially that the idea of fairness seemed aligned with population-based public health interventions, but that the ideas of protection seemed to be more of a special case. However, reflecting on it and exploring the sheer numbers of children who report maltreatment, I was struck by both the magnitude of the public health need in relation to protection and the relatively small response that is made by society, and indeed that even I who work with maltreatment on a regular basis am drawn to negate the size of the issue. Public health strategies, which could underpin greater social justice for children and families, seem to flow from the ideas discussed in this book.

Why is This Important for Policy?

Just as the Jesuit maxim 'give me a child for his first seven years, and I will show you the man' is much used colloquially, there is increasing evidence pointing to the vast significance of early experiences in determining future physical and mental health and also future earning potential and criminal justice outcomes.

Historically, there has been a lack of focus on long-term determinants of social justice for children and young people, in parallel to a lack of focus on the public health of children and young people, apart from vaccination and infectious diseases, with interest in these other areas only building over the last 15–20 years (Blair, 2010). We now know that even before birth, experiences in foetal life have lifelong and profound consequences on long-term health and well-being. Over the last 25 years there has been increasing evidence in terms of physical health, particularly cardiac disease, diabetes and stroke from the work of Barker, showing that decreased nutrition during pregnancy leads to a wide range of outcomes (Barker, 1992). More recently, there is increasing evidence that maternal stress and anxiety during pregnancy can be linked to mental health outcomes in childhood (O'Connor et al., 2003).

After a child is born, early experiences, development, health and well-being have wide-ranging effects on both health and opportunity across the whole of the life span. Angela J. M. Donkin sets out in her chapter on 'The Social Determinants of Child Health' (Chapter 3) the powerful evidence not only of the social determinants of health, but also, bringing in the evidence in relation to the lifelong effects of early experiences. She points out that optimal adult health requires not just addressing child health outcomes in terms of policymaking but also addressing the wider developmental outcomes for children as these impact on economic security in later life.

A further area where there has been a huge increase in knowledge over recent years is that of the impact of adverse childhood experiences (ACEs). While the long-term effects of abuse in childhood, particularly in mental health, have been postulated for some time, the studies using the ACE paradigm have broadened the work, finding links between adverse childhood experiences (as retrospectively reported by adults), such as parental illness, parental absence, divorce, neglect, physical and sexual abuse, and the adult health status. Clear dose-responsive effects were found across a wide range of adult conditions including substance misuse, suicidality, ischaemic heart disease, liver disease, alcohol misuse, smoking, sexual risk behaviour, violence, criminality and obesity (Felitti et al., 1998). It is interesting from a policy perspective that there were effects on both mental and physical health outcomes.

In a similar vein the chapter by Lorraine Khan on 'A Life Course Approach to Promoting Healthy Behaviour' (Chapter 11) sets out the links between early experiences and later behavioural difficulties and criminal justice outcomes. This is of particular salience as behavioural disorders such as conduct disorder are very common – up to 10 per cent of children and young people, giving a huge impact on society.

The fraction of disease burden, which can be attributed to early experience, is now understood to be very significant. In mental health, the proportion of adult disorders attributable to child maltreatment (and this was using very narrow definitions of child maltreatment) is estimated to be 25–30 per cent (Green et al., 2010; Bebbington et al., 2011; Varese et al., 2012). Given that 20 per cent of the population are thought to meet diagnostic criteria for a mental illness in any one year (Annual Report of the Chief Medical Officer, 2013), this is a potentially large proportion of illness burden, which could be targeted for alleviation.

Therefore, not only are the consequences large but also the potential gains through prevention or effect mitigation are equally massive and potentially larger than for any other area of public health. This is a key feature for policymakers in the health and well-being of children; there is a simply huge consequence of early experience as the effect multiplies through life. Perhaps unsurprisingly, the first and biggest conclusion from the Marmot Review and the commission on the social determinants of health was that 'giving every child the best possible start should be a policy priority' (2010).

Magnitude of the Problem

One of the considerations I had when reading the chapters on protection was the sheer magnitude of the numbers of children involved. There are 11 million children in England (Office for National Statistics, 2016). The National Society for the Prevention of Cruelty to Children research (NSPCC, 2011) suggests that approximately 25 per cent of 18–24-year-olds (equivalent to 2¾ million children) report that they have experienced severe maltreatment or victimisation over the course of their childhood. Other studies that look at maltreatment suggest similar figures through retrospective reporting (Bebbington et al., 2011). Studies of ACEs suggest that 10 per cent of the population experience more than four ACEs during childhood (Felliti et al., 1998).

Despite this large burden of maltreatment in our society, the number of children who receive help from social care remains relatively small: in 2016, 390,000 (Department for Education, 2016), although these children are mainly under the age of five so the relative proportion in that age group is likely to be greater.

The number of children involved in the court system is similarly small, with approximately 43,000 children being involved in public proceedings in 2016, with approximately 13,000 children being placed on care orders in 2016 and 165,000 children being involved in private court proceedings (divorce, contact, etc.) (National Statistics, 2017). In terms of the criminal courts there were 45,900 primary convictions for 11–17-year-olds in the year to March 2016 (Ministry of Justice, n.d.).

Given This, What Can We Take from This Book in Terms of Public Health Strategies? Or More Practically, How Can Policymakers Use These Ideas?

I return to the helpful distinction drawn by Amartya Sen between 'good health policy' and 'good policy for health': to achieve optimal health for a society, 'good policy for health' is required and policy across all areas needs to be aligned to promote health (Sen, 2010).

This book offers help in a number of ways. First, it explores areas that can be directly translated into policy and action. Second, it helpfully investigates the underlying themes that can be used to underpin the generation of policy, while taking children, families and a developmental perspective into account.

Public health strategies are often articulated in three parts: primary, secondary and tertiary prevention. Put simply, primary prevention tackles risk factors at a population level health; secondary prevention targets those in high-risk groups with preventative intervention; and tertiary prevention targets those who already have a disorder to prevent further complications of that disorder. Public health strategies can be broad, influencing policy over many policy areas, covering health promotion, the law, criminal justice, social support and child protection, in addition to healthcare commissioning.

In thinking about primary preventions, or universal interventions to improve the population health, this book makes very clear cases for policy targeting the social determinants of health, enabling children to have the best possible start. Angela J. M. Donkin helpfully sets out a section in her chapter articulating how policy can target the boarder social determinants. Similarly, Lorraine Khan makes this case clearly in her chapter on the life course approach to promoting healthy behaviour, noting the importance of promoting maternal mental health and also parenting interventions. It would also seem intuitive to intervene to prevent maltreatment of children at a population level; the evidence is less clear for what interventions might work. It seems likely that the parenting interventions that Lorraine Khan advocates would have broader benefits than purely behavioural outcomes. Similarly, good parental knowledge about parenting and child development and expectations, alongside awareness of, and early recognition of, child maltreatment has face validity.

In children and young people early interventions are often highly cost-effective but the links between interventions and final health outcomes are often not explicit in commissioning as the savings are often from another commissioner's budget; this is clearly articulated by Lorraine Khan in relation to behavioural problems, where early parenting interventions result in long-term savings for police and crime budgets.

Similarly, making investments to target early life experiences can have pay-offs over longer time frames than the policy or electoral cycle, and therefore may need to be strongly advocated for maintained funding, as they can be vulnerable to cuts, due to the lack of immediate impact. I would argue that this is a very significant obstacle to maintaining and sustaining good policy for children and young people.

Secondary public health interventions are those which target a high-risk group, reducing the chances that the consequences develop. Potential targets for this could be children with index maltreatment who are known to social services, children with known illnesses, children with known behavioural problems and perhaps, given the chapter of Angela J. M. Donkin, children who are socially deprived as well.

This is an area where there is a variable level of evidence for interventions depending on different risks and outcomes. For instance, there is clear evidence for intervening with children who have early behavioural difficulties and preventing the progression to conduct disorder as discussed by Lorraine Khan. However, there is a paucity of effective interventions to prevent poor adult mental health outcomes from, for instance, childhood sexual abuse, which has been linked to both psychosis and common mental disorders (Jonas et al., 2011; Bebbington et al., 2011) and also more broadly, adverse childhood experiences, which have been linked to poor adult mental ill health (Felliti et al., 1998).

There is often an interval between the exposure to maltreatment and the outcome of mental health difficulties, suggesting that there may be a possibility for intervention for this high-risk group. This is particularly demonstrated by the ACE studies described by Angela J. M. Donkin and others in this book where psychopathology in those exposed to abuse appears to get worse with age.

While this group would appear to be an ideal target for intervention, there is minimal actual evidence of effective interventions that reduce the risk of this group developing adult mental health problems. Helpfully, Broadbent, Mason and Webb (Chapter 8) advocate intervention planning through a developmental trauma lens, particularly looking at mothers who return to court multiple times, but these lenses would also, I suggest, be useful for this larger group of ACE-exposed children and young people. A clearer understanding and funding of interventions would be a direct and clear way of improving justice for this group, of which the first step would be the funding of research into possible interventions.

Similarly, a further theme expressed in several chapters is the role of the mental health of parents, particularly mothers, in relation to their children. Interventions in this area to prevent problems in their high-risk children or as yet unborn children can provide improvements across behaviour, health and well-being, as well as reducing maltreatment. This area again suffers from a disconnect between the costs of the interventions and the potential savings.

Lastly, I will discuss tertiary interventions, usually seen in classical public health terms as treating ill health and preventing the further complications of ill health. This book clearly articulates the possibilities of limiting further damage to children who have experienced severe maltreatment in relation to family justice for children, particularly concentrating on the special case of the Family Drug and Alcohol Court (FDAC) and its unique combination of health intervention and court decision-making. FDAC is a novel approach, offering a multidimensional treatment intervention as part of a problem-solving court, to achieve its outcomes (Chapter 9). It has a clear evidence base for improving the chances of children remaining with their birth families and not entering the care system, alongside greater stability for the children who are returned home compared to standard care proceedings. Additionally, it provides very significant financial gains, which can be achieved within two years of a case entering the court, making it arguably just, on both an individual and societal level. However, like other interventions described in this book it has been subject to a disconnect between the commissioner who pays for the court and clinical team and the services who benefit from savings leading to challenges in the funding stream despite a clear cost-effective evidence base.

Part of the FDAC intervention is the use of Video Interaction Guidance to improve the relationship between parent and child (Chapter 10). Video Interaction Guidance is included in the National Institute for Clinical Excellence (NICE) guidance on attachment (NICE, 2015) as an intervention for children who are at high risk of or who have attachment difficulties. It is an intervention that is relatively easy to deliver, and I would argue is one that could be provided much more widely to children who have been maltreated or who are at risk of maltreatment. There are very few evidence-based interventions for attachment difficulties, yet there is a strong evidence base for attachment difficulties having a large impact over the life course.

What are the Underlying Themes?

While this book helpfully explores areas that can be directly translated into policy and action, it also helpfully explores the underlying themes that can be used to underpin the generation of policy in other areas, while taking children families and a developmental perspective into account.

The editors have considered special topics, which have only been covered in a limited way elsewhere but are essential in thinking about developing policy for children and families. The chapters on the developmental perspectives on the development of autonomy (Chapter 14), the philosophical considerations of children (Chapter 4), children as citizens (Chapter 6) and the rights of children (Chapters 2 and 7) seem essential for policymakers to consider.

For me, however, this book exposes the tensions between the two ethical stances of rights-based (deontological) thinking and utilitarian thinking in both justice and policymaking. Deontological or rights-based ethics as put forward by Kant is founded on the premise that decisions about justice are based on an objective moral code, where each individual decision is considered on its own merits. Rights-based thinking is often enshrined in the law, legal safeguards and international conventions (Garbutt and Davies, 2011). In utilitarian thinking, as advanced by Jeremy Bentham, decisions are made in accordance with the good for the most. Bentham initially defined utility as the aggregate pleasure after deducting the suffering of all involved. Ideas such as QALYs (Quality Adjusted Life Years) have been a more recent development in measuring or comparing the relative good.

In a sense both individual medical consultations (doctor–patient) and court cases are primarily driven by a rights-based understanding where the decisions and outcomes are the product of the rights and best interests of those involved. Indeed, this book provides commentary on the United Nations Convention on the Rights of the Child (UNCRC) (Chapter 7), 'Foundations of Family Law' (Chapter 2) and 'Litigation for Failure to Remove' (Chapter 13), all of which examine the rights of the individual (Garbutt and Davies, 2011). This is in contrast to the much more utilitarian standpoint which is advocated in this book by the chapters on social justice and public health including social determinants, where the authors have sought to set out the determinants of the greatest good for all (Garbutt and Davies, 2011).

In terms of a public health agenda but also commissioning, policymaking and lawmaking agendas, there is a constant tension between the two ethical standpoints: both are important but they are difficult to balance and can seesaw. On a national level bodies such as NICE explicitly evaluate the spending of resources in terms of QALYs to measure relative benefit (NICE, 2012).

Finally, I Will Leave You with This Thought

'In the little world in which children have their existence', says Pip in Charles Dickens's *Great Expectations* (1861), 'there is nothing so finely perceived and finely felt as injustice.' A public health strategy for children and families could be seen as having justice at its heart. It will therefore be key that law, public health and evidence are aligned as much as possible to drive societal changes.

This book clearly sets out both the evident injustices that children experience in society but also the hidden injustices that society and policy have tended to forget, and which have become more evident (and evidenced) in recent years, such as social determinants of health, adverse childhood experiences and maltreatment, while also setting out underlying principles for policymakers to consider in making policy for children.

References

Annual Report of the Chief Medical Officer (2013) Public mental health. Department of Health England, London.

Banks, G. (2009) Evidence-based policy making. What is it? How do we get it? Australian Government, Productivity Commission.

Barker, D. (1992) *Fetal and Infant Origins of Adult Disease*. Chichester: Wiley-Blackwell.

Bebbington, P., Jonas, S., Kuipers, E., King, M., Cooper, C., Brugha, T. et al. (2011) Childhood sexual abuse and psychosis: data from a cross-sectional national psychiatric survey in England. *The British Journal of Psychiatry*, 199(1), 29–37.

Blair, M. (2010) *Child Public Health*. Oxford: Oxford University Press.

Department for Education (2016) Main tables B3 and C1. In Characteristics of Children in Need in England, 2015–16. Available at: www.gov.uk/government/statistics/characteristics-of-children-in-need-2015-to-2016 (accessed 8 June 2017).

Dickens, C. (1861) *Great Expectations*. London: Chapman and Hall.

Felitti, V. J., Anda, R. F., Nordenberg, D., Williamson, D. F., Spitz, A. M., Edwards, V., Koss, M. P. and Marks, J. S. (1998) Relationship of childhood abuse and household dysfunction to many of the leading causes of death in adults. *American Journal of Preventive Medicine*, 14, 245–58.

Garbutt, G. and Davies, P. (2011) Should the practice of medicine be a deontological or utilitarian enterprise? *Journal of Medical Ethics*; 37, 267–70.

Green, J. G., McLaughlin, K. A., Berglund, P. A., Gruber, M. J., Sampson, N. A., Zaslavsky, A. M. et al. (2010) Childhood adversities and adult psychiatric disorders in the National Comorbidity Survey replication I: associations with first onset of DSM-IV disorders. *Archives of General Psychiatry*, 67(2), 113.

Jonas, S., Bebbington, P., McManus, S., Meltzer, H., Jenkins, R., Kuipers, E. et al. (2011) Sexual abuse and psychiatric disorder in England: results from the 2007 Adult Psychiatric Morbidity Survey. *Psychological Medicine*, 41(4), 709–19.

Marmot, M. (2010) *Fair Society, Healthy Lives: The Marmot Review: Strategic Review of Health Inequalities in England Post-2010*. London: Department for International Development.

Ministry of Justice (n.d.) Youth justice annual statistics: 2015 to 2016. Available at: www.gov.uk/government/statistics/youth-justice-statistics-2015-to-2016 (accessed 7 June 2017).

National Statistics (2017) Family court statistics quarterly: October to December 2016. Available at: www.gov.uk/government/statistics/family-court-statistics-quarterly-october-to-december-2016 (accessed 7 June 2017).

NICE (2012) Guideline Manual Process and Methods (PMG6), November. Available at: www.nice.org.uk (accessed 7 June 2017).

NICE (2015) Children's attachment: attachment in children and young people who are adopted from care, in care or at high risk of going into care. NICE guideline (NG26), November.

NSPCC (2011) Statistics on child abuse. Available at: www.nspcc.org.uk/preventing-abuse/child-protection-system/england/statistics/ (accessed 8 June 2017).

O'Connor, T. G., Heron, J., Golding, J., Glover, V. and ALSPAC Study Team (2003) Maternal antenatal anxiety and behavioural/emotional problems in children: a test of a programming hypothesis. *Journal of Child Psychology and Psychiatry*, 44(7), 1025–36.

Office for National Statistics (2016) Table MYE2 in Population estimates for UK, England and Wales, Scotland and Northern Ireland, mid-2015.

Sen, A. (2009) *The Idea of Justice*. Cambridge, MA: Allen Lane and Harvard University Press.

Sen, A. (2010) Foreword. In J. P. Ruger, *Health and Social Justice*. New York: Oxford University Press.

Varese, F., Smeets, F., Drukker, M., Lieverse, R., Lataster, T., Viechtbauer, W. et al. (2012) Childhood adversities increase the risk of psychosis: a meta-analysis of patient-control, prospective- and cross-sectional cohort studies. *Schizophrenia Bulletin*, 38(4), 661–71.

Chapter

20

Looking Three Ways
Reflections on a Developmental
Perspective on Justice

Gwen Adshead

It is an honour and privilege to be asked to offer some comments and reflections on this rich collection of chapters. At starting, the editors stated that they wanted to explore the 'values, ideas and structures that promote justice for children and families', and they commissioned authors who had pertinent and rich experience to discuss their views utilising three perspectives: fairness, protection and autonomy. No one who has read this book could deny that the authors and editors have done excellent work, and provided valuable material that should inform those who have the heavy responsibility for making both policy and funding decisions.

What I would like to offer here are some thoughts that have been generated by reading this fascinating book; and some which are based on my own experience as a psychotherapist and psychiatrist who has worked in different kinds of legal fora for many years. As a psychotherapist, I am interested in how we grow our minds and identities during our earliest years; and how those minds and identities can and do change in response to events and relationships, internal and external. As a psychiatrist who works with offenders (including abusive parents), I am intrigued by what it means to perpetrators to make complex decisions that have life-changing effects for both their victims and themselves. I studied medical law and ethics as a junior psychiatrist, and in different ways I have tried to continue that study because it is so relevant to the work I do. It seems to me that what this book is discussing is ethical reasoning in action in relation to children and their families, by which I mean the process whereby we decide on actions that we consider to be good in ethical terms. The law tells us what course of action is legally good, and thus what we *can* do in law, within the resources that we happen to have, but we may still have qualms as to whether this is the right thing to do in ethical terms. The ethical reasoning process invites us to ask *how* we know what the right thing to do is; and poses another question about who gets to decide what is right.

Three Faces of Justice

Like the editors, I think it is possible to conceptualise justice in three ways: specifically, (i) justice as respect for individual rights, liberty and due process; (ii) justice as protection of the vulnerable in society; and (iii) justice as the promotion of the good life. I have previously argued (Adshead, 2014) that mental health services tend to emphasise different conceptions of justice at different times and in different ways; and I suggested that mental health services needed to utilise a pluralist account of justice, or run a risk of doing both harm and wrong to those patients we work with professionally.

I will use this triadic approach to my commentary, and start with some exploration of the concept of children's rights, especially in terms of their emerging identities and developing autonomy. I will add some comments on the use of law to protect children, and then link this with the idea of justice as the basis for the promotion of 'good enough' care for children. As many may know, the phrase 'good enough' was first applied to parenting by the well-known paediatrician and psychoanalyst Donald Winnicott, and it neatly encapsulates a practical idea of virtue in action, which is crucial to family law and justice.

Rights and Duties

The concept of individual human rights is a modern one, which arguably begins in a variety of religious accounts of individual accountability, and developed in the context of political revolutionary movements that challenged the idea that another human being could be an object or possession. Rights as absolutes gained legal and social ground in the twentieth century, especially in the post-war examination of human rights violations by Nazi government members, especially the Nazi doctors who had abandoned their therapeutic identity to experiment and kill vulnerable people. The European Convention on Human Rights was developed in this context as a protection against future such abuses.

It is however worth noting that the idea of human rights as an essential aspect of being human has been disputed; for example, Jeremy Bentham called the idea 'nonsense upon stilts' (Bentham, 2002), arguing that a system of moral reasoning could not be built this way because there was no way to derive rights from human status alone. Other critics of rights-based moral reasoning observe that there is no way to decide between two competing rights because each is presented as an absolute; nor is it clear how the scope of a right is to be assessed. Rights-based analyses tend to end up in adversarial discourses, which then naturally lend themselves for formal legal processes of representation and advocacy.

What rights-based discussions tend to omit is any discussion of relationships and social structures in which these rights are to be exercised; and this is especially problematic for children whose identity and personhood emerges from the matrix of relationships in which they 'live and grow and have their being' (with apologies to St Paul). If rights are based on individual identity, then they will emerge and develop as that identity develops; and this is a process that is not linear nor staged nor inevitably progressive. For example, the capacity to make moral decisions begins in late childhood but is a major developmental task in adolescence which engages a self-reflective process as part of an emerging self-narrative of identity (Day and Tappan, 1996; Tappan, 2010). This process is influenced by attachment security (van IJzendoorn and Zwart-Woudstra, 1995), which can change in adolescence, especially in response to family disruption and trauma (Sroufe, 2005).

It is no surprise that there is a strong relationship between attachment security and the capacity for a moral identity. Any exploration and expression of rights needs a secure psychological framework, which enables children and young people to develop the type of self-reflective function that is associated with coherence of thought and narrative identity (Blasi, 1993). At the same time, some studies of moral decision-making by adolescents have challenged the idea that rights awareness is the ultimate endpoint of a capacity for moral reasoning. In her groundbreaking study of teenagers discussing the choice to abort a pregnancy, Carol Gilligan (1982) found that they did not discuss this in terms of rights to choose and control over one's body, but instead couched their decision-making process in terms of the type of person they wanted to be, and the impact of their decisions on their relationships with those closest to them (their attachment figures). It seems to me that when judges talk of 'Gillick competence', what they are talking about is this capacity to think about oneself and others in a nuanced way, which can hold complexity and uncertainty.

As mental health professionals, we may therefore become anxious that children who lack attachment security may not be well placed to exercise their 'rights' because they lack attachment figures to help them to do so; or the insecurity of their attachment systems means that they struggle to develop a coherent narrative of moral identity as described above. We want children to be able to grow a capacity for moral reasoning which is a vital aspect of their narrative of themselves as moral decision-makers, what McAdams calls the 'narrative level of personality' (McAdams, 2009, 2013). As several authors in this book have indicated, adults concerned with children's justice may have particular anxieties about what level of competence is necessary to make really complex decisions like whether to have sex with someone, whether others are trustworthy, whether I can trust my own experience of my body, especially in the realm of sexual identity and choices; and whether to commit an assault that will end in someone's death. The chapters by Pearce and Coy (15) and Di Ceglie (17) in particular raise concerns that it is those especially vulnerable children and young people, who may have suffered trauma, loss and general insecurity of experience, who may be asked to make these especially complex decisions. For example, it is teenage girls who are placed in care because they have not been safe in difficult and sometimes dangerous homes, who appear to be most at risk of making risky decisions about trusting others, and/or getting pregnant (Chapter 15). The 700 per cent rise in gender dysfunction consultations over the last five years (as described by Dr Di Ceglie) is likely to include a sub-group of children whose experience of trauma, loss and insecurity will be a major contributing factor to their dilemmas about bodily identity, and how to 'do' their gender in the way that makes sense to them. In these cases, it is vital that a focus on 'rights' does not obscure the emotional complexity of what is at stake for these young people, and those they care for.

Protection

The value of rights-based discourse, as exemplified by the European Convention of Human Rights, is that it affirms the unique dignity and value of each person, regardless of age, sex, colour or nationality, and gives legal and moral status to our human identity as persons, not things. We see here the modern enactment of Kant's moral imperative that we should never treat people merely as a means to an end; humans are not things that we can use for instrumental purposes. This unique right of being human includes the freedom to be ourselves (as we define it) and the freedom to be left alone (Berlin, 1958) and it is this freedom from interference that is crucial to the protection of the vulnerable. Interference with the vulnerable is the leitmotiv of most human violence, whether as bullying, exploitation or physical attack; and this interference is driven by denigratory attitudes towards dependence, neediness and lack of power. Anyone who can exert power over another person (in whatever form) can be tempted to exploit that vulnerability; and legal powers exist to curb that unhappy human tendency.

In relation to children, evidence from studies of child maltreatment shows that sadly, it is biological parents or adults in caring roles, who present most risk of harm and exploitation in the early years. What seems to be common to child abuse perpetrators is a view of the child as a possession; where the word 'my' is used in the same way about a child as a person might say 'my car' or 'my shoes'. Abusive parents and carers will talk about their 'right' to treat their child in the way they choose, in absolute opposition to the idea that any rights they have are contingent on their duties to their children's welfare (as so beautifully expressed in this book in Chapter 2 by the Honourable Mr Justice McDonald). Parents or carers who have negative and derogatory attitudes towards children's neediness are at risk of seeing children as things that they have a right to treat as they like, not people to whom they have duties; and appear to be at greater risk of physically mistreating or neglecting children in their care. Maltreating parents often describe their children in hostile terms and as objects whose neediness makes them contemptible. I am reminded of a parent in a therapy group for maltreating and neglectful parents who commented prior to attending the group, that they 'had never really thought about their child as a person before'.

I would like to make a plea here for much better intelligence and understanding about child-maltreating parents, and how best to help them. Understandably legal, social and health services have focused on the needs of maltreated children, on facilitating rescue of children from abuse and trauma and provision of safe spaces where they can heal and repair. I am of course not suggesting that this attention and work should cease; only, that if we are serious about preventing the abuse of children, we must understand the people who do it and why. When it comes to parents who abuse their children in whatever way, we know that this is a minority of parents, most of whom have experienced abuse and neglect themselves, and who find themselves in hostile and helpless states of mind in relation to their children (Lyons-Ruth and Block, 1996; Lyons-Ruth et al., 2005). I was reminded of the importance of thinking about perpetrators of child abuse when reading the excellent chapter in this book about female genital mutilation (FGM) (Chapter 12); it is clear how much harm this practice does and it is satisfying to know that it is now illegal: but it seems to me that there is an urgent question about who is working with those who perpetrate FGM to stop their activities.

Other types of abuse might be identifiable at an early stage; it is hard not to grind my teeth with frustration when I read about millions of pounds spent on research into high-risk pregnancies that do not include any account of the riskiness of a mother's mind in relation to her baby, from conception to birth and thereafter. I am tired of seeing young women with personality dysfunction, whose babies are mindlessly conceived and who cannot care for them once they are born; whose babies are removed, but who are not then offered evidence-based therapies that might make a difference to the next baby, or might prevent the conception of an unwanted child who will be at high risk of abuse. There is evidence that abusive parents who have therapeutic interventions are at less risk of future maltreatment (Chaffin et al., 2004); actuarially, they should be good candidates for therapy because they often lack the other known risk factors (such as generally antisocial attitudes) for violence to others that make engagement in therapy difficult.

So why is it so difficult to find therapy for parents who struggle to care for their children? The question is rhetorical; the answer is that there does not appear to be any public concern about cutting services that provide psychological therapy for complex cases, nor any concern about the injustice of not providing services to people who need them. Take for example the welcome and valuable expansion of perinatal mental health services over the last two years, which is due entirely to the efforts and dedication of colleagues in perinatal mental health care, who have demonstrated the value long term of providing such services in terms of cost-offset. However, it is often asserted that these services are only funded for mothers with psychotic illnesses; they are apparently 'not funded' to provide a service for mothers with personality disorder. Such a position is massively unjust, and would not happen in physical health care: we may imagine the public outcry in response to a cancer service that was only funded to treat breast cancer and no other condition. But this position is also incoherent in terms of risk; we treat postnatal psychosis vigorously because it is a high-risk condition for both mother and child; but exactly the same is true for maternal personality disorder, especially in the first postnatal year.

A Good Enough Life for Children?

Defining the 'good life' for adults has preoccupied philosophers for centuries, and it is not easy to simply define what a 'good life' is for children; not least because we know that Tolstoy was wrong: there are many and varied ways to have happy human family life but only a few miserably predictable ways to be unhappy at home. Angela J. M. Donkin's chapter reminds us that although poverty is not always associated with unhappy childhoods, social deprivation and inequality can make life much harder for families to feel empowered to make good decisions about their families' health (Chapter 3). Evidence from the adverse childhood experiences (ACEs) studies conducted since the late 1990s show that exposure to more than four kinds of childhood adversity significantly increases the chance of poor physical and mental health in adulthood (Felitti et al., 1998). The worse and more numerous the adverse experiences, the more severe the outcomes; a recent study by Fox et al. (2015) of ACEs in young offenders in the US found that levels of childhood adversity were high in persistently violent young offenders compared to one-off offenders. In the Fox study, *each* type of childhood adversity conferred an increased risk of violent offending by a factor of *35*; only a tiny minority of persistent violent offenders had no childhood adversity at all.

So, enlightened self-interest alone should make politicians and health policymakers interested in reducing childhood adversity. There are active initiatives at national levels to reduce childhood adversity; the World Health Organisation are active in researching ACEs worldwide with a view to their reduction, and the US Centers for Disease Control and Prevention details research using ACEs on their website. Studies of UK populations have consistently found that about 10 per cent of the population have experienced four or more adverse childhood experiences, and are therefore at high risk of developing long-term physical conditions and debilitating psychiatric disorders, and becoming misusers of substances.

The difficulty is that childhood adversity is intimately bound up with parental adversity. The chance for a child to have a 'good enough life' is reduced if they have a parent in prison, who misuses substances, who is domestically violent or has a mental health problem; and unless they are genetically resilient, this exposure to adversity will increase their chance of a life characterised by what Fox et al. call 'downstream wreckage', a brutal metaphor for a brutal outcome. I have met the adult incarnations of these young men and women exposed to adversity who have become what Shakespeare called 'ruined pieces of nature', full of promise like every child, but who have been damaged because they missed out on all opportunities for rescue, repair and redemption.

When I talk of redemption, I am not thinking of the term in its traditional religious sense, but as Dan McAdams and colleagues use it to describe the process by which people manage to transform a negative or painful experience into something positive; not without effort, not without emotional discomfort, not without dogged persistence against tough odds. McAdams et al. (2001) suggests that there are possibilities for people to 'make good' out of bad experiences by reflecting on their experience and telling their story. This process can continue well into adulthood, and for the many people that I meet in my work, therapy has this redemptive quality. In the context of preventing childhood adversity, I reiterate that much childhood adversity could be reduced if parents who were struggling could get access to therapies that have been shown to change minds. There are interventions for battering fathers and mothers; interventions for parents who misuse substances, as described in the excellent chapter by Judith Harwin et al. (Chapter 9); interventions that could improve mental health that could be offered in prisons to people serving sentences, or better still as a condition of a non-custodial order.

These interventions are available and empirically validated; from an ethical standpoint in relation to resource allocation, it is getting harder and harder to justify *not* providing these interventions on a much bigger scale than currently. The benefits of these programmes can be identified directly, as described by Lorraine Khan (Chapter 11) and indirectly in terms of cost-offset later down the line. However, it appears that physical health costs and mental health costs are treated very differently in the public mind: there is apparently little public concern about spending millions of pounds on drugs that can only extend people's lives by months, but apparently a public reluctance to spend money on interventions that will improve mental health of future children and also save millions in the future. This seems bizarre given the evidence; and can only be attributed to a prejudice against offering help to men and women whose needs are hidden by their offender identity.

Meanwhile the ambivalence about child protection continues and focuses on child removal, not parental improvement. Consider this statement:

> We are at a pivotal moment in UK child health, when recent gains are likely to be lost. The Unicef report strikes right to the heart of a defining question for our times: what is the duty of the State in protecting and providing the best conditions for nurturing our children? Government policy can foster or hinder children's health, development and well-being. (Wolfe, 2014, p. 9)

with this:

> It matters not whether the parent is wise or foolish, rich or poor, educated or illiterate, provided the child's moral and physical health are not in danger... It follows that we must be willing to tolerate very diverse standards of parenting, including the eccentric, the barely adequate and the inconsistent... it is not the provenance of the State to spare children *all the consequence of defective parenting.* (Hedley J, in *Re: L (Care: Threshold Criteria)* [2007])

If it is not the duty of the state to protect its future citizens from defective care, whose duty is it? It is now a cliché to say that it takes a village to raise a child, but it is also true that children belong to no one and everyone: they belong to the future, a future that we have a duty to invest in. But it can start with small-scale activities, like the Pause project in Hackney, that supports young women to pause in their role as mothers; like the provision of a therapy group for parents who have had a child removed; like the provision of real and ongoing support to people who foster and adopt children; like the recent investment in perinatal services all over the UK. A good enough life for as many children as possible seems like a goal that no grown-up society would want to miss.

References

Adshead, G. (2014) Three faces of justice: competing ethical paradigms in forensic psychiatry. *Legal and Criminological Psychology*, 19(1), 1–12.

Bentham, J. (2002) Rights, representation, and reform: nonsense upon stilts and other writings on the French Revolution. In P. Schofield, C. Pease-Watkin, and C. Blamires (eds), *The Collected Works of Jeremy Bentham*. Oxford: Oxford University Press, pp. 317–401.

Berlin, I. (1958) *Two Concepts of Liberty*. Oxford: Clarendon Press.

Blasi, A. (1993) The development of identity: some implications for moral functioning. In G. G. Noam, T. E. Wren, G. Nunner-Winkler and W. Edelstein (eds), *Studies in Contemporary German Social Thought. The Moral Self*. Cambridge: Cambridge University Press, pp. 99–122.

Chaffin, M., Silovsky, J. F., Funderburk, B., Valle, L. A., Brestan, E. V., Balachova, T., Jackson, S., Lensgraf, J. and Bonner, B. L. (2004) Parent–child interaction therapy with physically abusive parents: efficacy for reducing future abuse reports. *Journal of Consulting and Clinical Psychology*, 72(3), 500.

Day, J. M. and Tappan, M. B. (1996) The narrative approach to moral development: from the epistemic subject to dialogical selves. *Human Development*, 39(2), 67–82.

Felitti, V. J., Anda, R. F., Nordenberg, D., Williamson, D. F., Spitz, A. M., Edwards, V., Koss, M. P. and Marks, J. S. (1998) Relationship of childhood abuse and household dysfunction to many of the leading causes of death in adults: the Adverse Childhood Experiences (ACE) study. *American Journal of Preventive Medicine*, 14(4), 245–58.

Fox, B. H., Perez, N., Cass, E., Baglivio, M. T. and Epps, N. (2015) Trauma changes everything: examining the relationship between adverse childhood experiences and serious, violent and chronic juvenile offenders. *Child Abuse and Neglect*, 46, 163–73.

Gilligan, C. (1982) *In a Different Voice*. Cambridge, MA: Harvard University Press.

Lyons-Ruth, K. and Block, D. (1996) The disturbed caregiving system: relations among childhood trauma, maternal caregiving, and infant affect and attachment. *Infant Mental Health Journal*, 17(3), 257–75.

Lyons-Ruth, K., Yellin, C., Melnick, S. and Atwood, G. (2005) Expanding the concept of unresolved mental states: hostile/ helpless states of mind on the Adult Attachment Interview are associated with disrupted mother–infant communication and infant disorganization. *Development and Psychopathology*, 17(1), 1–23.

McAdams, D. P., Reynolds, J., Lewis, M., Patten, A. H. and Bowman, P. J. (2001) When bad things turn good and good things turn bad: sequences of redemption and contamination in life narrative and their relation to psychosocial adaptation in midlife adults and in students. *Personality and Social Psychology Bulletin*, 27(4), 474–85.

McAdams, D. P. (2009) The moral personality. In D. Narvaez and D. K. Lapsley (eds), *Personality, Identity, and Character: Explorations in Moral Psychology*. New York: Cambridge University Press, pp. 11–29.

McAdams, D. P. (2013) The psychological self as actor, agent, and author. *Perspectives on Psychological Science*, 8(3), 272–95.

Sroufe, L. A. (2005) Attachment and development: a prospective, longitudinal study from birth to adulthood. *Attachment and Human Development*, 7(4), 349–67.

Tappan, M. B. (2010) Telling moral stories: from agency to authorship. *Human Development*, 53(2), 81–86.

Van IJzendoorn, M. H. and Zwart-Woudstra, H. A. (1995) Adolescents' attachment representations and moral reasoning. *Journal of Genetic Psychology*, 156(3), 359–72.

Wolfe, I. (2014) Disproportionate disadvantage of the young: Britain, the Unicef report on child well-being, and political choices. *Archives of Disease in Childhood*, 99(1), 6–9.

Legal Case

Hedley J, in *Re: L (Care: Threshold Criteria)* [2007] 1 FLR 2050.

Index